Culture, Capitals and Graduate Futures

In a time of too many graduates for too few jobs, and in a context where applicants have similar levels of educational capital, what other factors influence graduate career trajectories? Based on the life history interviews of graduates and framed through a Bourdieusian sociological lens, *Culture, Capitals and Graduate Futures* explores the continuing role that social class as well as cultural and social capitals have on both the aspirations and expectations toward, and the trajectories within, the graduate labour market.

Framed within the current context of increasing levels of university graduates and the falling numbers of graduate positions available in the UK labour market, this book provides a critical examination of the supposedly linear and meritocratic relationship between higher education and graduate employment proposed by official discourses from government at both local and national levels.

Through a critical engagement with the empirical findings, *Culture, Capitals and Graduate Futures* asks important questions for the effective continuation of the widening participation agenda. This timely book will be of interest to higher education professionals working within widening participation policy and higher education policy.

Ciaran Burke is Lecturer in Sociology at Ulster University, Northern Ireland.

Society for Research into Higher Education (SRHE) series

Series Editor: Jennifer M. Case, University of Cape Town
Jeroen Huisman, University of Ghent

Published titles:

Intellectual Leadership in Higher Education: Renewing the Role of the University Professor
Bruce Macfarlane

Strategic Curriculum Change: Global Trends in Universities
Paul Blackmore and Camille B. Kandiko

Reconstructing Identities in Higher Education: The Rise of 'Third Space' Professionals
Celia Whitchurch

The University in Dissent: Scholarship in the Corporate University
Gary Rolfe

Everything for Sale? The Marketisation of UK Higher Education
Roger Brown with Helen Carasso

Literacy in the Digital University: Critical Perspectives on Learning, Scholarship and Technology
Robin Goodfellow and Mary R. Lea

Researching Student Learning in Higher Education: A Social Realist Approach
Jennifer M. Case

Women Leaders in Higher Education: Shattering the myths
Tanya Fitzgerald

Writing in Social Spaces: A social processes approach to academic writing
Rowena Murray

Digital Technology and the Contemporary University: Degrees of digitization
Neil Selwyn

Stepping up to the Second Year at University: Academic, Psychological and Social Dimensions
Edited by Clare Milsom, Martyn Stewart, Mantz Yorke and Elena Zaitseva

Culture, Capitals and Graduate Futures
Ciaran Burke

Culture, Capitals and Graduate Futures

Degrees of class

Ciaran Burke

LONDON AND NEW YORK

First published 2016
by Routledge
2 Park Square, Milton Park, Abingdon, Oxon OX14 4RN
together with the Society for Research into Higher Education
73 Collier Street
London N1 9BE
UK

and by Routledge
711 Third Avenue, New York, NY 10017

Routledge is an imprint of the Taylor & Francis Group, an informa business

British Library Cataloguing in Publication Data
A catalogue record for this book is available from the British Library

Library of Congress Cataloging in Publication Data
A catalog record has been requested

ISBN: 978-1-138-84053-9 (hbk)
ISBN: 978-1-138-84054-6 (pbk)
ISBN: 978-1-315-73281-7 (ebk)

Typeset in Galliard and Gill Sans
by Florence Production Ltd, Stoodleigh, Devon, UK

Printed and bound in Great Britain by
TJ International Ltd, Padstow, Cornwall

To my wife, Sydney Lanier Burke –
partner, friend, copy editor

Contents

Series editors' introduction

This series, co-published by the Society for Research into Higher Education and Routledge Books, aims to provide, in an accessible manner, cutting-edge scholarly thinking and inquiry that reflects the rapidly changing world of higher education, examined in a global context.

Encompassing topics of wide international relevance, the series includes every aspect of the international higher education research agenda, from strategic policy formulation and impact to pragmatic advice on best practice in the field. Each book in the series aims to meet at least one of the principle aims of the Society: to advance knowledge; to enhance practice; to inform policy.

Ciaran Burke's book will be an asset to the series in that it explores an important topic – inequalities in higher education by social class – using a sociological lens. Although this topic already has an expansive treatment in the higher education literature, the novelty of Burke's work lies in his shifting of the focus from access to graduate trajectories. He seeks inspiration in and builds upon the work of Bourdieu, authoritatively engaging with key concepts of habitus, capital, field and reflexivity. Using a biographical narrative interview method, he reports findings from his study on graduate careers in Northern Ireland. This volume offers new impetus to the argument that while attention to widening participation in higher education continues to be important, this should be supplemented with institutional strategies and governmental policies that address persistent inequalities once working class students have gained access to higher education, for access for these students does not necessarily imply successful entrance to the graduate labour market.

Jennifer M. Case
Jeroen Huisman

Acknowledgements

There are a number of people to whom I owe a great deal of thanks and – without whose help, support and guidance – this work would never have been completed. First to my respondents, the 27 individuals who shared their life histories with me, without whom there would have been no research. A special thanks to colleagues and friends: Bob Miller, Matt Wood, Nicola Ingram, Nathan ('conceptual *tour de force*') Emmerich, Jenny Thatcher, Tamsin Bowers-Brown, Sarah Hannaford-Simpson, Justyna Bell, Ciaran Acton, Maire Braniff, Jessica Abrahams, Neil Wilson, Tom Hughes, the SRHE book series editors and the Routledge team. A final thank you for the constant support from my family and, in particular, my wife, Sydney Lanier Burke.

Abbreviations

11+	Academic Transfer Exam (Primary School to Grammar/ Secondary School)
BCC	British Chambers of Commerce
BIS	Department for Business, Innovation and Skills
BNIM	biographical Narrative Interview Method
CBI	Confederation of British Industry
CIPD	Chartered Institute for Personnel and Development
DfE	Department for Education
DfEE	Department for Education and Employment
DfES	Department for Education and Skills
DEL	Department of Employment and Learning
DETI	*Department of Enterprise, Trade and Investment*
DFP	Department of Finance and Personnel
ECA	Extra-Curricular Activity
FE	Further Education
GBCS	Great British Class Survey
HE	Higher Education
HEA	Higher Education Academy
HEI	Higher Education Institution
HESA	Higher Education Statistics Agency
HEFCE	Higher Education Funding Council for England
HEI	Higher Education Institution
NILT	Northern Ireland Life and Times Survey
NS-SEC	National Statistics Socio-Economic Classification
OECD	Organisation for Economic-Co-operation and Development
ONS	Office for National Statistics
QAA	Quality Assurance Agency for Higher Education
UCAS	University and Colleges Admissions Service

Introduction

The emergence and development of post-industrialization, illustrated by Daniel Bell (1973), has ushered in a number of significant and lasting changes to the labour market. Within Organisation for Economic Co-operation and Development (OECD) countries, the main economic sector has shifted from production to service and communication. Mass produced products created via a Fordist model of production have made way for smaller scale, niche products, produced by creative employees operating under a greater deal of autonomy within a post-Fordist model, characterized by progression and change rather than routine. The change in organizational hierarchy and management has also witnessed the decline of 'hard' labour and the rise of service-based labour, placing a greater emphasis on inter-personal skills and emotional labour (Hochschild, 1983). Another central facet within Bell's thesis is the emergence of a knowledge economy. For Bell, the university would replace business enterprise as the primary economic institution. The workforce within a post-industrial society requires advanced education and training in order to 'succeed' within this new system.

Teichler (1999) highlights that the labour markets within many OECD countries have gone through a period of adjustment. The employment sector within these countries has witnessed the decline of agricultural and industrial labour – in contrast to an increased requirement for computer literacy and generally higher levels of knowledge – for a market characterized by an increased pace and the need for a workforce that can update its skills per the needs of the economy. The emergence and establishment of a knowledge-based economy defined by Brown *et al.* as one 'driven by the application of new technologies, accelerating the shift to high-skilled, high-waged European economies' (2008: 131) has become a central goal within post-industrial societies. As Brown and colleagues further note, a knowledge-based economy, or what they term a knowledge economy, is a central feature of European economic policy, citing the European Commission as aspiring to hold the 'most competitive and dynamic knowledge-based economy in the world' (2003, cited in Brown *et al.*, 2008: 131). While there have been debates concerning the true reach of the knowledge economy and the lasting grip that traditional organizational structures have, reducing multi-skilling to multi-tasking, quelling the extent to which employees are afforded autonomy and therefore questioning the relative empowerment of a highly skilled workforce (Rinehart *et al.*, 1997), higher education (HE) is understood to play a prominent role in access to employment and increased life chances. This shift can be seen through the meritocratic narratives within social policy and the rapid expansion of the higher education system.

The expansion of the UK higher education sector, which began with the *Robbins Report* (1963), has steadily grown. Figures from Brooks and Everett (2009) place the percentage of 19- to 20-year-olds attending university at the beginning of the 1960s at 6 per cent; this number has continuously risen to 47 per cent in 2012 (Heath *et al.*, 2013). An obvious and immediate consequence of the expansion in student numbers is the level of university graduates. According to the Office for National Statistics (ONS) (2013b), the percentage of graduates in the UK has more than doubled between 1992 and 2012. In 1992, graduates accounted for 17 per cent of the UK population; in 2012, they accounted for 38 per cent. In spite of the meritocratic narratives running through much of UK social policy, the level of graduate jobs has not kept up with the number of graduates, questioning the assumed linear relationship between higher education and graduate employment (Brown and Scase, 1994; Tomlinson, 2013). Recent findings from the Futuretrack study (Purcell *et al.*, 2013) and ONS (2013b) reported that 40 per cent and 47 per cent of graduates, respectively, are not in graduate employment. From these figures, it is clear that the expansion of higher education has not translated into a 'guaranteed' return for investment.

The research on which this book is based took place in Northern Ireland. While Northern Ireland is often seen as a unique region of the UK, owing to its particular history and composition, there are a number of parallels between the Northern Irish and general UK labour markets, allowing for the extrapolation of findings and analysis to a much wider audience. The findings and commentary will add to a growing international focus on the issue of graduate under-employment and, in particular, the disparity of access to capitals based on class background, including research based in Europe (Barone and Schizzerotto, 2011), Africa (Tagoe, 2009) and North America (Mullen, 2010). In addition to contributing to internationally based sociological discussions, this research will examine the policy initiatives leading to the expansion of higher education and the subsequent implications stemming from higher education's central position with future economic strategies, a trend that both Teichler (1999) and Wilton (2008) identify as being common with most OECD countries.

Northern Ireland has very similar levels of general employment to the UK; at the time this research was concluded, the Northern Irish unemployment rate was 7 per cent (DETI, 2012b), compared to the national unemployment rate within the UK of 8.4 per cent (ONS, 2012). This similarity in labour market experience is also apparent when examining graduates' employment trajectories. The percentage of the 2006/2007 cohort of Northern Irish graduates who were employed three and a half years after graduation was 88 per cent (Martin, 2013). This number can be compared to the UK average, for the same cohort, of 86.4 per cent (HESA, 2011). Additionally, Atfield and Purcell (2014) observed very similar attitudes and expectations of Northern Irish university students compared to other UK students. Differences, however, arise in terms of average wages and public/private sector divide: in Northern Ireland, average weekly earnings in April 2011 was £360, while, in the rest of the UK, average weekly earnings for the same time of year was £403.90. Earnings for all employees in Northern Ireland were 89.1 per cent of the UK's average (DFP, 2011). In Northern Ireland, 30.8 per cent of employees are employed in the public sector (DETI, 2012a), compared to the UK average of 20.6 per cent (ONS: 2012).

In the context of increasing participation rates and high levels of graduate underemployment, this research was interested in examining which graduates enter the graduate labour market and more specifically, what variables direct these pathways. Adopting a sociological approach – in particular, the theoretical lens of Pierre Bourdieu (1972/1977)[1] – this research asked: *Are strategies that graduates use to secure employment influenced by social class?* This project was, in part, an extension of previous research applying Bourdieusian social theory to education pathways (Reay *et al.*, 2005; Bradley *et al.*, 2013) toward graduate trajectories. As such, it was interested in whether graduates' aspirations and expectations and subsequent strategies within the labour market were influenced by social class. Building on previous work examining hierarchy within educational institutions – in particular, the classed attitudes and experiences – the research was keen to examine whether there were differences in graduate trajectories based on the Higher Education Institution (HEI) attended. In an effort to not force findings into assumed classed patterns based on previous educational research or focus solely on one variable, the research was cautious to consider the extent that other aspects of identity – gender and ethno-national identity – account for trajectories.

The research on which this book is based was conducted between 2009 and 2012. The primary form of data collection was the biographical narrative interview method, supplemented by demographic questionnaires. The theoretically constructed research sample, consisting of 27 respondents (Appendix A), accessed through gatekeepers and a snowball sampling, was stratified by institution for first degree, gender and social class (Appendix B). In addition, respondents were Northern Irish and had attended a Northern Irish HEI for their first degree, 'Southern' or 'Northern',[2] and graduated in a non-vocational subject between two and ten years before the research.

Structure of the book

Chapter 1 provides a discussion of Bourdieu's conceptual tools, offering a detailed and critical examination of the three central conceptual tools – habitus, capital and field – tools that were applied within the research. It then moves on to provide a wider discussion concerning debates within current social theory on choice and reflexivity. It presents and compares the late modern and critical realist position, advocating the development of a fluid system of relations and the collapse of social structures, with a general Bourdieusian position, advocating the reproduction of social structures and the continuing influence of class on the choices that individuals understand themselves to make. Once these positions are presented and debated, the chapter will detail the approach to choice, informed by reflection, used within the empirical research. It will conclude with a discussion on the epistemological issues the research faced and the empirical processes employed.

Chapter 2 will provide the research context for the empirical study by discussing previous research and explaining where it fits within the growing body of work, questioning education and social mobility. Here I propose that graduate employment research should be understood as a sub-area of educational research; graduate employment is understood as the marker of a successful university graduate. As such, this chapter is divided into two sub-sections: the first sub-section provides an analysis of previous educational research, specifically secondary level and higher education, proposing either a human capital or social closure position. The focus of this sub-section is on educational research that has questioned the classed nature of access and experience of education. The second sub-section is an examination of previous research concerning graduate employment. Looking at both large-scale quantitative research projects and smaller qualitative studies, this section – similar to its predecessor – considers previous studies that advocate either a human capital or social closure position when examining the classed nature of graduate employment trajectories.

The book then moves on to provide an account and analysis of empirical findings before offering a discussion of the social policy implications from this study. Chapter 3 discusses the aspirations/expectations and trajectories of respondents who were in graduate employment at the time of the research. By comparing the respondents' aspirations/expectations and trajectories during their time in education and since graduating from university, this chapter demonstrates the role of class – or, more specifically, habitus and capitals – on their ability to enter the labour market. Chapter 4 essentially complements the previous chapter, charting the educational and employment trajectories of respondents who were not in graduate employment at the time of the research. Once again, via a Bourdieusian lens, the role of habitus and the directive and destructive influence of capitals – when they are held in insufficient amount or incongruent to the labour market – are examined to provide an account of the social barriers graduates face when attempting to enter the labour market.

Chapter 5 approaches the empirical findings from a different angle. While Chapters 3 and 4 stratify the respondents by employment status and consider the specific influence of habitus and capitals on each of their particular trajectories, this chapter discusses the general/collective classed nature found within the graduate employment trajectories. It demonstrates the way class affects aspirations/expectations and the ability to negotiate the graduate employment market. The chapter then moves on to provide a 'paired graduates' section, where graduates who attempted to enter similar forms of graduate employment with very different outcomes are directly compared to reinforce the continuing influence of social class. It concludes with a discussion on the influence of gender, institutional capital and ethno-national identity.

A central element of the research in this book was a critical assessment of widening participation strategy. It questions the validity of understanding access – specifically, to university – to equal success and reminds the reader of the continuing support that working-class university undergraduates require if they are to successfully enter the graduate labour market. Chapter 6 provides a discussion of the history and current higher education policy context before making a number of recommendations on the role that higher education should take up in order to truly foster social mobility. The book concludes with a reflection of the findings and possibilities for moving forward within higher education and graduate employment.

Notes

1 Appreciating the chronology of the publication of Bourdieu's work in French is a useful way for non-Francophones, such as myself, to have a greater understanding of his work. This will become more obvious as I discuss his comments on education and how they changed over time (Chapter 2). As such, each reference will include first either the French publication date or, as Bourdieu's articles have been reproduced countless times in various formats, the first publication date and the date of publication of the text I am referencing.

2 The universities where students read for their degrees were provided pseudonyms. Southern is a pre-1992 university, which is a member of the Russell Group. Northern is a post-1992 university.

Chapter 1

Sociology of 'choice'

Sociological enquiry, at its fundamental level, is the relationship between structure and agency, individual and society or choice and regulation in everyday practice. In C. Wright Mills' seminal work *The Sociological Imagination* (1959), he challenges social researchers to accept and appreciate the role of both structure and agency and critically and empirically examine how these work together to engender practice. The focus of this book, and the research that formed its basis, is to question the directive influence of social class on graduate employment trajectories within a society that is increasingly characterized as populated by individuals making choices and, in large part, directing their own pathways based on levels of capital – in particular, educational capital they have amassed for themselves and by themselves.

In order to effectively examine the influence of social class and meet Mills' challenge to appreciate the relationship between the individual and society, the research applied the theoretical position of the French sociologist Pierre Bourdieu. The scope of Bourdieu's work covers areas such as education, employment, cultural consumption, art, television, politics and anthropology, and, as such, he has established and applied a large set of 'thinking tools' with which to discuss these areas of enquiry. As a precursor to this chapter, a brief discussion concerning the rationale of Bourdieu's theoretical project and, in part, a defence of my own rationale for adopting this particular theoretical lens would be prudent. Equally concerned with the reduction of practice to a mechanical reaction associated with the anthropology of Levi-Strauss and the ephemeral status phenomenologists, such as Merleau-Ponty, had ascribed to social structures, Bourdieu offered a *structural constructivist* model of practice adopting elements of both positions but also going beyond the limitations of each view. In an *Outline of a Theory of Practice* (1972/1977) – Bourdieu's first theoretical publication – he offered not a theory of practice but rather a theory of the generation of practice that seeks to reconcile both structure and agency. In order to explain the amalgam of structure and agency, Bourdieu began to develop certain tools: *Habitus, Capital* and *Field*. Bourdieu displays his triad in schematic form '[(habitus) (capital)] + field = practice' (1979/1984: 101), in an effort to demonstrate their *interpenetrative* relationship.

The purpose of this chapter is not to provide an inventory of Pierre Bourdieu's conceptual toolbox.[1] Instead, this chapter comments on how I understand his conceptual tools and applied them in my empirical research, specifically in relation to the directive role of social class and that of choice – or, in a theoretical context, *reflexivity* – on graduate trajectories. While Bourdieu is 'good to think with' (Hodkinson *et al.*, 2000), there are certain limitations to Bourdieu's theory, as 'borrowing the emperor's clothes can leave one looking very naked' (Nash, 1999: 172). As such, I intend to discuss how I have adopted and progressed, rather than simply applied, certain conceptual tools. Once this theoretical groundwork has been laid, the chapter will move to demonstrate the effectiveness of Bourdieu's – albeit altered – logic of practice. This effort will be achieved through considering and, to an extent, defending Bourdieu's position on choice and reflexivity. The chapter will provide a critical discussion on various attempts at different models of reflexivity, from Ulrich Beck (1992, with Beck-Gernsheim, 2002) and Margaret Archer (2007, 2013), and hybridized models of habitus and reflexivity, from Andrew Sayer (2005) and Will Atkinson (2010a, 2010b). This section of the chapter will then offer an account of my own position on the role and influence of ordinary reflection, as discussed by Greg Noble and Megan Watkins (2003), as an aspect of Bourdieu's logic of practice.

This chapter will conclude with a discussion on the relationship between social theory and empiricism and the specific research design and empirical processes employed in the research study, primarily, biographical narrative interview method (BNIM). It will specifically describe how this approach challenged and informed a theoretically driven project. This section will discuss how the BNIM is suited to create an opportunity to observe the directive influence of Bourdieu's conceptual tools.

Habitus

'Definitions'

The habitus is perhaps the most widely used and most generally misunderstood of the concepts[2] within the Bourdieusian toolbox. Bourdieu by no means coined the term;[3] nevertheless, it is a central conceptual and empirical element in his theory. The concept of habitus was born from the rejection of alternative models of practice, namely those that rested either on structure or agency. It was the habitus, Bourdieu explains that, 'allowed me to break away from the structuralist paradigm without falling back into the old philosophy of the subject of consciousness' (1985: 13).

Providing a definition of habitus has proved quite challenging, certainly thanks, in part, to the interpenetrative relations between structure and agency within the habitus. The most often cited definition of the habitus is 'systems of durable, transposable *dispositions*, structured structures predisposed to function as structuring structures' (Bourdieu, 1972/1977: 72, emphasis in original). This explanation of the habitus as a set of durable dispositions appears to be quite structuralist; however, there are more subjective and individualistic understandings of the habitus. For Bourdieu (2002), the habitus is not understood as reductive, nor its practice monolithic; rather, habitus, while being an open concept, is built upon limitations. This position is further elaborated through this definition of habitus as 'a durably installed generative principle of *regulated improvisations*' (1972/1977: 78, emphasis added). In other words, the habitus is attempting to fuse these two concepts together. The habitus is a set of generative improvisations – however these improvisations are framed – and, therefore, are constrained/regulated by the structure in question.

The habitus is formed through experiences related to our material conditions as well as influences from sources like the family, peer group and the educational system influencing levels of strategic action or practical mastery. The durable dispositions and the generative improvisation, albeit regulated, are understood to mould our aspirations and expectations, our 'subjective expectations of objective probabilities' (Bourdieu and Passeron, 1970/1990: 156). The habitus was intended to provide an escape from the Cartesian philosophy of the rational agent who, through intentional strategy, can choose the best means to maximize their goal (Bourdieu, 2002). While there are conflicting definitions of or comments on the habitus, it was meant to resemble real life, and we should understand, as Reay argues, 'there is an indeterminacy about the concept [habitus] that fits in well with the complex messiness of the world' (2004b: 438). This point – of the 'subjective expectations of objective probabilities' founded by the habitus, along with capital, which I shall discuss next – is a crucial element of how habitus was applied within this research. Thinking about attitudes, the subjective expectations, through the habitus is useful when examining aspirations and expectations of university graduates. This approach provides an opportunity to consider their genesis and progression, as well as how they work alongside and through capital and field.

As a conceptual tool, habitus exists as both an individual and collective model. According to Nash (1999), there are two forms of habitus: the specific and the general. The general habitus is concerned with large-scale statistical regularities and provides Bourdieu with the apparatus to explain statistically relevant social generalizations and reproduction without having to discuss individual cases. The specific habitus, however, is individual and used to consider individual practices. Reay (2004b) discusses the multifaceted and seemingly contradictory position of considering the habitus at both the individual and the collective level. From this perspective, the habitus becomes a complex multifaceted and multi-layered concept; it is formed through the individual's history but also through the collective histories of the family and the wider social group/class. At times, the habitus appears quite individualistic while, on other occasions, demonstrating a uniform or group dimension. Bourdieu (1972/1977) defends the notion of a group habitus, arguing that, while it is impossible for all members of a social group to have the same experiences – which in part form the habitus – it is more likely that members from the same group will have similar experiences and exist in similar conditions than members from different social groups. Habitus is most influential when in group form, the homogeneity of self-presupposed shared norms – attitudes and dispositions – provides an opportunity for significant directive influence. A plural appreciation of the habitus provides us with an opportunity to consider both the social structure and the socially structured individual while not reducing their relationship to a zero-sum situation.

The habitus is a 'thinking tool'; as such, the level of habitus a researcher adopts or appreciates is based on the empirical challenge at hand. It has certainly been the case with regard to the progression of the 'institutional habitus' and the 'familial habitus' (Reay, 1998; Reay *et al.*, 2001; Reay *et al.*, 2009b; Ingram 2009, 2011; Burke *et al.*, 2013). Appreciating the habitus at different levels or heights was critical to my research. While I was considering the relationship between a graduate's habitus and capital in relation to a field at an individual level, I also framed that discussion in the wider context of class habitus through discussing the role of habitus via classed conceptual groups.

Progression through critique

While I intend to discuss the critiques of Bourdieu's model, his logic of practice and his position on choice/reflexivity in a subsequent section of this chapter, there are a number of specific critiques of the habitus that I think will offer a greater insight at this juncture. Bourdieu's reaction to such criticisms will also provide a fuller understanding of his position of the habitus and how it was applied throughout the research. A charge often brought against the habitus is based on the reading of 'durable dispositions'; it is seen as being structurally deterministic (DiMaggio, 1979; LiPuma, 1993; Mouzelis, 1995, 2007; Goldthorpe, 2007). In his now notorious critical publication on Bourdieu, Jenkins (2002) argues the habitus removes any influence agency may have over the structure and, therefore, over practice. He is equally critical of the apparent stable nature of dispositions, which, for Jenkins, begs the question of how to account for social change. Through comments such as these, the habitus appears to share a similarity with Foucault's (1978) concept of the soul – a durable and all-encompassing prison of the self – or, perhaps, with Durkheim's (1893/1982) social facts – forming outside of the individual's consciousness and ruling from above.

Bourdieu, when presented with similar charges by Wacquant (1992a), argues that at the centre of these critiques is the problem individuals (lay and academic) have with the idea that we are, at least in part, structurally constrained. Habitus 'collides head on with the illusion of (intellectual) mastery of oneself that is so deeply engrained in intellectuals' (Bourdieu, 1992b: 132). Individuals like to think of themselves as freethinking reflexive individuals in charge of their own destiny, while the habitus is firmly based on an appreciation of structural influence. Bourdieu attempts to show there is a pragmatic relationship between structure and agency and to give a realistic, but non-reductionist, account of the role they play.

In addition to Bourdieu's defence that a site of hostility toward the habitus is that individuals enjoy the sense of autonomy and choice, the habitus is also open to change. The habitus is formed by the environment; therefore, a change in environment could lead to an altered habitus (Bourdieu, 1992b). Bourdieu is cautious to point out that an environment strong enough to affect the habitus is unlikely, as it would require a significant push to change such a strongly embedded element of practice and, due to the habitus, we are more likely to encounter experiences that reassure rather than question the habitus. With regard to actors who share a similar position in the social space but have divergent end results, Bourdieu (1979/1984) proposes that the relationship between social class/position and practice is based not only on the influence from their family or conditions in the formative years of their lives but also on trajectory from experiences along the way. This point demonstrates the role of environment on the habitus and how it can develop with the appropriate circumstances. Whatever the next stage of an individual's life is, it will be influenced by the previous stage and so on, as the habitus is an incomplete creation, constantly being added to. It is the generative principle within habitus that provided an escape from structural determinism.

In support of Bourdieu, DiMaggio (1979) and Reay (2004b) accept and maintain that the individual's habitus is open to change; it is this appreciation that saves Bourdieu from a Parsonian trap.[4] As Atkinson (2010a) has pointed out, however, the habitus' ability to change can be difficult to appreciate; nevertheless, the possibility of change based on exposure to new environments and new experiences in the habitus is a central facet of my research. To provide a greater opportunity for this to be realized, I have adopted Reay's (2004b) 'permeable habitus' model. This reading sees the habitus as being able to react to the context of its surroundings. It is this permeability that provides an opportunity for the influence of new environments and experiences. While Bourdieu discusses the influence of experience on the habitus and, arguably, intended for a more permeable understanding of the habitus than some commentators have granted, the contribution from authors such as Reay is that she essentially 'says it out loud' – there is no ambiguity concerning either the permeability of the habitus nor on the role of experience in (re)shaping it.

In order to provide a bridging mechanism between structure and agency, habitus requires a certain level of malleability. Above all else, the habitus is a thinking tool; its plural understanding of structure and agency is replicated in its plural application by researchers. As such, it is important to clarify that the habitus, applied in this research, was understood as a set of dispositions, expectations and aspirations created and influenced by sources such as family, peer group and the educational system that, along with capital and field, influence practice. While at times being empirically (heuristically) understood on an institutional, collective or classed level, the habitus is specific to the individual. Via its permeable character, the habitus is open to alteration through new experiences and environmental change, however unlikely these experiences and environmental changes may be.

Capital

Forms of capital

In order to have a thorough appreciation of Bourdieu's theory of practice, an understanding of the forms and roles of capitals is necessary. For Bourdieu (1983/2004), three essential forms of capital are economic, cultural and social. Economic capital is measured by levels of monetary capital: savings, investments, property, etc. Cultural capital is understood to include personal tastes, knowledge and skills.[5] Social capital is based on the combination of actual or potential contacts that can lead to a form of exchangeable credit. The amount of social capital an individual has is based on the size of the contact network and the position within the social space each contact inhabits. As such, Bourdieu suggests, social capital is not an autonomous form of capital, independent from economic and cultural capital. The composite, or fourth, form of capital is symbolic capital – essentially, legitimate levels of these capitals. Symbolic capital is the most powerful form of capital, as those people who possess it can shape the doxa, the norms (that benefit the dominant group) or common sense of the field. Economic capital is the root of the other forms of capital; however, these forms of capital, with their specific character and manner, are not reducible to economic capital alone. Multiple forms of capital allow us to appreciate capitals other than economic while also remembering their economic influence.

These forms of capital allow us to 'plot' an individual's position within social space, moving beyond merely economic indicators. There are three dimensions that need to be taken into consideration when placing individuals within social space: 'volume of capital, composition of capital, and change in these two properties over time (manifested by past and potential trajectory in social space)' (Bourdieu, 1979/1984: 114). Crossley (2008) comments that, through mapping social space, we are able to place individuals within social groups based on similar levels of capital and attitudes. Crossley warns us, however, that we must remember these groups are only created 'in theory' or, what Bourdieu calls, 'classes on paper' (*ibid.*: 92). Similarity of positions within social space does not guarantee similar or collective practices or attitudes. A similar position within the social field, however, does suggest similar life chances and attitudes. While it is not guaranteed, individuals within similar positions are more likely to socialize with each other than with those who possess differing positions.

According to Bourdieu, levels of capital and subsequent positions within the social space are crucial for understanding levels of aspiration and expectation. Similar to 'subjective expectations', understood to be moulded by the habitus, levels of capital are thought to enable or restrict what individuals think or know they can achieve – the '*field of the possibles*' (1979/1984: 110, emphasis in original). Capital has a tendency to reproduce itself in almost its exact form and contains a certain longevity to its influence; it is capital that influences individuals to essentially cap their aspirations, to make us understand certain trajectories as 'not for the likes of us' (*ibid.*: 471). Appreciating *all* forms of capital is crucial for a Bourdieusian project. Oliver and O'Reilly (2010), researching on 'life-style migration' from the United Kingdom to Spain, report that the occupational classed distinctions that had been an issue for their respondents before they immigrated had largely receded. Other aspects of class – other forms of capital – such as attitudes and taste, however, became more important and assumed the role of class barrier.

Class in the UK

Stemming from the post-war boom, the UK has been subject to sustained debates concerning classed identities and classed inequalities within society.[6] A central tenet within Bell's (1973) post-industrialization thesis was the establishment of hierarchies no longer based on patronage or nepotism but on skills and credentials. This prediction, along with increased flexibility and transitory working patterns for all, coupled with higher standards of living and increased connectivity via the Internet, led critics such as Ulrich Beck (1992, 2007) to equate the collapse of occupational structures with the collapse of class groups. These processes and progressions have created a 'multifaceted' individual that can no longer be classified; class will, according to Beck, 'recede into the background relative to the new emerging "centre" of the biographical plan' (1992: 131).

The reading of class as dead, kept alive only by those who research it and therefore relegated to a 'Zombie category' (Beck and Beck-Gernsheim, 2002) prompted quite a critical response. The emergence of 'cultural class analysts' formed a new and, in a sense, progressive approach to class analysis (Skeggs, 1997, 2004; Reay, 1998, 2000; Savage, 2003; Crompton and Scott, 2005; Atkinson, 2010a). According to Atkinson (2010a), there are two central components to the cultural class analysts' multifaceted nature of class. First, this approach appreciates the increasingly complicated classed relations in contemporary society, and, therefore, has moved away from large-scale quantitative projects to in-depth qualitative research. Second, they have tried to move beyond simplistic occupation-based classification or understanding of social class to focus on the combination of economic capital (Savage, 2000), cultural capital (Skeggs, 2005) and social capital (MacDonald *et al.*, 2005). The strength in a cultural class approach, according to Savage *et al.* (2014), is that it addresses the central flaw in continuing with a traditional Marxist understanding of social inequality based on economic relations. Whereas previous models can be articulated through the relationship between those who own the resources of production and those who work in them for a disproportional wage, contemporary post-industrial models are not as neat. We need a messy theory to account for our messy world. From this perspective, both Savage (2000) and Lawler (2005) suggest that Beck's understanding of the relationship between the individual and social class is based on an outdated appreciation of social class, therefore missing the point.

The most recent development for Bourdieusian inspired class analysis is Savage *et al.*'s (2013) *Great British Class Survey (GBCS)*. Savage, along with an expansive team and in association with the BBC, attempted to provide a map of contemporary class identities within the UK. Examining economic, social and cultural capital, Savage's team created a new 7-class model.[7] The *GBCS* has received some critical attention, not least from *Sociology*'s (2014) special issue on the 'British Social Class Debate', featuring commentaries from Bradley, Dorling, Mills and Rollock. Bradley (2014) provides quite a constructive commentary, arguing that the model is flawed on three main counts: it is gradational rather than relational; it contains highly selective cultural capital markers; and it contains an incoherent model of latent class analysis. At the other end of the spectrum is the highly critical – verging on aggressive – reading from Mills (2014) questioning the fundamental rationale behind the entire project. Savage *et al.* (2014) have begun to respond to the critics, a central argument being that the *GBCS* findings have only scratched the surface thus far; the debates within *Sociology* are based on the initial findings/overview from Savage *et al.* (2013). There is still quite a lot to come from this project. At this early stage, a clear achievement from the *GBCS* is to return our attention back to the continual issue of social class. Importantly, these approaches, echoing previous comments from Scott (2002), do not ignore the role of older structures, such as economic capital.

From the 1970s to 1990s, British and American pop culture was littered with programmes demonstrating a clear class identity. The joke was often found within the tension and unease a character felt when trying to occupy a 'higher class' position in social space. Whether it was Basil Fawlty's attempts to run an establishment free of 'riff-raff', Hyacinth Bucket's tireless efforts to enter the 'candlelight supper class' or Roseanne Conner's message to middle America articulating the plight of a growing population ignored by policy makers and mainstream media, class was thought *then* to have clear boundaries and experiences. What Savage *et al.*'s arguments show is that everyday life is still very differently experienced for distinct classes. The subsequent chapter will examine research that demonstrates the role of class in educational and graduate trajectories, but, for a clear indication of the visceral affinity the UK still has for class, we need look no further than the events surrounding the incident between the then Chief Whip Andrew Mitchell and the Metropolitan Police in 2012. The allegations were that Andrew Mitchell swore at police officers upon leaving 10 Downing Street. The public reaction was not in response to Mitchell swearing at the police but that he had called them 'plebs'. Almost instantly, there were campaigns across the country announcing 'PC Pleb' and 'Pleb and Proud'. Members of Mitchell's own cabinet, including Eric Pickles, then Secretary of State for Communities and Local Government, identified themselves as plebs. This episode of a relatively privileged individual belittling someone on classed grounds demonstrates how our apparent classless society is only skin deep; it only takes one jibe to open up old wounds.

Class within a Northern Irish context

There has been a distinct lack of research concerning class identity in Northern Ireland (Smyth and Cebulla, 2008). What has concerned most authors is ethno-national identity and its effects on what is still seen as a divided community in Northern Ireland. In contemporary Northern Ireland, however, with the decline in traditional Protestant industries such as ship-building and Section 75 of the *Northern Ireland Act 1998* (employment equality legislation), Catholics and Protestants experience similar levels of employment and similar, economically defined, classed positions. In 2007, the Northern Ireland Life and Times Survey (NILT) (ARK, 2007) reported that over twice as many people think that there is no occupational advantage now for one ethno-national identity over the other. Additionally, Miller (2004) argues that there is much less evidence now showing that levels of mobility can be linked to ethno-national identity. He does remind us, however, that gender is still an issue, with fewer women in employment that is considered both full-time and high in status.

Life chances and trajectories are heavily classed within Northern Ireland. As such, similar classed experiences, as demonstrated by Scott (2000), are evident in Northern Ireland, in areas including health, education, well-being, life chances, etc. Northern Ireland is a continually divided society; however, this divide is one based on class. The persistent focus on the Troubles in Northern Ireland has 'clouded the relationship between community conflict and local inequalities, lifestyle preferences, beliefs, and more complex notions of identity' (Moore, 2007: 401).

Putting capital to work

Capital and field are generally seen as 'second tier' conceptual tools to habitus (Reay, 2004b). Within Bourdieu's schema of practice, capital shares an equal footing with habitus. The multifaceted nature of capital, the opportunity for drastic shifts in levels and the subjective interpretation of forms of capital in differing contexts perhaps affords the agency that some see as missing from habitus, providing a more concrete account of the genesis of social change. It is clear that, in reaction to the commentators such as Beck, the cultural class analysts have adopted a Bourdieusian understanding of class. Savage (2000) argues Bourdieu's work provides a much more flexible and dynamic approach to class than many British authors. The continuing application of Bourdieu's approach demonstrates its continuing relevance within British class analysis. This approach to capital is how I understood and applied it for the purposes of my research. Each form of capital, while generated from an economic base, has its own specific form, content and consequences. An individual's position within social space corresponds to their inter-related levels of capital and, along with the habitus, shape dispositions, aspirations and expectations. In addition to the inter-related levels of capital, gender and ethno-national identity need to be given an opportunity to be appreciated, rather than being simply understood as 'other'.

In order to establish a measureable 'baseline' of class identity, I employed the National Statistics Socio-Economic Classification (NS-SEC) model, recorded using the self-completion questionnaire. To expand this preliminary position, I also used family background and asked respondents to self-identify with a particular class group. Once I had established an initial class identity for each respondent, I moved on to levels and forms of economic, social and cultural capital. Following from Bourdieu's own position, all capitals were examined in relational distance from necessity. Economic capital was the most straightforward of capitals to measure. Respondents were grouped by access to economic resources such as savings accounts but also investments and property. Social capital was not measured only in terms of individuals the respondents knew, but also how they used their social contacts. For example, two respondents could use their social contacts to find employment; if one found employment in a solicitors' office and one in a newsagents, the first respondent demonstrated higher levels of social capital. Finally, cultural capital, the most difficult to measure, as it is open to charges of selectivism (Bradley, 2014), was measured by its absence or self-identification. A respondent may feel comfortable in a middle-class environment, such as university, while, alternatively, a respondent may feel uncomfortable in a middle-class setting, such as a formal dinner. These environments are too highly selective but are offered only as examples. Feelings of discomfort were experienced in a number of settings; however, a constant theme was the respondents overtly placing these environments outside of where they felt they belonged.

Field

More than merely a playground?

Field, the final instalment of Bourdieu's theory of practice, is perhaps the least understood and, certainly, the variable that is offered the least attention. Thomson (2008) suggests that, when considering social phenomena, simply understanding what was communicated or what occurred in a situation is not sufficient to fully grasp what was happening. Where the social phenomena occur, the social space or *field*, is also of great importance. From a Bourdieusian perspective, our understanding of the field should go beyond where interactions and processes occur and encompass the context in which the object of study has been previously understood.[8] Similar to the concept of habitus, the idea of field was created in an attempt to move beyond the constant tension between structure and agency. The field is not disconnected but, rather, an active site where both structure and agency play a role. Thomson points out that Bourdieu's field did not refer to *le pré* (a calm meadow) but, rather, *le champ* (battlefield), a context in which the strongest survive. For Bourdieu, all action within the field is competitive; actors or players within this field use forms of strategy – levels of practical mastery – to maintain or advance the position that they hold within the field. The accumulation of capital is both the desired result of the game and the genesis for how it is played. Players will have different forms of capital entering a game; if their form of capital is suited to the game, then they will thrive and accumulate more capital.

The field is not merely some static or pre-built structure; it is the very basis of Bourdieu's triad. The field provides a dynamic context for the habitus and capital, as it is a site of constant struggle and competition. Within the field, agents act with respect to their position (based on capital) and their dispositions (based on habitus). Generally speaking, Bourdieu understands position and dispositions to be complementary to one another, commenting that, when the habitus encounters a field or a position within a field they are meant to be in, 'it is like a "fish in water" . . .' (1992b: 127). At times, however, there may be tensions, with possible negative consequences for the agents involved. The crucial point is that the relationship between the habitus, capital *and* field needs to be constantly appreciated in order to fully examine a particular social setting or research object.

An example of the dynamic character of field can be found in what Bourdieu referred to as 'hysteresis of habitus' (1972/1977: 78). As the field progresses or shifts, there can be a lag, or a gap, between an agent recognising the structural shift and creating a more effective strategy to move within the new field. Hysteresis represents this new 'lack of fit' between the habitus and the field. As such, the field does not act merely as a 'playground' for the habitus, it can move and develop, requiring the habitus to 'keep up'.

In the context of this research, I was primarily interested in the field of education – particularly higher education – and the field of graduate employment, two fields that commonly and easily interact with each other. It is important to appreciate previous comments on the fields of study; as such, in Chapter 2, I discuss the discourses surrounding (higher) education and subsequent employment. Within these fields, there is both struggle and competition over resources and positions; however, the dominant members of these fields are in an advantageous position, via habitus and capital, making it more likely they will be able to reproduce their own privileged and influential positions.

Reflexivity – challenging the determinism of structure?

Bourdieu's theoretical project has come under a considerable amount of criticism. The common denominator between various critics (Jenkins, 2002; Archer, 2007) is structural determinism. Many commentators see Bourdieu's tri-part system, unfortunately focusing on the habitus as a system void of agency, returning us to the iron cage through an emphasis on practical mastery – pre-reflexive action. At the centre of this debate toward the charge of structural determinism is Bourdieu's position concerning reflexivity – the role or influence of the consciousness over bodily and structural constraints embedded in the habitus. Many Bourdieusian modernisers (Reay, 2004b; Sayer, 2005; Atkinson 2010a, 2010b; Lahire, 2011) suggest that Bourdieu's position on the role of consciousness, framed by the concept of pre-reflexive action, is unclear and, therefore, untenable.

Bourdieu (1992b) defends his position toward consciousness as a reaction or protection against Rational Action Theory. Concerned with the level of reflexivity afforded to individuals he attempted to ensure that the structural influence on reflection was not forgotten. Bourdieu talks quite positively and overtly about consciousness, describing the habitus as 'a structured principle of invention' (2002: 30); invention, or the role of consciousness, is seen as the other side of the coin to practical mastery, defined as symbolic mastery. In other words, habitus is generative and, therefore, does not come with 'no assembly required'. The issue remains, however, of how to approach or understand consciousness and reflexivity.

Late modernity: reflexive individuals

The specifics and etymology of late modernity lies closer to a Giddensian stance. Social theory has forever played havoc with semantics and required the combination, conflation and the occasional looking the other way to reach a point of application. In this view, I read late modernity, as authors such as Savage (2000) and Atkinson (2010a) have done before, as an umbrella term for Beck's reflexive modernity (1997, with Beck-Gernsheim, 2002), Bauman's liquid modernity (2000, 2001) and Giddens's late modernity (1991, 1992), all of which are theoretical positions grounded in various levels of empirical research considering the composition of contemporary Western society, the collapse of traditional structures and the development of reflexive individuals. I have decided to focus on Ulrich Beck's work to examine and critique the late modern position, as Beck is seen as the most aggressive adversary to social structures (Atkinson, 2007b) and is also featured most often in debates concerning education (Reay *et al.*, 2005; Tomlinson, 2013).[9] Beck's particular take on contemporary society and the relationship between structure and agency is provided through his concept of reflexive modernity (1997). Essentially, Beck's model characterized contemporary post-industrial society as a constantly changing one, where previous social structures have either waned or collapsed and where the process of individualization has occurred where individuals are required to draw their own barriers and form identities out of the rubble that was modernity.

Two central processes have occurred in order to foster this shift into reflexive modernity: the establishment of far-reaching welfare states (Beck, 1997; Beck and Beck-Gernsheim, 2002) and global risks (Beck, 1992). For Beck, the development of welfare systems – including access to education, health and legal representation – has addressed some of the overt barriers previously experienced by some social groups. Providing access to these services gives individuals an opportunity to start from a relatively level playing field, certainly providing more choices than prisons and poorhouses of the Dickensian era. The second process is global risks; indeed, *Risk Society* (1992) is where Beck largely found fame within English-speaking countries. The general argument is that, as the world develops into a post-industrial society, dangers and risks change, multiply and cross borders – both social and national. These new risks do not just affect one class group; we breathe the same air and drink from the same well. Global risks transcend previous structures and require all individuals to make choices. Beck's characterization of the 'European project of democratically enlightened industrialization [. . .] disintegrating and losing its foundations' (1997: 13) is predicated on these two processes.

Beck's model does not advocate an absence of structure; reflexive modernity becomes a new structure. Within Beck's model, social inequality still exists, as risk society does not advocate egalitarianism but it is a system of 'capitalism without classes' (1992: 88). The inequalities within society, however, are no longer fixed and experienced by certain groups or classes of individuals but, rather, are subject to movement as circumstances change for all (Beck and Beck-Gernsheim, 2002). Economic levels fluctuate, depending on an individual's life stage; therefore, changing economic disadvantage can no longer point to a social group, as market experiences are open to change. Within reflexive modernity, everyone has the opportunity to be dominant but also dominated.

Beck has amassed a number of critiques (Ball *et al.*, 2000; Reay, 2000; Savage, 2000; Reay, *et al.*, 2005); however, the most thorough and theoretical critique comes from Atkinson (2007b, 2010a), with Beck (2007), himself, praising Atkinson for finally taking up a sustained debate with his theoretical position, before, of course, highlighting the inaccuracies in Atkinson's reading. For Atkinson (2007b), a fundamental weakness in Beck's thesis is that Beck is often unclear and contradictory in the definition of individualization and lacks clarity on the definition of operationalization. The issue with Beck's contradictory comments is specifically concerned with the level of agency; Atkinson points out that Beck talks of re-embedding and dis-embedding. This comment suggests very different levels of structure, where an agent either breaks with previous structures but then folds back into a social system, albeit altered, while the other denotes a permanent departure from structure to a state of individualization.

The second key issue with Beck's model that Atkinson highlights is the account of the genesis of individualization. A central institution in engendering the dis-embedding of previous social structures like class is the wealth of social provision provided by Western welfare societies, such as access to education, providing individuals with certain choices. The form and level of reflexivity an individual may demonstrate is based on the duration and composition of one's education. The educational resources afforded to provide reflexivity may only be applicable or available to the few, the 'resource rich'. This process would, then, alter the concept of individualized reflexivity to a pre-reflexive disposition on the dominant to make choices and choose paths to maintain their social position. In a similar vein, the other key process leading to reflexive modernity, global risk, is also dependent on resources. Beck's position on the transcendence of structures via global risks also does not consider the role of resources, access to specialists, medicines and the ability to leave an area immediately threatened by a global risk are all founded on resources. Beck's account fails to resolve the contradiction between the process of measures that engender individualization and access to these processes being largely based on resources.

Beck's reflexivity is a form of action available to and performed by the few; the few are demarcated in terms of class. Ball *et al.* (2000) and Reay (2000) are highly critical of what they term Beck's 'triumph of individualisation', as it creates the idea of free agents and then blames them for their choices – choices that many would argue they are not free to make. There have been increases in life chances, synonymous with Zweig's (1961) *Embourgeoisement* thesis, and we have witnessed the development of global risks that now threaten everyone. In the rush to account for contemporary society, characterized by a multifaceted nature, late modernity fails to acknowledge the significance of social structures. There is the danger that we will leave the concept of previous structures behind but, in fact, still carry that particular baggage.

Morphogenetic society: meta-reflexives

In previous work from Atkinson (2010a), Margaret Archer has been drafted into late modernity, in the redubbed 'reflexive school', to provide a neat reading of her position as complementary to that of Beck *et al.*[10] In one sense, she is a logical addition to the group; however, it needs to be highlighted from the outset that Archer is not a late modern theorist. Her specific brand of critical realism sees itself as a departure from the concept (Archer, 2013). Rather, Archer's project, similar to that of late modernity, is to examine post-industrial society, the collapse of traditional structures and the consequences for individuals, in particular, the heightened role of agency.

Within the structure/agency debate, Archer charged previous positions of having reduced one over the other or confusing both elements, labelling these positions as downward conflation, upward conflation and central conflation.[11] In an attempt to distance herself from previous models and, according to her, crimes of conflation, Archer defines her position as 'centrism' (1996: 80), accepting that individuals shape structure/culture while being affected by that structure/culture in a relationship that does not conflate either side. To achieve this most coveted site, Archer developed the concept of morphogenesis, based firmly on the notion of interconnectedness – neither can survive without the other. Archer's morphogenetic model operates through a three tiered process: the structural and/or cultural system influences the action of the socio-cultural system; there are relationships between individuals and groups within the socio-cultural system; these relationships affect or elaborate on the structural and/or cultural system.

For Archer, a unified or centralist theory approach to the relationship between structure and agency provides a more appropriate and useful view on the role and influence of each. In order to appreciate social change via the morphogenetic process, Porpora (2013) suggests we should consider the cause and effect – and everything in between – of developments such as the Internet. It was made by individuals, providing a new form of cultural conditioning and leading to new and different forms of interaction that altered (elaborated) that culture. These changes can be seen in how we order food, watch television, connect with friends/family and spend our free time.

Reflexivity is a crucial element to Archer's morphogenesis model, as Steve Fleetwood comments, 'in short, *reflexive deliberation, via the internal conversation, is the mechanism linking structure to agency*' (2008: 184, emphasis in original). In a trio of publications – *Structure, Agency and the Internal Conversation* (2003), *Making Our Way Through the World* (2007) and *The Reflexive Imperative in Late Modernity* (2012) – Archer creates three ideal types of reflexives; *communicative, autonomous* and *meta-reflexive*, through which internal conversations are acted. For Archer, the form of internal conversation in which we partake – the type of reflexive we are – is quite subjective; it is 'to have a particular life of the mind, which thinks about the self in relation to society and vice versa in a particular way' (2007: 100).

To briefly summarise, communicative reflexives are those whose thoughts are worked through and completed via external conversations with other people, their confidants. They tend to reduce their aspirations and accept a static trajectory of social immobility through external conversation. In contrast to the communicative reflexive is an autonomous reflexive, one whose important conversations are entirely self-contained and is able to reflect on situations and actions and come to conclusions – as the name would suggest – autonomously. The autonomous reflexives in Archer's study are commonly thought to be upwardly mobile. Meta-reflexives are understood to essentially reflect on reflections and 'internal conversations'. A key difference between the autonomous reflexive and the meta-reflexive is that the former is task-oriented while the latter is value-oriented. Meta-reflexives, Archer continues, are concerned with issues of morality, and, while autonomous reflexives, as people of action, take responsibilities for their actions, meta-reflexives take responsibility for their differing levels of action and inaction. It is through the ability to be reflexive that social and cultural interaction and elaboration can take place. Reflexivity is the heuristic device Archer employs to account for agency within society; crucially, the 'greater' the form of reflexive, the greater the level of agency. According to Archer, we all have elements of the three ideal types of reflexives – it is the dominant strand that defines us.

Important to Archer's overall project is the contention that communicative reflexives, understood to be most likely to reproduce relations, are declining in the face of increasing levels of both autonomous and meta-reflexives, pointing to a future characterized by increased social mobility. In the concluding book of Archer's reflexivity trilogy (2012), she posits that this trend is creating the conditions required for a morphogenetic society. Archer argues that, contrary to previous historical periods, we are now in a situation where 'structure and culture have come into *synergy* with one another with far reaching morphogenetic consequences' (2013: 13, emphasis in original). In effect, what Archer is saying is that, in previous periods, structure worked above culture, resulting in morphostasis or 'cultural/social maintenance', but, since roughly the 1980s, culture and structure are coming together through the conditions of late modernity, globalization and increased welfare, engendering morphogenesis. To take one example in more detail, a great deal of one's identity is born through the nation state; for many, nationality is a central element of defining who you are. Within the context of post-industrialization, we have witnessed an increase in migratory patterns where individuals do not stay in one place but increasingly become 'global citizens'. For Archer, removing a central component of identity formation leads to the establishment of a more malleable process of identity formation. At this stage, Archer is careful to produce her thesis as a question of whether we have reached this period, but it is also clear that it is the end goal.

For Archer (2013), the progression into a symbiotic relationship between structure/culture and agency is not as a result of entering the liquid phase of modernity but, rather, through the generative consequences of increased variety operating through a non-protectionist narrative. As various phenomena are introduced to the cultural/social system, there are increased opportunities for new and radical connections to be made, replacing previous conditions and/or creating new ones. The emergence of a morphogenetic society will be demonstrated through the reduction and collapse of previous institutions/structures, pointing to an adequate level and speed of social change. These include the reduction/loss of inter-generation continuity, routine practices, social classes, cultural capital and governing bodies defined by geographical locations.

Archer's model can be critiqued on three counts: role of agency, conditions for morphogenetic society and the continuing role of 'traditionally structured' institutions. Considering the tri-part system of morphogenesis (conditioning, interaction and elaboration), it appears that the real influence over the process occurs during the interaction stage, the portion of the model where agency/the individual takes the lead. My critique is shared by Zeuner (1999), who also charges Archer with placing too much emphasis on the socio-cultural stage, or interaction stage. A caveat or reaction to this critique could be that the result of morphogenesis could be to 'modify or sustain' (Porpora, 2013: 28); however, the decision of the outcome appears to be very much concluded within the socio-cultural phase. As such, Archer accords too much influence to agency within her model of practice. To use her own terminology, she is guilty of upward conflation.

In a similar vein to the critique offered against Beck, the conditions Archer understands are facilitating the development of a morphogenetic society and those that demonstrate its establishment have not taken place or still carry with it elements of modernity. Take the example of globalization: there has been a development of a global identity; this shift has not spelled the end of the nation state and role of nationality in identity formation. Again, similar to the critique against Beck and related to the conditions for a morphogenetic society, Archer accounts for the increased numbers of autonomous and meta-reflexives – for which we can read increased reflexivity – through increased globalization and the access to higher education – a feature of an established welfare society. Both of these movements, however, are subject to resources. A thorough 'experience' of globalization – certainly the form to which Archer alludes, constant migration and globetrotting – are dependent on resources, an observation that is clearly overlooked in her model. Archer is correct is arguing that there has been a breakdown in national borders, the most significant of which is the collapse of the Soviet Union and the establishment of the European Union, which not only opened up trade but also unfettered migration. The majority of a population, however, does not continually change their geographical or national position; global citizenship is often open only to the elite. Our lives have been influenced by other national cultures through advances in travel and communications, but national identity still stands. Indeed, while the European Union shows a move toward a European identity, one need look no further than the most recent European Union (2014) elections to appreciate the prevalence of national identity across Europe. Additionally, the educational system, a traditionally structured (classed) institution, is central to not only the establishment of morphogenetic conditions but also the establishment of both autonomous and meta-reflexives (Archer, 2007: 97). Again, in parallel to Beck's key fault, Archer has produced a model where reflexivity, following the logic of morphogenesis, the ability to change the cultural and structural system, is based on resources, which are not evenly available to all.

Hybrid models: mundane reflexivity, mundane consciousness and the reflexive habitus

Many of the critiques levelled at both Beck and Archer have focused on the continuing presence and influence of class and structural inequalities, suggesting the continuing relevance of a Bourdieusian position. Adams argues that authors such as Beck do not realize that 'the concepts of reflexivity, rationality, and other Enlightenment terms, are ways of "embedding" the individual in a particular cultural framework' (2003: 226). Nevertheless, the issue remains that Bourdieu was unclear about what exactly consciousness *is* and *how* it works within his model.

Over the past few years, there have been attempts to 'hybridize' the habitus with reflexivity (Adams, 2006; Elder-Vass, 2007), while preserving the richness of Bourdieu's social theory. Adams (2006) develops Bourdieu's (1992b) comment that, in times of crisis, the habitus may take a rational form. Drawing on work by McNay, Adkins and Sweetman, he questions whether, as a result of the emergence of late modernity, these crises may be becoming more common. Through the increasing prevalence of crises, there will be greater social and cultural change and, as such, the environment that influences the habitus to become reflexive will 'seep' into the habitus. The habitus still retains its central facets and processes, but now reflexivity is understood as a disposition within it. Adams suggests that the relationship between reflexivity and habitus is one where reflexivity may be generating choices and a change in practice. The resources required, however, to realize these practices and to translate new ways of thinking are still based in the habitus; as such, reflexivity will only ever be partly realized.

Two more developed and certainly convincing attempts to overtly account for the role of consciousness within the habitus model come from Sayer (2005) and Atkinson (2010a, 2010b). Sayer (2005) argues that class affects not only our ability to partake in certain actions or our distance from resources but also how we view other people and, in turn, how we view ourselves; as social actors, we are always evaluating and are, therefore, conscious of ourselves. For Sayer, class goes beyond simple distribution of wealth or material possessions and, instead, covers such things as evaluations as to what a good lifestyle is and what kind of person you should aspire to be. While it is easier to accept the social norms of the society and avoid the – at times – painful consequences of challenging social norms and hierarchies, the influence or inspiration for such resilience can stem from reflective morality. At times, our moral consciousness will be in conflict with the class system based on inequality.

For Sayer, the habitus assumes a social actor's compliance. As such, resistance to this influence is understood to occur only in special or specific situations. Sayer maintains that we must adapt the concept of habitus, particularly with regard to its normative orientation; this comment is in a bid to demonstrate how resistance can be central to the creation and formation of the habitus. Individuals may be able to 'consciously override' (2005: 23) the influence of the habitus. If we fail to appreciate it, then, according to Sayer, we are lost to determinism. While behaviour and action do involve habit, they also involve understanding and evaluation. To illustrate this point of habit and cognition, Sayer comments that, while we stop at a red traffic light because we are socialized to stop, we also understand why.

To distance himself from previous late modern models, Sayer adopts the term 'mundane reflexivity' to discuss individuals' understandings of their everyday lives – the how and why we do things. He argues that, while it is dangerous to assume that a lay person possesses the same level of reflexivity as that of a social scientist,[12] it is also deterministic to assume that they have none. Adopting Archer's (2003) internal conversations, he explains how his mundane reflexivity is realized or generated. It is not only possible for an individual to reflect on their position but also to attempt to change it. This shift, according to Sayer, is evident in Bourdieu *et al.*'s *The Weight of the World* (1993/1999) with regard to the case study of the young French Algerian woman discussed by Sayad (*ibid.*: 580–589). The young woman in question manages to break free of her patriarchal family and *create* a new life for herself; for Sayer, it is an example of how reflexivity can overcome the habitus.

Sayer is careful to place his comments on the resources and tactics of resistance supplied by moral dispositions within a Bourdieusian model that appreciates the influence of structure, acknowledging that the process of lay reflexivity may be overrun by 'other obstacles or forces' (2005: 29). He tempers this argument by commenting that the fact that individuals attempt to break out of their constraints shows they are reflexive. For Sayer, there is no need to abandon the habitus, seeing it as the only concept that allows us to understand the structure of dispositions while appreciating their generative power. He proposes, however, that we supplement the concept through a 'recognition of the close relationships between dispositions and conscious deliberation, the powers of agency and mundane reflexivity, and by addressing actors' normative orientations, emotions and commitments' (*ibid.*: 50–51).

An appreciation of mundane reflexivity and conscious action as created through resistance, emotions and ethical dispositions is Sayer's attempt to add a more conscious element to Bourdieu's habitus model. The ethical dimension of the habitus is created, he concludes, by socialization. How it is expressed, however, cannot be explained or reduced to interests. The ethical actions of an individual are not always self-serving; they can be for the welfare of another or a group of individuals. Ethical dispositions will vary by social position, but they will also cut across them.

Similarly, for Atkinson (2010a), the undeveloped or un-theorised habitus is not open to reflexivity or consciousness. It understands action to be based on unconscious or pre-reflexive dispositions leading to an understanding of objective possibilities, generated from their position in the social space, 'captured in the phrase "that's not for the likes of us", to refuse what they are refused in reality anyway' (*ibid.*: 50–51). Contrary to how Bourdieu is typically received, Atkinson (2010b) comments that rational action or reflexive practice is actually, albeit subtlety, at the centre of Bourdieu's project. For Bourdieu, Atkinson argues, the level of rational action is based on an individual's habitus and position within social space. The generative character of the habitus creates or generates both more automatic forms of practice but also 'intentional actions' (*ibid.*: 12). In a bid to separate this position from social theorists who understand reflexivity to be created *ex nihilo*, Atkinson adapts Sayer's (2005) 'mundane reflexivity' to 'mundane consciousness' – the everyday consciousness and thought patterns influenced and generated by the habitus.

According to Atkinson, it was the result of a lack of clarity that Bourdieu did not fully expand his position on intentional thought, rather more often discussing logic of practice and structure over our agency. He suggests, however, that Schutz's 'subjective stocks of knowledge' can help to illuminate the reflexive or conscious character of the habitus (2010b). For Atkinson, there are certain crossovers between the habitus and stocks of knowledge: they both represent our means to understanding the social world and products of past experiences. The crucial difference between the two is that stocks of knowledge are what Atkinson describes as 'multi-layered'; in effect, they have levels of knowledge created by past experiences but also a conscious layer. Through repetition of actions, however, these conscious practices appear to be second nature, releasing the need to discuss or consider them while retaining the influence of thought. Atkinson maintains that the habitus is still a central component of action, but it is infused at this point with stocks of knowledge. Applying his model, an individual's field of the possibles – essentially, what they think they can do and the choices which are open to them in an everyday or mundane sense – demonstrates both intention and consciousness. Where the model differs from Beck or Archer is that the individual's reflexivity is structured by the habitus.

There are certain issues surrounding both Sayer and Atkinson's contributions; difficulties arise when the authors attempt to implement their models in practice. Sayer's account provides agency with too much influence over the structure and the habitus. His model is based on a discussion of the life history of a young French Algerian woman 'Farida' (2005: 30). She retells stories from her childhood, living in a strict, patriarchal Muslim household. She explains the events that led her to leave her family home and compares her life now with her old family life; it appears as if she has completely reinvented herself. This story, Sayer argues, demonstrates the power of the mind over the habitus. It is important, however, to note that Farida did not make the break from her family life unaided (Sayad, 1993/1999). She explains that the catalyst for her exodus came from her cousin insisting that she come to stay with her in her home for a few days. It was only when her cousin had removed her from this environment was she able not to go back. Second, Farida has seemingly changed her identity; she tells of having to relearn social conventions. This effort is quite Bourdieusian in itself: the habitus is open to change in the context of environmental change. The events that led Farida to leave her family home were not entirely of her own making, and her ability to change her identity was based on specific necessity; therefore, it is not appropriate to build a general model from her life history in the way that Sayer does, as he fails to acknowledge the significance of social structures.

Regardless of my reservations, these authors highlight the need to appreciate consciousness within a Bourdieusian model. This call has been reinforced or strengthened by the recent translation of Bernard Lahire's (2011) *The Plural Actor*, which suggests that, while the rationale behind the habitus was to bridge the divide between practical and symbolic mastery, the habitus is too often understood to operate exclusively through practical mastery and structural influence. Lahire argues that, as in times of crisis, the habitus can become rational. There must be a conscious stream within the habitus; if the habitus cannot accommodate it, then it means that not all action can be accounted for by Bourdieu's model. Lahire reiterates the need for a form of compromise to include reflexivity. Otherwise, in the context of a continued call and need for an account of the conscious individual, 'the tool [habitus] ends up breaking' (*ibid.*: 147).

Rushing the net: developing the concept of reflective strategy

Bourdieu (1980/1990), in an effort to illustrate his point with regard to practical mastery or the feel for the game, offers examples such as tennis and chess, where success or failure is reliant on our feel for the game, as sports characterized by speed do not provide an opportunity or time for reflexivity. The analogy of tennis is a commonly used example (Sayer, 2005; Atkinson 2010a; Lahire, 2011) to develop concepts of consciousness. The central argument of each author is that, while hitting the ball at the right speed at the perfect angle is almost automatic or 'natural', a great deal of *conscious* effort went into conditioning the body to produce this skill. Noble and Watkins (2003), adopting the term 'ordinary consciousness' or 'ordinary reflection', offer a more developed position with regard to the sporting analogy through adopting a sports science model of 'levels of awareness'. Such ordinary reflections are not critical or reflexive, they do not engage with issues of social location and power struggles. Instead, they are concerned about what an agent has done and is able to do; 'they are about putting daily conduct into discourse' (*ibid.*: 531). For Noble and Watkins, Bourdieu's position (those who have a feel for the game do not need to objectively create their strategy as it is essentially *part* of them) is quite limited. They argue that levels of awareness, ordinary reflection, can be seen in pre-determined strategies and an appreciation of the game that has just been played. Athletes require a goal, an ideal toward which to work. While these goals are embodied to the extent that, during a game or a match, they become almost automatic, the authors remind us that they are based on a conscious plan fostered through reflection.

Noble and Watkins' comment on the role of consciousness within sport form the basis of my own theoretical development with regard to consciousness and action. In a sense, for Bourdieu, all practice can be understood as strategic practice, with some strategies better or more effective than others. To be clear, Bourdieu was cautious not to conflate the common-sense term 'strategy' with his specific conceptual tool (1989/1996, 1997/2000). Rather, he understood the conceptual form of strategy to be 'objectively orientated "lines of actions" that obey regularities and form coherent and socially intelligible patterns' (Wacquant, 1992b: 25). Within Bourdieu's model of structure and agency, strategy should be understood as neither objective nor subjective, as 'one can refuse to see strategy as the product of an unconscious program without making it the product of a conscious and rational calculation' (Lamaison, 1986: 112). The unconscious element of strategic action, the practical mastery or feel for the game, belongs to the habitus; however, the (mundane/ordinary) conscious element, also bound to the habitus is, to an extent, generative and creative. Individuals do play an active role in their action, though it will be founded by certain attitudes and dispositions from their habitus. As the habitus determines them and they determine their action, Reay comments, 'choices are bounded by the framework of opportunities and constraints the person finds himself/herself in, her external circumstances' (2004b: 435). This concept is what Bourdieu means when he defines the habitus as 'the unchosen principle of all "choices"' (1992b: 137); however, he argues that this position only appears deterministic from a superficial understanding of the habitus. He writes that, 'failing an analysis of such subtle determinations that work themselves out through dispositions, one becomes accessory to the unconscious of the action of dispositions, which is itself the accomplice of determinism' (*ibid.*).

It is within a model that appreciates the continuing influence of the habitus with regard to consciousness that I place my own understanding. The mundane reflexivity, fostered through internal conversations, suggested by Sayer (2005) is not influential enough to *break* the habitus in the manner that Sayer proposes it can. It is the habitus 'blip' (Bourdieu, 1997/2000) or the crisis that causes rationality (Bourdieu, 1992b), that explains these findings. When forced to be reflexive, we can be. I am reminded of Samuel Beckett's comment that he would often write in French and then translate back into English, as writing in his second rather than native language required him to think. I find my own model closer to Atkinson's (2010b) in the sense that I wish to understand the role of the mind or the individual's subjectivity within the habitus. I join Atkinson in attempting to move away from the term 'reflexivity', even in its mundane form. I find Noble and Watkins' (2003) ordinary consciousness or ordinary reflection more useful than Atkinson's mundane consciousness.

My understanding and application of reflection is that it is comprised of two central parts: an individual understanding what they have done and how they have done it *and* understanding what they are capable of doing in the future. An individual who objectively understands what they have done points to a certain level of symbolic mastery, while understanding what they are capable of demonstrates their subjective expectations. Where my own and Atkinson's model truly part ways is in our position toward the habitus. Atkinson fuses the habitus with Schutz's stocks of knowledge in an attempt to escape the charge of structural determinism. I would argue that Reay's (2004b) permeable habitus model provides sufficient opportunity to escape this charge. Ordinary reflection is bound to the habitus; as the habitus changes through change in environment and experiences, so, too, does the level of reflection. The permeable habitus allows it to happen over time rather than being based on an arbitrary crisis that may engender a level of rationality.

My own understanding of the place of reflexivity within Bourdieu's theory of practice is that it simply does not have one. This statement does not mean that reflexivity is absent from Bourdieu's social theory; there is reflexivity within the (theory of) practice of sociology (Bourdieu *et al.*, 1968/1991; Bourdieu, 1992b; Deer, 2008). This epistemic reflexivity allows us to break from common sense and critically examine social relations and processes. The problem is that Beck and Archer place this form of epistemic reflexivity into everyday (lay) society, creating the illusion of '*homo calculans*' (Bourdieu, 2002: 32), without appreciating that a critical and total understanding of *your own* life course, including a combination of the subtle processes and influences out of your control, is an untenable goal. Individuals do not choose their lifestyles as Beck (1992) asserts but, rather, have a larger selection from which to choose based on their resources. Instead, ordinary reflection is founded through the habitus, allowing the habitus to 'work' on itself (Noble and Watkins, 2003) while appreciating the structural constraints on agency. If we return to Bourdieu's schema of practice, [(habitus) (capital)] + field = practice, we can read practice as strategic action, comprised of both practical mastery and symbolic mastery, demonstrating both the unchosen and chosen principles of choice as being generated by Bourdieu's conceptual tools. Times of crisis may carry a more reflexive character of the habitus; however, change or progression of ordinary consciousness/reflection will more commonly be influenced through a changing habitus via a permeable understanding of the concept.

Empirical considerations of the habitus: from paper to people

The final portion of this chapter will explain my empirical approach to locating and tracking Bourdieu's logic of practice. It is all very interesting to provide a discussion on social theory and various positions on reflexivity, etc., but, unless one can empirically record and then demonstrate the relationship between structure and agency, they remain just that: discussions. As such, I will offer some remarks on the importance and need for a working relationship between empirical research and social theory within social research. Then I will discuss the empirical qualities of the habitus and what I was generally looking for in order to track its influence. Finally, I will discuss the empirical process used in order to observe, track and report on the role of habitus.

Theory and empiricism: a match made somewhere . . .

A key issue for social researchers is that, while they are interested in studying and understanding the social world, they are also social actors, existing within that social world (Hammersley, 2000). As such, they have been socialized to accept certain cultural practices and beliefs forming a 'common-sense' understanding. Bourdieu *et al.* (1968/1991) caution their readers against the dangers of being too comfortable in the social context that they are researching. A tacit understanding of a research environment, while helpful, is often an obstacle a researcher must overcome. To counter this obstacle, Bourdieu *et al.* comment that an epistemological break with preconceptions or common sense is necessary for effective research.[13] Common sense is so deeply embedded within our pre-reflexive understanding that, in order to create a *break* with our most tacit and trusted preconceptions, we must quite literally force ourselves to be objective. The application of a critically theoretical approach can aid researchers in creating such an epistemological break.

With this acceptance of the role of theory within research, we, as researchers, *now* need to protect our analysis from any theoretical bias. The epistemological break is intended to safeguard against common sense. Bourdieu (1992a), however, warns his readers of the 'double bind', where a researcher applies social theory to create an epistemological break only to replace common sense with 'learned' common sense. In other words, if you apply Karl Marx to critically understand society, you will inevitably only understand society through Karl Marx. Empirical research, when applied with theory, can provide the tools to foster a 'radical doubt' and create a break with 'learned' common sense. The interpenetrative relationship creates an opportunity for theory and empiricism to not merely complement each other but to *question* each other, fostering an environment for epistemic reflexivity. This approach provides theory with a role in the empirical process, both in data collection and analysis, but also creates an environment to present findings that will force us to, if not re-evaluate, certainly question our theoretical position.

Habitus: empirical appearances and opportunities

Accepting the role of social theory within the empirical process and appreciating the relationship between theory and method as interpenetrative helps us to realize the strength and application of the habitus as an empirical tool. Once again, adopting Reay's concept of a 'permeable habitus' can further increase the opportunity for its empirical application. Reay (2004b) comments that Bourdieu intended the habitus to be employed in an empirical context much like it would theoretically – as a heuristic device used to account for and understand both structure and agency. Just as structure and agency inform each other, so, too, do theory and research. Meeting the epistemological challenge as set by Bourdieu and appreciating the habitus is a complicated task, as dispositions, values and norms are often so tacit they go unnoticed; they are, therefore, difficult to observe and measure, as is the ever-changing and interpenetrative relationship between the individual and society. Bourdieu (1986/1987) suggests that one approach is to seek out and focus on beliefs and behaviours that are constantly repeated.

At this juncture, there is a danger of focusing only on observable actions and, once again, falling into the trap of structural determinism. As I have previously discussed, practice, bound to habitus, is both practical mastery and symbolic mastery that takes the form of ordinary reflection, engendering an understanding of not only why and how an individual did something but also what they are capable of in the future. As such, ordinary reflection is the narrative signifier of the level of symbolic mastery an individual is able to apply to a situation. In addition to recording levels of repetition and their outcomes denoting various levels of practical mastery, one also needs to record levels of symbolic mastery to have a clear appreciation of the habitus' influence. Symbolic mastery can be recorded through observing levels of ordinary reflection; these levels can be measured through the relational depth of understanding an individual offers to account for previous actions and future plans.

Biographical research: unearthing the habitus

A longitudinal study would be the preferred approach to observe levels of repetition and ordinary reflection. Constraints on both my time and research budget, however, like many social researchers, necessitated me to adopt an alternative form of data collection that still provided the rich and nuanced data required. As I have argued elsewhere (Burke, 2011), the BNIM provided such an opportunity.

Biographical research is a well-established tool within social research with a number of sub-fields;[14] however, it is the specific mechanics of the BNIM (Schütze, 1992, 2008; Rosenthal, 2003; 2005) that provides an opportunity to observe both practical and symbolic mastery in a (epistemic) reflexive manner. Rosenthal (2005) provides a brief but comprehensive guide to the working of a 'traditional' BNIM interview. The interview is comprised of three parts, often referred to as sub-sessions; in the first of these interviews, respondents are asked to 'tell their life story', at which point the interviewer is instructed to offer no stimuli (verbal or physical) to interfere or interrupt the respondent's main narration. The second interview is very much focused on the main narration, and interviewers are allowed to only ask for more information or clarification on something mentioned by the respondent. Finally, the third interview can be much more akin to a semi-structured interview where the interviewer can ask questions based on previous responses or literature/theory that informed the research. Approaching this form of data collection from a theoretical position – what Miller (2000) refers to as a neo-positivist BNIM interview – does two things. It first allows a researcher to form a theoretically influenced research question but forces them to 'sit on their hands' and allow empirical findings to question, dis/confirm or alter their position, providing the break with common and learned common sense. Second, the BNIM essentially acts as an ethnographic interview, providing extremely rich data that creates the opportunity to mark and trace a repetition of actions/beliefs, but the passive nature of the interview also allows the researcher to record levels of symbolic mastery and reflection.

Conclusion

This chapter has offered a discussion of Bourdieu's thinking tools and, more importantly, an account of how they were used to think with in relation to this specific research. Choice – the role of agent – is a fundamental issue within sociology and has been a constant issue with which theorists and researchers have wrestled. In the context of post-industrialization and an increased sense of individualization, there is the danger that a common-sense understanding of the individual, to borrow a phrase from Archer, 'making their way through the world', will prevail without a clear appreciation for the continuing role of social structures – in particular social class. I have presented my own position with regard to choice or reflexivity, essentially arguing that a much more appropriate term, from Noble and Watkins, is ordinary reflection. Reflection is comprised of an understanding of previous actions and an appreciation of required subsequent actions. It is the cognitive process involved in playing the game, similar to practical mastery; this symbolic mastery is bound to habitus and capital and reacts within a certain field. This model provides space for social structures, access to recourses, to influence the choices that people make and shares a number of features with Beck and Archer's models, i.e. based on resources, despite their best efforts to move beyond traditional structures.

This chapter has deliberately offered a discussion of Bourdieu's thinking tools and different positions concerning choice in a largely abstract context. The next chapter will focus specifically on the opportunity for and level of choices available for individuals within higher education and the graduate labour market. By examining competing discourses around the mobilizing effects of education, central to Beck and Archer's theses, it will consider the application of Bourdieusian social theory to illuminate the two fields of interest to this research.

Notes

1 For a comprehensive introduction and elaborated glossary, see Webb *et al.* (2002) and Grenfell's edited work, *Pierre Bourdieu: Key Concepts* (2008).
2 Reay (2004b) offers an account of the troubling increased application of habitus in social research without much thought for the theory.
3 For a 'history of the habitus', see Nash (1999) and Maton (2008)
4 Parsons (1966) comments that the changing patterns or the evolution of structural norms can only take place on a grand scale.

5 Cultural capital can be further appreciated as three distinct forms: *embodied* – which Bourdieu explains as 'long-lasting dispositions of the mind and body'; *objectified* – which is understood 'in the form of cultural goods (pictures, books, dictionaries, instruments, machines, etc.)'; and *institutionalised* – 'a form of objectification [. . . that] confers entirely original properties on the cultural capital which it is presumed to guarantee' (1983/2004).
6 It is not the purpose of this chapter, or anywhere in this book, to provide a history of class analysis. For those interested in such discussions, see Savage's (2000) work.
7 Elite, established middle class, technical middle class, new affluent workers, traditional working class, emergent service worker and precariat.
8 Bourdieu's first use of the term 'field' was in 1966's *Champ Intellectual et Projet Creater*, and, as his career progressed, the concept became increasingly central to his research. It was translated into English as 'Intellectual Field and Creative Project' (1966/1971a).
9 For a thorough critical reading and examination of Bauman and Giddens, please see Atkinson's (2007a, 2008) articles.
10 Curiously, Atkinson, before solidifying his position in class, *Individualisation and Late Modernity: In Search of the Reflexive Worker* (2010a), provided a thorough and critical account of each of his 'Reflexive School' authors, with the exception of Archer. This is a common occurrence within British sociology – there is much more focus on Beck, Bauman and Giddens to the detriment of Archer. As a social theorist providing critical insight into the composition for society for over 35 years, Archer certainly deserves to be considered alongside these authors.
11 Downward conflation is when the action is an afterthought to structure. Contrastingly, upwards conflation is when action is placed above the structure, and central conflation is where structure and agency are combined in a manner which renders both useless as they essentially cancel each other out.
12 Indeed it is dangerous to assume a social scientist possesses an equal level of reflexivity in their 'lay' life as they do in the field.
13 There are quite clear parallels between Bourdieu *et al.*'s position and that of Durkheim's. In *The Rules of Sociological Method*, Durkheim's first principle rule for the observation of social facts is 'one must systematically discard all preconceptions' (1893/1982: 72). The parallels and, indeed, influence of Durkheim becomes more apparent as Bourdieu *et al.* (1968/1991: 93–96) use this very principle to demonstrate the need for such a break.
14 Miller (2000) and Merrill and West (2009) offer a chronological account of its progression.

Chapter 2

Setting the scene

Introduction

This chapter will provide the social and cultural setting in which this research took place. Here I propose that graduate employment research should be understood as a sub-area of educational research; graduate employment is understood as the marker of a successful university graduate. As such, this chapter is divided into two sub-sections. The first provides an analysis of previous educational research, proposing either a human capital or social closure position. As the bulk of sociological research is critical toward meritocratic discourse, often located within government policy, the focus of this sub-section is on educational research that has demonstrated the classed nature of access and experience of higher education through Bourdieusian social theory. The second sub-section is an examination of previous research concerning graduate employment, providing a discussion of the current composition of the graduate labour market. Looking at both large-scale quantitative research projects and smaller qualitative studies, this section, similar to its predecessor, considers previous studies that advocate either a human capital or social closure position when examining the classed nature of graduate employment trajectories. The chapter concludes with a discussion on the break between higher educational research demonstrating the role of social class and its empirical counterpart, applying similar arguments to graduate employment trajectories. It will offer some suggestions on how to fully equip graduate employment research with the same critical gaze toward education's mobilizing effects that has characterized educational research within many post-industrial societies. The chapter, however, begins with an examination of Bourdieu's position on the socially reproductive nature of the education system before considering how his conceptual tools have shaped a large section of the sociology of education.

Bourdieu and the education system

Within Bourdieu's theoretical model, where dispositions, provided by the habitus, operate or arbitrate between structures and practices, it is crucial to understand how these structures produce or influence the production of agents that are pre-disposed to practices that will reproduce these structures. The sociology of education, and specifically the sociology of higher education, can make a substantial contribution to this understanding (Bourdieu, 1973). As Robbins (1998) reminds us, Bourdieu did not purport that the education system creates privilege; rather, it works with or against practical mastery, the 'feel for the game', and it works with the habitus. The education system fosters both social and cultural reproduction, but it does not create it.

For Bourdieu (1967/1971b), scholarly institutions transmit forms of thought, expressed and understood on different levels of consciousness; therefore, the sociology of the institutional transmission on culture is a central facet to the sociology of knowledge. In other words, if forms of thought are transmitted by educational institutions, then, to understand knowledge, we must look to these institutions. Building on the work of Panofsky, Bourdieu understood the education system as a 'habit-forming force' (*ibid.*: 194). The school system, whether an individual has had direct or indirect contact with it, will influence our dispositions or master patterns that will, in part, direct how we interpret and act in cultural situations; the education system (in)forms the habitus. In time, these master patterns become 'second nature' or unconscious; the thinker owes these unconscious generative patterns to their education. It is these unconscious interpretations and approaches to cultural situations, influenced and reinforced by the education system that, in part, allocates position in social space or membership of a certain group.[1] To temper this position, Bourdieu was sensitive to not reify the educational system but was conscious to give the education system the attention and premise it deserves, understanding its role in shaping culture.

Bourdieu's first significant empirical study in education came with Jean-Claude Passeron in the publication of *The Inheritors* (1964/1979).[2] The central interest of this study was the classed nature of participation in higher education. The crux of their argument was that economic dis/advantage was not enough to explain what they call 'educational death rates'; rather, differences in attitudes and ability in higher education can be explained or traced by social background.

The classed disparity in participation was seen to be directed by the family. The child of a professional will understand entry into university as being normal or part of their destiny, as they have been raised in an environment where a university education was commonplace within their family. This attitude is in contrast to the industrial worker's child who is forced to get 'second-hand information'. Students from middle-class or professional families will feel more comfortable within the educational setting. Comfort or anxiety within higher education and the ability to effectively understand and act on the connection between certain subjects and occupations is based on an assumption of previous knowledge and cultural practices. The education system rewards students who, due to their middle-class or privileged social background, came to the institution with previous knowledge, thereby reinforcing social inequalities without ever mentioning them. Lower-class students do not possess the same previous knowledge – they have but 'scholastic culture' (Bourdieu and Passeron, 1964/1979: 19) – in the sense that all their knowledge and all their capital is created by the educational system itself. Teachers were seen as the primary source of information for working-class children, whereas their middle-class counterparts often called on the experiences of their family to plan their own educational trajectories.

The Inheritors concludes with a call to arms; Bourdieu and Passeron saw that turning a blind eye to social inequalities within education requires and, thus, allows the inequalities within education to be explained as natural differences in ability. It is this discourse of natural ability that allows the educational system to appear to treat every student like equals when, really, only certain social groups who share the same culture as the educational system will do well within its walls. The solution, however, can be found within the educational system; Bourdieu and Passeron proposed a system that would allow for a hand up for social disadvantage or what they termed 'social handicaps' (1964/1979: 69). Robbins (1993), writing on *The Inheritors*, comments that, for this period in Bourdieu's academic development, the position that the education system could be used to create a fairer or equal system was extremely important. As the system of education in a society is linked to that society's system of thought (Bourdieu, 1967/1971b), it could be the starting point for fostering a more egalitarian society.

Curiously, in the epilogue that follows *The Inheritors*, the tone changes from a hopeful or positive comment on how to engender educational change and, therefore, social change to understanding the education system as 'the bamboozling of a generation' (Bourdieu, 1979: 83).[3] This epilogue does not appear in the original French publication but was added to the 1979 English translation. This swift change in tone demonstrates the progression in Bourdieu's position toward the educational system.[4] It marks a change from Bourdieu's 'Algerian view', where 'radical pedagogy' could alleviate such educational and subsequent social inequality, to a more fatalistic position of social reproduction within the educational system and greater society (Robbins, 1993: 153–154). Bourdieu's two major empirical studies to this effect were *Reproduction* (with Passeron, 1970/1990) and *The State Nobility* (1989/1996).

The bureaucratization of the market brought with it a more (hierarchically) structured and organized division of labour (Bourdieu and Boltanski, 1973/1978). With this introduction of rational structuring and recruiting came an increased focus on qualifications from the more prestigious *grandes écoles*, which were (almost) essential for entering positions of power. The inculcation of capital by the *grandes écoles* essentially replaced the inculcation of the upper-class family in the previous phase; the class position that was once passed down from father to son through inheritance is now transmitted through the school system.

According to Bourdieu and Passeron (1970/1990), the education system is a tool for reproducing social relations. Through processes such as the type of language teachers use and the architectural design of the buildings, the education system expresses and reinforces the cultural values of the dominant social group.[5] Students who possess a similar level of cultural capital, i.e. students from the dominant group, will typically do very well within the education system. Students from the lower classes, however, will not carry a complementary form/level of cultural capital and, therefore, struggle in comparison to their dominant classmates. As a result, working-class students will have reduced and capped levels of aspirations and expectations inculcated via the educational system.

This course of social domination is fostered through the process of symbolic violence, an acceptance that the norms and values of the ruling class are the status quo and, further, that those norms and values are 'not for the likes of them'. Status or social norms of class stratification are transmitted in a school system that is superficially meritocratic. It is, indeed, the meritocratic discourse of the school, through things such as scholarships, that provides symbolic violence with its influence. The power of a system comes from agents not realising they are being oppressed. The educational system can distance itself from the overall power relations and structure, making it look like the school is working in the interests of the pupils and not another field, such as the economic market or politics. It perpetuates this appearance by allowing only a few into the dominant group, placating the larger social group.

For pedagogic action (with pedagogic authority) to work, Bourdieu and Passeron argue there needs to be pedagogic work, which they define as 'a process of inculcation which must last long enough to produce durable training, i.e. habitus, the product of internalization of the principals of a cultural arbitrary' (1970/1990: 31). This event is not a lapse in some schools or an old-fashioned practice, it is an institutionally operated system of oppression that strengthens class divides and lessens the opportunity for social mobility (Collins, 1993). Bourdieu and Passeron propose that the education system's right to transmit what is valid would be questioned if the process of institutionalization had not all but removed dissent within society. There are many institutions in which to transmit symbolic violence; however, second only to the family, the education system 'underlies the structuring of all subsequent experiences' (Bourdieu: 1972/1977:87). As such, pedagogic work is essential to moulding the habitus.

The central role of the sociology of education, as understood by Bourdieu (1973), is to discuss the relationship or process between cultural reproduction and social reproduction. It does this through observing the role of the education system in reproducing the relations of symbolic power between classes by observing its role in reproducing the distribution of cultural capital. Merely allowing everyone access to middle-class institutions, however, will not create mobility or enhance lower classes' cultural capital; individuals must be able to profit from or take advantage of these forms of capital. Simply letting people into the schools is not enough, as the education system reproduces the inequalities that have been created by previous influences on the habitus.

Robbins (1998) comments that Bourdieu's contribution to the sociology of education was intended to make us question our everyday or common-sense understandings about the educational system, forcing researchers to be somewhat pragmatic, not giving in to the hope that we are already free agents.

Social mobility and education: discourses and research

Mobility discourses

The dominant, binary theories concerning the relationship between education and occupations are human capital theory and social closure theory. Human capital theory, which can be accredited to Becker (1964) and Schultz (1971), proposes that, in a knowledge economy, a high educational level, such as a university degree, can be exchanged for higher status jobs and higher salaries. Schultz argues 'knowledge is our most powerful engine of production' (1971: iv), and investment in human capital includes things such as 'schooling and higher education, on-the-job training, migration, health and economic information' (*ibid.*: 8). For Schultz, this point was a crucial development, as he understood economists to have been too prescriptive with the concept of capital goods by failing to see knowledge and practical skills as forms of capital. This position is further illustrated in studies by Blau and Duncan (1967) and Boudon (1974), who suggest that, as entry and participation within higher education rise, social inequality would, proportionately, drop. Human capital theory, founded upon a meritocratic discourse, is the dominant narrative within current UK politics. Recent policies (Cabinet Office, 2009b, Cabinet Office, 2011) clearly demonstrate the understanding that education is the central entry point to social mobility.

Social closure theory – proposed by Collins (1979) and Murphy (1988) and demonstrated through studies by authors such as Halsey *et al.* (1980) – occupies the other side of the binary position. The relationship between credentials and occupations is one built on inequality and exploitation to reproduce or even increase the position of the dominant group in society. The worldview or concept of a meritocratic society is responsible for the creation of rules concerning entry into powerful positions. In the context of graduate inflation, it is social status in addition to credentials that will 'tip one's favour' in the labour market.[6]

It can be dangerous or misleading to adopt a pure form of either of these positions, as the employment market is much more complex than either side is willing or, perhaps, able to appreciate (Tyler, 1977; Payne, 1987; Smetherham, 2006). Human capital theory assumes a functionalist relationship between the education system and the occupational structure; it also assumes that graduates will get jobs, ignoring the supply-and-demand relationship between people and employment. Social closure theory, Smetherham comments (2006), is equally dangerous to accept without question, as it does not discuss the working-class students who 'make it' or other contributing variables, such as gender or race/ethnicity.

Social inequality among school children has been a concern within the UK since before the Second World War. An attempt to address social inequality could be witnessed through the introduction of the 1944 Education Act, crafted in the same philosophy that was to become human capital theory, intended to reduce reproduction of social inequalities through mass inclusion to secondary level education. Social inequality, however, still continued into the latter half of the twentieth century. Foster *et al.* (1996), charting the developments of educational research after the 1944 Education Act, explain that there was an increasing understanding that differences in educational ability can be linked to the family background. This theory demonised the family, claiming that they had not prepared the student for academic success. In reaction to this growing position, a 'new sociology of education' emerged that was primarily concerned with the type of education students received in school and what specific attributes it took to be successful. A key argument from this new school was the knowledge that schools transmit and reward runs in parallel to that of the ruling class; 'schooling came to be seen as involving the imposition of a dominant culture on subordinate groups' (*ibid.*: 11). A truly reflexive sociological gaze was placed on the relations within the educational system, as researchers began to understand that selection based on ability, and selection based on background were interpenetrative.

In the wake of the re-emergence of right-wing politics in the UK, however, educational research discussing social frictions felt by the working classes (Jackson and Marsden, 1966) or educational social inequalities (Hargreaves, 1967) was replaced with a preoccupation toward test scores and academic standards. The sociology of education began to focus less and less on white, working-class boys and, instead, looked at issues concerning ethnic minorities and girls (Foster *et al.*, 1996). The same rhetoric was applied to the study of gender or racial disadvantage, only the subject matter had changed. The shift away from social inequalities also spelled the decline of sociology's influence in the public/policy conscience.

Educational trajectories and the continuing role of class

Despite mass participation within higher education – 47 per cent of 18- to 30-year-olds were in HE in 2011 (Heath *et al.*, 2013) – there has been very little progression in social relations within the educational system, and the reality is that the educational system still serves the interests of the middle classes (Reay, 2004a). The gap between the rich and the poor, or middle class and working class, is understood as an individual's problem, created through either lack of effort or lack of talent. This common-sense understanding, or 'spontaneous sociology' (Bourdieu *et al.*, 1968/1991: 39), of the mobilizing effects of the educational system is a central issue demonstrating the need for the application of social theory in mobility research. Reay *et al.* (2005) add that, while there is a changing or a changed understanding of class identity and, indeed, an agreed complexity that must be addressed, we must not let this distract us from the persisting problem of class inequality within the educational system. This issue is not confined solely to the UK; Gábor (2008), Barone and Schizzerotto (2011) and Mullen (2010) discuss the continuing classed nature – despite educational expansion in light of increased industrialization – of educational trajectories within Europe, North America and parts of Asia, including capitalist and communist countries, suggesting, at the most, a weak level of social mobility.

While the human capital discourse forcefully ran through the veins of the British Parliament, and her subsequently regionally devolved Sisters, social closure theory experienced a clear resurgence in the UK. The form of social closure theory, like many positions in UK sociology stemming from the 1990s onward, was one of nuance and measurement. While its focus was on the socially reproductive element of the British education system, there was an appreciation of greater flexibility and change within the structure (Brooks, 2005). There are clear parallels between the cultural class analysts and this reformed social closure position, with many researchers, such as Diane Reay and Stephen Ball, from one realm occupying the ranks of the other. As such, an adaptation of Bourdieusian social theory has been applied by many of these researchers to examine social class and educational trajectories – more specifically, entrance to higher education and the type of institution attended.

Educational 'choices'

Reay and Lucey (2000, 2004) suggest that the transition from one stage of education to the other is an important but also risky point in a student's life; this risk is only increased for the working-class student. Individuals are relationally positioned to the institutional habitus of their school or college based on the level their family and peers' habitus complement or question that of the institution (Reay *et al.*, 2001). In other words, the ease of transition into the educational system will be influenced by class background and the level to which this complements or questions the norms and values of the educational system. Recent research (Leathwood and Hutchings, 2003; Reay *et al.*, 2005; Sianou-Kyrgiou and Tsiplakides, 2010; Bradley *et al.*, 2013), has examined the role of class in whether a student intends to advance to university and also where they intend to read for their degree. Bradley *et al.* (2013) report that their working-class student sample displayed a strong sense of uncertainty and anxiety with regard to going to university and were seen as perhaps settling for less than they could have achieved, stemming from a cramped field of the possibles. Contrastingly, the middle-class students expected to attend university, as their parents had done before them. There was an understanding and a comfortable feeling that their cultural capital would flourish within the university walls, what Ball *et al.* term, 'social class "in the head"' (2002: 52). Additionally, Reay (2012), comparing research in the late 1990s with current research, found clear parallels in both the classed experience/nature of educational transitions.

A fundamental barrier affecting working-class students' trajectories is economic constraints. Reay *et al.* (2005) report that, for their working-class sample, this barrier was felt in a number of ways; first, students would only choose or consider universities that were geographically near – generally in the same socio-economic area – as they could not afford transport or accommodation. Second, material constraints meant that more working-class students had part-time jobs in their final years at school. Two-thirds of Reay *et al.*'s working-class sample had part-time jobs, which compares to one-third of the middle-class sample. Additionally, Louise Archer (2003b) comments that working-class students are more likely to drop out of university because they are preoccupied with paying back their student loans. In the wake of the recent tuition fee increase, this issue is set to only worsen, as Bradley *et al.* (2013) report on the apprehension of their working-class respondents expressed in relation to increased university tuition fees. Evans (2009) reminds us, however, that financial barriers preventing students from living away from home and attending 'better' universities should not be understood in isolation. She found that working-class students who had opted to live with their parents during university and lived within a reasonable distance to elite Russell Group universities[7] in London still did not consider applying to these institutions.

For Bourdieu, the family is the key player in habitus formation, understanding that it 'underlies the structuring school experience' (1972/1977: 87), placing parents as key actors in forming their children's attitudes toward education. As such, the classed relationship between parents and the educational system is important to appreciate (Ball *et al.*, 1997; Conway, 1997; Lareau, 1997; Reay and Lucey, 2004; Ingram, 2009). Reay and Lucey (2004) argue that understanding structural constraints are crucial to examining parental 'choice'; they suggest that the social exclusion experienced by ethnic minorities and lower classes need to be explained. In terms of secondary level schooling, the middle classes have a greater choice due to their position within the field. The authors report that middle-class families with high levels of economic capital were able to move to more prestigious catchment areas and, therefore, fall within the geographical boundaries in which schools are permitted to select students. In contrast, they found little working-class aspiration to relocate in order to gain access to a more prestigious school; they were concerned with leaving their community behind. For those middle-class families who could not afford to relocate to a more prestigious catchment area, they were more likely than their working-class counterparts to enter their children for the selective school exam. In other words, they displayed a greater understanding of and ability to 'play the game'. This body of research was careful to stress that their findings did not suggest that working-class parents are any less concerned about their children's education, but the choices they make are directed by structural constraints. The extent to which parents understood how to 'play the game' and the subsequent consequences were also present within higher educational trajectories. Middle-class families spend a great deal of time ensuring that their children have a smooth trajectory from secondary to higher education (Brown and Tannock, 2009). In the shadow of meritocracy, Reay comments that the middle/upper classes work tirelessly to ensure that their children 'have a better chance of a fair chance than other people's children' (2013:666). The ability to create smooth trajectories requires resources, an extended understanding of the game and increased levels of practical mastery. To further illustrate this point, Bradley *et al.* (2013) discuss the classed levels of practical advice parents could offer their children in university access and experience. Working-class students received emotional support but lacked practical support through their parents' reduced understanding of the game, 'formed' by their own working-class habitus.

Additionally, Brooks (2003) discusses the importance of social peers when choosing HEIs. She suggests that, while families are influential on a student's decisions, the role of friends requires us to take a 'two-step interaction' approach between family and friends. Through the working-class students making collective decisions, they are reinforcing their working-class habitus. As Reay *et al.* (2001) and Ingram (2009) point out, the collective habitus is more difficult to break from[8] and, thereby, reinforces the cultural barriers. As discussed in Chapter 1, Bourdieu (1992b) comments that the habitus can be altered through a change in environment; however, the individual, the habitus, is more likely to remain in an environment that will not question but reinforce it.

Stemming from Bourdieu and Passeron's comments on the school's role in habitus formation, research (Leathwood and Hutchings, 2003; Reay *et al.*, 2005) has examined different levels of support within different institutions. The general findings have been that there are clear differences between state-run and private schools regarding support and advice. In their research, Leathwood and Hutchings found that state schools often advised their students to consider a further education (FE) trajectory instead of the students' preferred pathway of continuing on to Advanced Level (A-Level).[9] The authors point to this advice as a clear example of symbolic violence where the state-run school, housing mostly working-class students, has essentially capped their students' aspirations and expectations. These findings mirror Willis' (1977) previous observations that careers classes reproduced class identity by informing the working-class students about what they should expect when they leave secondary education.

Gilchrist *et al.* (2003), in an effort to understand the typical characteristics or variables that would encourage students from lower classes to attend higher education, found a much higher propensity of lower middle-class respondents who were planning to go to university or were considering it, in relation to members of the skilled and unskilled working classes. The tendency to go to university fell as the social classification did. The authors report that respondents from the lower middle-class are 3.8 times more likely to apply for university than their working-class counterparts. If a respondent experiences positive encouragement from their parents and friends, they are 15 times more likely to apply for university; students with a high level of confidence are 12 times more likely to apply for university. The greatest single influence was economic necessity; students who felt they needed to earn money sooner rather than later were 27 times more likely to *not* apply for university. Gilchrist *et al.* create, in relation to their sample, an avatar of the most likely applicant:

> Someone from the lower middle-class, with good educational qualifications, receiving encouragement from family and peers, with access to information on HE at school or college who believes they have the ability to succeed in degree study and who positively chooses university over earning money.
> (*ibid.*: 90)

The authors comment that a student exhibiting all these aspects is 57,000 times more likely to apply for university than someone who lacks these attributes.

Almost in spite of the above literature, the shifts in the social architecture, individualized educational policies, discussed by Beck and Margaret Archer, form part of the contemporary context for educational trajectories. There is much more choice now in terms of courses to study and subsequent employment routes. In the context of this choice, Atkinson (2010a) questions the extent to which individuals are able to deliberately or reflexively choose, from a range of options, the educational trajectory that is best suited to them and whether it is influenced by the habitus/mundane consciousness. The logic is, if the educational trajectories of his respondents transcend class through creating dispositions and paths not linked to a particular class pattern, it will strengthen the reflexive school's position; however, if the ability to succeed is inherent on possession of high levels of capital, regardless of the state practices to become classless, then, indeed, class shall prevail. Each of his classed groups largely followed trajectories that reproduced positions and routes of family and peers, understanding these trajectories as 'natural'. For Atkinson, the list of possibilities understood by the respondents and the 'choices' they made concerning them were provided or framed by their forms of capital, their habitus. The structural constraints on conscious thought, or the subjective expectations, are based on the objective reality of their position within social space.

An often-cited counter position to this argument is found in Paul Willis' (1977) *Learning to Labour*. Willis discusses the role that working-class lads play in rejecting the cultural norms of the school and, therefore, removing themselves from the institution and a socially mobilizing trajectory. Rather than passively accepting the hidden curriculum within the school and recognising its culture as legitimate or symbolic, they created their own subculture. The significance of Willis' study is that he was seen as giving action to the working classes and not simply understanding them as passive actors. Wacquant comments that Willis has been seen as the agentic saviour of educational research, protecting the subjective role of the individual from reproduction theorists such as Bourdieu and Passeron; however, Wacquant suggests that Willis' position is complementary to Bourdieu and Passeron's comments with regard to symbolic violence and social reproduction. He writes, 'active resistance by students can, and often does, objectively collude with the reproduction of class and gender hierarchies' (1992a: 80, n24). In other words, a student's active, rather than passive, withdrawal from the education system assists in the social reproduction through education, and it does not empower individuals.

Binary education system and binary choice?

In addition to issues of reading for a degree, a common manifestation of the level of educational aspiration or expectation can be found through a student's attitudes to pre-1992 universities and post-1992 universities.[10] To retain their niche in the current situation of graduate inflation, graduates must utilize some other aspect of their education or character to secure employment. Leathwood and Hutchings (2003) suggest that, as competition grows in the graduate market, students look to the institutional capital of their institution to re-balance the deficit. According to Ross (2003), there was a clear sense of arrogance felt between the pre-1992 and post-1992 universities, with post-1992 universities widely regarded as vocation-based and of a lower status to the 'old' universities. Vocational paths to higher education were and remain seen as a working-class strategy and not for the middle classes, and traditional academic routes are still seen to be of greater value.

Access to university – certainly, the disposition to apply – is heavily classed. It is not only access to university that is classed but also access to specific universities (Egerton and Halsey, 1993). Inequalities are complex and, therefore, cannot be solved by merely adding more university places. Reay *et al.* (2005) found a great deal of unease among their working-class sample with regard to older, more prestigious universities. They quote one respondent as saying, 'what's a person like me going to do in a place like that?' (*ibid.*: 91). The authors reveal that this attitude was commonly expressed throughout the working-class sample. This comment is a haunting illustration of Bourdieu's 'not for the likes of me' – the students refuse themselves entry, or even the process of applying, as they do not think they are good enough for such institutions.

More recently, Reay *et al.* (2009a) question the presence of differing attitudes of working-class students across different types of HEIs. They were interested in whether the students interviewed wanted to conform to the university life, resist the wider university experience or simply feel validated, as well as how much they fitted into the university and how much they felt that they stood out. Reay *et al.* report that there were very different institutional habituses across the four institutions. HEIs treat students very differently: some are more independent, creating a culture of where students almost hide what they have done, to one where academia is the central theme, allowing students to relish hard work. A key point of Reay *et al.*'s argument is the complexity of learner identity and social identity – that 'there is no perfect fit and these different types of learners cannot be mapped neatly onto different types of institution' (*ibid.*: 13).

As with entering university, the family and educational system play an equally influential role on what type of university to which a student will apply. Reay (1998) comments that her respondents understood some universities as better than others. In addition, students felt that going to a certain institution would provide them with something more than educational capital, an edge over other students. The middle-class respondents were more comfortable making this distinction and were confident in their ability to attend these elite institutions. The attitudes could be intersected and further fractured by ethnicity and family educational history; the general trend of classed attitudes, observed through state-run and private, persisted. Reay argues that the influence of the educational system, the institutional habitus, plays a central role in the disparities between respondents. She reported that the privately educated students explained that their schools had, over a number of years, engrained an expectation to attend an elite university and to expect high academic credentials. Contrastingly, the students who attended the FE college were encouraged to 'think locally' and consider one of the two local, less prestigious, universities with which their FE college had links. Again, students who attended the state-run school understood that their school provided 'little support'. Reay recorded a classed level of parental advice. Parents who had experienced university were able to give their children advice while the working-class group members who had no relatives with a higher education background were unable to avail of this advantage. This dichotomy is an extension, or an element, of the previous comments concerning classed differences in parental levels of strategy and legitimate practical advice that could be utilized by their children.

In what could be understood as an extension of this study, Reay *et al.* (2005) examined how different institutions, stratified by class, affect student choice. They considered the role or influence of the careers service in different schools and colleges, the contrasting curriculums offered between state and private schools and the importance of connections within the field of higher education – essentially, the closeness between certain schools/colleges and universities. Similar to previous findings, Reay *et al.* reported that private schools have greater resources for careers advice, offered more traditional or 'academic' subjects on their curriculum and had greater contact with elite universities, while state schools were connected to local, non-elite, HEIs. The teachers in the private schools had also attended prestigious universities, including Oxford and Cambridge, while teachers in the state schools did not. This point, Reay *et al.* suggest, increases the level of presumption and expectation for a similar trajectory to that of your teacher. The effects were clearly demonstrated in the contrasting levels of students who applied to Oxbridge (Oxford and Cambridge) from the private and state schools. Reay *et al.* conclude that they found very little evidence of calculative or individualized choices in terms of higher education; however, within the private schools, there was evidence of what could be deemed objective reflection or calculation of choices. It could be explained as due to their position within the field because they have the greatest understanding of the rules.

In contrast to this social closure position, Chowdry *et al.* (2008), using quantitative research methods, report that entries into elite university, compared to lower-status universities, were not based on social class but on poor grades. Mangan *et al.* (2010) suggest the disparity between Reay *et al.*'s position and Chowdry *et al.*'s can be explained through a misleading measurement of social class on Chowdry *et al.*'s behalf and the superficial nature of quantitative data. While entry into the elite institutions may be based on academic qualifications, the distinction between entry into an elite institution and a non-elite institution can be partly explained by social class. In light of their own research, Mangan *et al.* report that social class is strongly associated with the type of university to which a student will apply. They comment that students do not – what could be described as reflexively – choose a university based on its status and their social class; rather, indicators of social class influence how students choose to which university they apply.

Social class and education within a Northern Irish context

In some respects, class stratification within the education system appears to be more prevalent within a Northern Irish context. A central phase and process in the Northern Irish educational system is the academic transfer test (11+),[11] an exam that is heavily classed, leading to an unbalanced and elitist academic selection process (Archer, 1970; Leathwood and Hutchings, 2003). This exam has largely been disbanded for decades in England and Wales; however, the legislation to disband the exam in Northern Ireland was only recently passed, taking effect in the academic year 2008–2009. While it will take at least eight years to have a university student from Northern Ireland that was not affected by the 11+, it could take even longer, as what will permanently replace it is still unclear, and the ethos and culture that it created within schools that only accepted high marks or were characterized as institutions for students with low marks may continue for many years to come. As at 2015, there is still no new policy in place for the Northern Irish education system, private entrance exams have been established, requiring private tutoring and, perhaps, increased fees, creating greater and unregulated inequality.

The educational system in Northern Ireland, according to Smyth and Cebulla (2008), is largely seen as stratified by ethno-national identity; however, they argue that class is a much more divisive factor. Educational success is essentially mirrored for both Catholics and Protestants; in relation to the transfer exam, secondary level education and higher education, the divide is found in class backgrounds. A similar case has been made in relation to gender. Osborne (2004: 73) reports that there was a very small gendered difference when looking at children who did not sit the 11+. There was a significant difference in terms of children who were entitled to a free school meal to those who did not.[12] From this finding, Osborne contends that the 11+ is more classed than it is gendered.

Connolly and Healy (2004a) consider the specific ways symbolic violence can be transmitted in a Northern Irish school. The authors report that a working-class primary school let very few of their students sit the academic transfer exam, understanding that their students did not have the ability to pass. To convey the tacit nature of symbolic violence, the working-class students who did not take the academic transfer exam did not acknowledge that they were prevented from sitting an exam, seeing it as natural. Bourdieu and Passeron argue that treating reasons for a student eliminating themselves from a course or exam as due to a personal choice is somewhat naïve, as, if it were based on choice, the spread would be more even between social classes; rather 'the subjective expectation which leads an individual to drop out depends directly on the conditions determining the objective chances of success proper to his category' (1970/1990: 156). Connolly and Healy found the opposite situation in a middle-class primary school. They suggest that it fostered greater levels of aspirations for these young (middle-class) students. They report that, even at 10 and 11 years old, none of the middle-class sample were considering leaving school once they had passed the compulsory age for attendance (16 years of age) and instead planned to continue on and complete their A-Level studies. In a similar study looking at 7–8-year-old working-class girls in Northern Ireland, Connolly and Healy (2004b) report that aspirations toward education and future careers were eclipsed by aspirations of motherhood and marriage. The authors suggest that a key influence on this trend was the girls' local neighbourhood; their environment, from which they seldom ventured, formed their dispositions – their habitus.

Narratives of individualization

While most of the discussed literature clearly demonstrates the influence of social class and the damaging impact it can have on students' educational experiences and trajectories, the students interviewed commonly offered a narrative of individualization and choice (Reay and Lucey, 2000, 2004; Reay, 2012). Many of the students in Reay's (with Lucey) studies demonstrated a neo-liberal sense of individualization, understanding that their trajectories were up to them and that no one else was to blame for their failings. This attitude, Reay suggests, illustrates how symbolic domination/violence operates through discourses of individualization. This form of higher educational research typically ends at graduation; however, a key question is whether students, with an increased sense of individualization and personal responsibility, fare well in the graduate labour market. The second half of this chapter discusses these issues and examines the role of class in graduate employment.

Graduate trajectories

Graduate employment statistics

There have been a number of large quantitative studies examining graduate employment trajectories within the UK. These studies have generally supported a human capital theory understanding of the mobilizing effect of education, particularly in terms of entering the labour market. Elias and Purcell's (2004) *Seven Years On* survey on graduate employment trajectories reports that nearly 80 per cent of UK graduates find a graduate job within seven years of leaving higher education. Similar figures have been reported from successive Higher Education Statistics Agency (HESA) Destination of Leavers Surveys (2007, 2009) and also reports focusing on Northern Ireland (Martin, 2013). Brennan *et al.* (2003), commenting specifically with regard to graduates who read English, report that between three and four years after graduation, 66 per cent of English graduates are in stable graduate employment. Studies such as these publications – specifically, Elias and Purcell – have been heavily criticised. Brooks and Everett (2009: 334) suggest that Elias and Purcell's statistics can be questioned due to their 'broad' definition of graduate employment – in particular, their criteria for 'niche graduate'. Mason (2002) reminds us that non-graduate positions do not become graduate positions simply because more graduates are entering them. The subsequent issue is that each of the other surveys discussed above adopted Elias and Purcell's model of graduate employment, thereby casting doubt onto regularly cited and consulted statistics agencies.

Perhaps the strongest dismissal of previous studies has come from the studies' own architects. Elias and Purcell (2011) explain that they had found a significant number of graduates 'crowding' into non-graduate jobs. These positions did not utilize their levels of skills nor have a discernible promotion route. As such, the authors reclassified graduate employment to focus much more on graduates' opportunities to use their academic knowledge and transferable skills. Purcell *et al.* (2013), reporting on the final stage of Futuretrack – a longitudinal study of students accessing, experiencing and leaving higher education – comment that a significantly higher number of graduates were experiencing difficulties entering the labour market than in the previous decade. Purcell *et al.* found that 60 per cent of graduates were in graduate employment, effectively doubling the level of graduate underemployment, from Elias and Purcell's (2004) figure of 20 per cent, to 40 per cent in 2013. The authors are careful to point out that the doubling of graduate underemployment in the last ten years cannot solely be attributed to the re-classification of graduate employment. Running their 2013 findings through the classifications used for the previous research, Purcell *et al.* found that an 8 per cent rise could be accounted for, but the remaining 12 per cent rise in graduate underemployment was due to other factors. This more recent research more closely reflects student attitudes. Highfliers (2010) reports that only 36 per cent of final year students, interviewed in March, who were set to graduate in the summer of 2010, expected to get a graduate job, with that number dropping to 25 per cent when only arts and humanities subjects are taken into consideration.

Social mobility and graduate employment

Despite the critical questions posed to human capital theory from the above research, there are numerous studies (O'Leary and Sloane, 2006; Chowdry *et al.*, 2008; Gudgin, 2008) supporting their meritocratic discourse. For Chowdry *et al.*, regardless of increasingly high numbers of graduates, a degree still brings more security, increased employability and, therefore, better life chances. A central element of increased life chances is increased wages; O'Leary and Sloane (2006) argue that a university graduate would earn, on average, £149,761 more over the course of their life than a non-graduate. The concept of meritocracy is often expressed, if not in terminology then certainly in spirit, through the OED triangle (Devine and Li, 2013). The basic premise, assuming that the relationship between class origins and educational attainment will decrease, is that the relationship between educational attainment and class destination will increase, and, most importantly, the relationship between class origins and class destinations will decrease. Despite increased belief in meritocracy, successive studies (Savage and Egerton, 1997; Breen and Goldthorpe, 2001; Bukodi and Goldthorpe, 2011; Devine and Li, 2013) have argued that, while ability is important, class remains an influential variable on destination. In other words, education does not provide increased levels of social mobility outweighing the impact of social origin on social destination. Comparing findings between the 1991 British Household Survey and the 2005 General Household Survey, Devine and Li (2013) report that more people had higher levels of education in 2005; however, there is still a marked difference in levels of education by social class. Subsequently, people are now in 'better' jobs and enjoying comparatively increased life chances, but there are still clear connections between social background and occupational trajectory.

There has been a renewed focus within sociology demonstrating the classed nature of (graduate) employment (Furlong and Cartmel, 2005; Brooks and Everett, 2009, Hebson, 2009; Hodkinson *et al.*, 2000; Atkinson, 2010a). Furlong and Cartmel (2005) comment that the graduate labour market is a complex interplay between many different and competing elements, including the degree read and the institution the graduate attended. They argue that graduates from lower social groups face greater difficulties. Their respondents expressed quite low aspirations and negative or indifferent feelings toward the use of a degree, despite having graduated from university. These low levels of aspiration could be observed in the (much lower than average) wage expectations. One reason for this low wage aspiration, they suggest, is due to their local disadvantaged area; the expectation of graduate earnings reflect the earnings of their area. Additionally, many of the working-class students interacted with other working-class students, reinforcing working-class expectations of wages (collective habitus) and limiting opportunities to foster social links while at university. Low wage expectations and apprehensions about using their degree translated into graduates entering non-graduate jobs in order to have immediate financial resources for daily essentials.

A classed disparity in attitudes to being unemployed upon graduation was evident in Brooks and Everett's (2009) research. The authors suggest that the graduates who were the least concerned about being unemployed were graduates from more prestigious institutions who were seen as possessing a relatively larger amount of cultural capital. They argue that for those coming from a more prestigious institution or from a family who have experience of higher education, the graduate market may influence graduates to wait and not merely settle for a lower job; access to higher economic capital allows graduates to adopt this course. The respondents in Brooks and Everett's study who had entered or been forced into temporary work saw this as a normal process, something that can be expected. This explanation could be interpreted as a continuation of the lower-class attitudes of 'that's not for the likes of us', while, due to their higher level of capital and position in the social space, the options available to middle-class graduates allow them to create a strategy that is more in line with the game. A fundamental issue when examining the choices people make is the origin of their choices. In the context of the transition from education to general employment, Atkinson (2010a) contends that social background and levels of capital play a directive role. Contrary to the reflexivity theses, as proposed by Beck and Beck-Gernsheim (2002) and Margaret Archer (2013), middle-class respondents were in a much better position, due to their capitals, to navigate an increasingly de-structured labour market. In many instances, respondents' trajectories, similar to their educational routes, reflected and reproduced the trajectories of their family and their social background.

In the late 1970s, Tyler argued that there had not been a great shift in rewards (money, occupational status) through qualification expansion. He suggests this observation points to 'the deep-seated tendencies in the social system to allocate rewards on the non-meritocratic [. . .] basis of family background' (1977: 44). According to Tyler, if meritocracy is on the rise, then entry into the elite would become based on one's efforts and the fruits of their labour. The correlations between a father and a son's occupation would become less structured, and there would be a rise in the lower end of the salary level (to show that mobility is everywhere, not just for the mobile). The above literature, however, has demonstrated that, even if life chances are improved by education, pointing to a meritocracy, the gap between social groups and the importance of capitals has not diminished.

The classed nature of graduate occupational trajectories is not isolated within the UK (Wyn, 2008) or Western society (Mirana, 2008; Tagoe, 2009). Tagoe (2009), commenting on graduate employment in African countries, argues that entry into the labour market is enhanced by 'human capital', skills and abilities; it is the universities' – and higher education institutions in general – responsibility to develop this human capital. According to Tagoe, previous studies on graduate employment in African countries reported a large proportion of graduate jobs – some as high as 50 per cent – were secured not through credentials but through contacts. Social capital was a central facet in securing graduate employment. Previous studies also highlighted a general theme: humanities graduates were much less likely to find employment than students who had studied science. Wyn discusses the results of a cohort of Australian students from the Life-Patterns program.[13] He reports, through the emerging notion of a changing and de-structured society, graduates from higher socio-economic backgrounds seemed to be able to make sense of the changing nature all the quicker and to their betterment.

The restructuring of the (fuzzy) labour market

In the past, professional occupations or graduate positions would have been characterized as relatively stable. In contemporary post-industrial society, there is a great deal of movement or fluidity within professional occupations, where having a number of jobs or positions in a relatively short time is becoming quite normal (Savage, 2000). Two central characteristics of post-industrialization (Bell, 1973; Castells, 2000) are an increasingly de-structured and temporal labour market and the shift toward a knowledge economy. There has been a distinct increase in skilled highly technical jobs requiring advanced education coupled with a greater expectation of service to the detriment of routine, 'blue collar', semi-skilled professions. Between the year 1994/1995 and 2009/2010, the percentage of people in the UK employed in 'manufacturing' positions dropped 38.5 per cent, whereas 'other business activities/research' increased 61.5 per cent and 'education' increased 46.8 per cent (Elias and Purcell, 2011: 3).

As I have previously discussed in the introduction to this book, the emergence of the knowledge economy, in part, instigated the turn toward mass participation in higher education. The new social hierarchy was thought to be based upon credentials and not on heritage; the university provided access to routes previously reserved for the middle classes. Phil Brown's (2003, 2006, 2013) concept of the 'opportunity trap' illustrates the current situation within the graduate labour market. Essentially, individuals attempt to 'get ahead' of other individuals within a congested market. The problem is that the resources individuals typically use to get ahead, educational capital, are the very thing causing the congestion. This issue was exacerbated by the 2008 financial crisis, but it existed long before it and was created by a multitude of factors, not least by the limited capacity of the labour market to house increasing levels of graduates. As more and more people enter university, the degree becomes devalued, putting graduates in the difficult position of navigating a de-structured labour market within a knowledge economy, where academic qualifications are increasingly losing their value. Brown *et al.* (2003) are careful to remind us that, while there has been a shift from meritocratic to market principles within the education system, educational credentials are still of paramount importance. Applicants need to be educated in order to enter the race; the authors quote a human resources manager in their study as saying, 'academic qualifications are the first tick in the box and then we move on' (*ibid.*: 120). When educational capital is no longer the deciding factor, graduates need to employ other forms of capital in order to stand out and form strategies to successfully negotiate the graduate labour market; a common denominator between forms of capital and strategies is social class (Brown, 1997).

A fundamental aspect of calling in other capitals and forming appropriate strategies is understanding the changing nature of the graduate labour market, entry to which is only open to the university educated but by no means guaranteed by their qualifications. There has been a wealth of research examining students' and recent graduates' understandings of the labour market (Brown and Scase, 1994; Tomlinson, 2007, 2008; Wilton, 2011; Morrison, 2014). In Brown and Scase's (1994) study, they questioned to what extent students still view the transition from higher education to employment as a meritocratic process differentiated by different types of universities – essentially, a proxy for social class. The middle-class respondents demonstrated a strong understanding of the market, appreciating the devaluation of a degree and setting strategies to rebalance this deficit. Contrastingly, the working-class respondents did not understand the market as well and were intending to enter positions within the bureaucratic sector, which were fast declining.

The image of students as savvy customers who appreciate the changing nature of the (higher) education and the (graduate) labour market is a growing image within social research (Du Bois-Reymond, 1998; Hodkinson, 1998; Hodkinson *et al.*, 2000; Evans, 2007; Stokes and Wyn, 2007; Tomlinson, 2007, 2008). Indeed, Tomlinson compares his own study to that of Brown and Scase (1994) to demonstrate students' increased understanding of the devaluation of degrees and the need for other credentials to create an employable identity or 'graduateness' (2008: 52). Building on Holmes' (2001) work on graduate identity, Tomlinson suggests that his findings demonstrate an increasingly individualized approach to graduate employability. Adopting Beck's reflexive modernity thesis, he concludes that students are reflexively creating their own identities. An issue with Tomlinson's argument is that his sample was completely comprised of middle-class respondents. As I commented in the previous chapter, a central element that fosters reflexivity in Beck's model is welfare provision – in particular, access to education. As such, education is a key ingredient in the formation of reflexive modernity. Access to education, however, is highly classed (Reay, 2012), meaning that the reflexive individuals in Beck's thesis are middle class; rather than transcending social class, reflexive modernity reinforces it. The same can be said about Tomlinson's findings, as the middle-class students demonstrated a greater understanding like the middle-class cohort in Brown and Scase's (1994) study. While Tomlinson is correct in demonstrating increased market sensibilities within UK undergraduates, it can only be said for middle-class undergraduates. My point is strengthened by Tomlinson's (2007, 2008) observations that some of his conceptual groups had lower aspirations than others, linked to their relational position within the middle-class nexus, such as being first generation university students. In other words, lower middle-class students had a lower understanding of the market. Additionally, Hodkinson *et al.*'s (2000) 'horizons of action' and Du Bois-Reymond's (1998) 'choice biographies' are inherently classed. For Hodkinson *et al.*, practice is influenced by three factors: habitus, interaction with others and key turning points. The issue, however, is that the likelihood for interaction with others and key turning points significantly altering the habitus is very low.

In the context of educational capital losing its value, the logical reaction would be to try to make up for lost earnings with another form of capital. Indeed, the importance and classed nature of capitals within graduate employment has enjoyed a sustained interest within British social research (Brown and Hesketh, 2004; Smetherham, 2006; Tomlinson, 2007, 2008; Bathmaker *et al.*, 2013; Morrison, 2014). Apart from economic capital, which can decide a graduates' trajectory depending on their access to other sources of financial support, the two key capitals that graduates have been found to employ are cultural and social capital.

Increasingly, employers are no longer concerned with merely academic qualities and hard skills but an orientation/disposition to work, and personal and organizational skills beyond their technical abilities (Brown and Hesketh, 2004). As such, soft skills are becoming more and more important for successful entry into graduate employment. Morrison (2014) considers the classed dimension to soft skills, which arguably fall under Bourdieu's definition of cultural capital, and the difficulties working-class graduates face due to their prevalence within post-industrialization. Working-class students, within his study, demonstrated an appreciation of the importance of soft skills – in this case, speaking, as they put it, 'properly' – but they also expressed concerns of their ability to follow through with these skills, limiting their employment potential. Students identified both class and gender as barriers to work, especially in work outside of vocational parameters of their degree – in this case, teaching.

Equally as important to cultural capital is social capital, or being able to utilize social contacts as a means to increase your chances of getting a graduate job. Knowing someone in a particular company or a member of an interview panel is a very direct way to use social capital; however, as an increasing number of degrees include some form of work placement/internship, the opportunities to employ social capital have increased, as have the negative consequences for those who cannot (Bathmaker *et al.*, 2013). Discussing some findings from the *Paired Peers* project, the authors demonstrate the classed nature of internships, as a number of working-class students expressed frustration of not being able to find a reputable internship, whereas their middle-class counterparts had their choice of a number of options. As placements/internships constitute a large element of a degree, this problem translates into a substantial element of a student's overall degree classification being decided by social capital and not educational capital.

Another key strategy to rebalance devalued credentials – again, based on the level of appreciation of the graduate market – is to enhance your profile by getting involved in other activities that can be placed on a CV. There is an increasing focus on both the importance and classed experience of extra-curricular activities (ECAs) (Tomlinson, 2007, 2008; Bradley and Ingram, 2012; Bathmaker *et al.*, 2013; Purcell *et al.*, 2013). Going back to Tomlinson's (2007, 2008) thesis on 'graduateness', ECAs were a key resource that students could use in order to create their own identity. It was a way of regaining lost capital through degree devaluation; in a sense, they were advocating a form of neo-human capital theory where individuals still invest in their education for later rewards, but the capitals invested in during education have been extended. There is a marked difference, however, in participation rates by social class, with middle-class students making up the bulk of those students involved (Purcell *et al.*, 2013). Non-participation had quite clear consequences; while Purcell *et al.* did not observe a significant relationship between ECAs and general employment, a substantial percentage of graduates who partook in ECAs were in graduate jobs. Bathmaker *et al.* (2013) found that there were economic and cultural barriers to working-class students joining ECAs. Some students were under time pressures from jobs, while others were concerned that they, through their working-class background, would not fit in at these events. Working-class students were often involved in activities that would not result in transferable capitals.

Research from Smetherham (2006) clearly articulates the importance of other capitals. She reports a disparity in terms of graduate earnings on entry into the graduate market based on gender; however, there was an even larger disparity in terms of institutional hierarchy. She comments that graduates with first-class degrees from 'elite' institutions were four times as likely as their equally qualified counterparts from lower-status institutions to enter a graduate fast track trainee programme. On entry into the labour market, twice as many graduates from elite institutions were in a position where a degree was a formal entry requirement compared to graduates from a low-status university. Smetherham concludes that her findings point to a complicated transition from school to work and one that human capital theory is unable to explain.

The human capital position is that credentials are like currency; they are exchanged for employment and life chances. Within this system, as Bell (1973) predicted, social class and other structural barriers are transcended by the 'color of their qualification'. These qualifications are what is most important to employers and, therefore, on what applications are based, creating an 'access equals success' situation. In the context of mass higher education – and mass graduates – the currency of credentials becomes devalued, and equal importance is placed on technical ability (hard skills) and personality traits (soft skills). With an emphasis on soft skills, socio/cultural background re-surfaces as a key influence on occupational trajectories. As Skeggs (2004) argues, the working classes cannot 'fill-in' a perceived cultural deficit with increased technical skills, as everyone applying for a position has similar levels of technical skills. In addition to few soft skills, working classes do not partake in ECAs in order to acquire the necessary 'economy of experience' (Brown and Hesketh, 2004), nor do they form the required social networks to call on in the congested market or to form their own graduate identity. There has been some research discussing the working-class students using their own working-class identity to counter these effects (Lehmann 2009; Bradley and Ingram, 2012). In Bradley and Ingram's study, their working-class students demonstrated a form of 'resilience'. These students understood that they could mobilize the personal resources they previously used to gain access to university, such as hard work and determination, and avoid the 'opportunity trap' (Brown, 2003). It is an encouraging sign to see working-class students using their 'working-class work ethic' to address social reproduction; however, the issue still stands that hard work and determination will reap rewards, but it will most likely be the academics – and not cultural or social capital – which are increasingly the deciding factor in an educated work force.

There are clear parallels with the research on the classed nature of graduate employment and the previous research on the influence of class on (higher) educational trajectories and experiences. A key difference is in the direction and level of social theory to consider empirical findings. Bourdieu is often referenced in these graduate employment studies, but, bar a few exceptions (Hodkinson, 1998; Hebson, 2009; Atkinson, 2010a),[14] his thinking tools are not thoroughly applied – certainly not to the extent that they have been in educational research. A likely reason for this is that, while Bourdieu's theoretical and empirical work spanned a number of sub-disciplines, he is often seen primarily as a sociologist of education. Additionally, there is the issue of how relevant in today's fast-paced market is a social theorist whose most profound work was written in the 1960s and 1970s. This attitude is the position seen in Brown *et al.* (2014); they question the salience of Bourdieu's understanding that the educational system reproduces class position through qualifications. They have a perfectly valid point: in the context of degree devaluation, what more can we learn from these works? The critiques, however, from Brown *et al.* are quite clearly discussed by Bourdieu in the 1970s. In addition, he offers an account of how his thinking tools can be used to understand the current situation higher education and the graduate labour market is experiencing. The final section of this chapter will consider the often overlooked Bourdieusian literature concerning graduate employment in the context of degree devaluation.

Bourdieu and graduate employment

Social inequality, via the reproduction of individual's positions within social space and fostered by the educational system, does not end with entry into higher education. There are clear signs from Bourdieu (and colleagues) that the dispositions, aspirations and expectations framed by the habitus and forms of capital play as significant a role after graduation as they did before. A clear example is the differing levels of salaries from graduates with the same qualifications (Bourdieu and Boltanski, 1973/1978). Graduates who have quite low levels of *a priori* economic and/or social capital will only have their educational capital to exchange for monetary rewards, essentially creating a scholastic class. For graduates who have high *a priori* economic and/or social capital, they will have greater access to positions of power within a company, and their salaries will be independent of their levels of qualification. Bourdieu and Boltanski clarify this position in their notes, writing, 'It follows that outside the strictly educational market, the degree is worth what its holder is worth economically and socially . . .' (*ibid.*: 225). In short, when qualifications are equal among those in the employment market, social and economic capital are deciding factors. With the ever-growing level of university graduates, this observation is increasingly relevant.

Bourdieu (1973: 97) offers the example of graduates from the *école des hautes études commerciales* who were largely recruited into the Parisian business world. He writes that their subsequent success varied in terms of how they got their first position – through family connections – and not in terms of where they were placed in their final exams. As such, the value of academic qualifications can vary once the individual leaves the education market; the true value depends on the previous levels of capital inherited from their family background.

The importance of previous levels and forms of capital is supplemented by the changing face of the (graduate) labour market. Bourdieu and Boltanski suggest that, as employment becomes more 'fuzzy' (1975/1981: 145) – either from a change in industry resulting in new forms of employment or from weaker definitions of employment, which is characteristic of recent developments in graduate occupations – the greater the role of other forms of capital, such as cultural and social, not replacing educational credentials but supplementing them. It is the dominant class habitus, whether intentional or not, that provides a bodily hexis employers seek (Bourdieu, 1973).

Bourdieu (1979) comments that the devaluation of qualifications, through educational expansion, and the changing face of the labour market, has had a number of consequences; the most obvious or important, we are told, are the strategies that agents employ to maintain the value that their qualifications previously had or to secure the position that their qualifications previously promised in relation to entry into the (graduate) labour market. This need to reproduce their educational capital is felt greatest by the scholastic class, as they invest the most in education. According to Bourdieu, the devaluation of qualifications may be difficult to accept or negotiate due to hysteresis of habitus.[15] [16]

The structural lag between opportunities and the ability to adapt in order to grasp them causes previous understandings of a qualification's value to be applied to a new qualification market without any appreciation of the market's altered dynamics. Hysteresis is more forcefully experienced by those individuals who are most removed from the educational system and who are not widely informed about the qualification market. One of the more valuable forms or aspects of knowledge associated with cultural capital is an appreciation of how the game works – in this case, how the qualification market fluctuates, providing the holder of such cultural capital an inherited knowledge of how to play the game. In terms of the educational market, holders will know how to get the best return, which disciplines to avoid and in which disciplines to invest, based on the current qualification market and not based on an understanding of a discipline's previous market value or an assumption that qualifications should create or reinforce previous status. Via hysteresis, lower-class graduates with these, now devalued, qualifications, do not understand the drop in value; they assume or award a value to it that is not objectively or externally accepted. Bourdieu suggests the hysteresis of habitus explains why working-class students still put a premium on educational capital, as can be seen in the working-class students' rationale for not taking part in ECAs (Reay *et al.*, 2009a; Redmond, 2010; Bathmaker *et al.*, 2013). It is these students, however, who are most detrimentally affected by educational expansion or graduate inflation, as they have no other form of capital to exchange for a (graduate) employment position. There is a disparity between aspirations that are created through attending university and the opportunities to realize those aspirations. This tension or frustration will be felt at different levels, depending on the continuing value of an agent's qualification and their social origin. Middle-class graduates enter the graduate labour market based not on their qualifications but rather on their 'real-social-qualifications' (Bourdieu, 1979/1984: 88).

Conclusion

This chapter has demonstrated the largely socially reproductive nature of access to higher education, in terms of if an individual goes to university and where they go to university. While the UK – and many other post-industrial countries – has witnessed a move toward mass higher education, it has not signalled an end to social exclusion and elitism within the HE sector. A large number of researchers have adopted Bourdieu's thinking tools in order to articulate the subtle but brutal process of social reproduction. Education is still highly classed; if we were to follow Beck or Margaret Archer's logic, a fundamental cog within the reflexive project is bound by resources and previous social structures, thus reproducing access of 'choice' to the few.

In the context of the knowledge economy, the university is seen as the main arbitrator of social mobility. As such, we have witnessed an influx of more students in higher education than ever before, resulting in higher levels of graduates than ever before. A direct consequence is a congested graduate market characterized by devalued degrees and significantly more graduates than graduate positions in an increasingly de-structured labour market. An increasing amount of research has discussed the need for other forms of capital – *a priori* capital, such as social or cultural – or neo-human capital theory, where individuals still invest in their education but expand what type of capitals are available to them during their time in education, such as ECA. A growing body of research has argued that the multi-faceted nature of higher education has forced the development of the reflexive student, required to foster their own graduate identity from a number of different resources. Access to these resources, however, and the dispositions required to successfully apply them are heavily influenced by social class.

Findings from social closure research on graduate employment mirrors that of similar research focusing on higher education. These parallels point to the consequence of a socially reproductive educational system: a socially reproductive graduate labour market. The mirroring of findings also demonstrates a link between higher educational research and graduate employment research. A key difference is that graduate employment research generally does not provide a thorough application of Bourdieusian social theory, which has been the foundation of most critical sociology of education. This chapter has provided a discussion of often referenced but seldom applied comments from Bourdieu concerning graduate employment and indicates how graduate employment research would benefit from reflecting on these comments and applying specific thinking tools, such as hysteresis of habitus. Additionally, an application of Bourdieusian social theory, popular with cultural class analysts, in graduate employment research helps maintain a connection between a new phase of class research and employment studies. The next three chapters, based on my empirical findings, illustrate the classed nature of graduate employment and heuristic qualities of Bourdieusian social theory.

Notes

1 This argument is from 'Systems of Education and Systems of Thought'. It was one of the first glimpses the English-speaking world had of Bourdieu's considerable contribution to the sociology of education. This essay, along with 'Intellectual Field and Creative Project' (1966/1971a) can be found in Michael Young's (1971) *Knowledge and Control: New Directions for the Sociology of Education*.

2 Derek Robbins (1993) provides us with the social context of this study of entrants into state university. He explains that, at that time, France was witnessing an increasing split, in terms of social inequalities, between urban and the rural populations.

3 Bourdieu and Passeron had parted ways by the mid-1970s; therefore, Passeron should not be cited as a co-author of the epilogue.
4 It is unfortunate that, due to *The Inheritors* being published in English after *Reproduction*, the progression of Bourdieu's position with regard to education can get lost.
5 Bernstein (1971, 1973) makes a similar observation in relation to speech patterns within the educational system. He argues that there are essentially two patterns of speech: the 'Restricted Code', which is a basic level of language common among the working class, and the other 'Elaborated Code', a more advanced and sophisticated level of language often found within the middle classes. As the educational system, Bernstein argues, operates and transmits via the Elaborated Code, the working-class students are at a constant disadvantage, creating a situation of social reproduction. See Gorder (1980) and Collins (2000) for further discussion on the similarities and contrasts between Bourdieu and Bernstein.
6 Similar binary positions are offered by Brown (1997), discussing the technocrat discourse and social closure discourse, and Brown *et al.* (2003), comparing Consensus Theory and Conflict Theory. While in the minutia of social theory, these discussions offer nuanced readings; the inevitable 'broad stroke' approach to theory in empirical research reduces their impact. As such, it is equally appropriate and useful to discuss human capital theory and social closure theory.
7 Russell Group universities are the 24 leading universities in the UK for teaching and research.
8 The authors were discussing institutional habitus; however, the main principle applies.
9 FE courses are typically understood to be more vocationally based compared to the academic nature of A-Level courses.
10 In 1991, a government white paper, *Higher Education: A New Framework* (DfE, 1991) was published, giving polytechnics university status, expanding the number of universities and, therefore, university students. Universities that existed before this time are generally referred to as 'pre-1992' or 'old' while universities established afterwards are generally referred to as 'post-1992' or 'new'. An account of the various higher education policies can be found in Chapter 6.
11 The 11+ was an exam students sat in their final year of primary school. The results decided whether children attended an academically focused grammar school or a secondary school understood to carry a stronger vocational focus. The secondary education system in Northern Ireland did not exclusively operate under this binary system, however these were the two most common types of institution.
12 Entitlement is offered to low-income families.
13 This was a longitudinal study concentrated in the state of Victoria; the survey interviewed members of the community who had left secondary school in 1991.
14 Research from Bradley and Ingram (2012), Bathmaker *et al.*, (2013) and Bradley *et al.*, (2013), comprising findings from the *Paired Peers* project, does clearly apply Bourdieu's thinking tools; however, their findings only point to possible implications and not actual graduate experiences.
15 Hardy (2008) provides examples of Bourdieu's work involving hysteresis of habitus. These examples include: marriage strategies of peasant farmers in the Béarn, displacement of identity during the Algerian war, entry into the academic profession and social suffering and poverty. I have not been able to find a discussion on hysteresis of habitus in graduate employment from the secondary literature.
16 This argument, almost word for word, can also be found in *Distinction* (Bourdieu, 1979/1984) and class*ement, déclassement, reclassement* (Bourdieu, 1978).

Chapter 3

Graduate employed

Providing a thick(er) description

'Thick description' is most notably attributed to Geertz (1973). The salient concept contends that we need to know more than merely what or why an individual does something; we must also understand the context in which it is performed. Geertz tends to be overused and misunderstood within the qualitative tradition. For Hammersley (2008), there are two issues with Geertz's approach. First, how do we decide what is important to the description, who should be studied and, similarly, what theoretical framework should be applied? Second, how do we separate the understanding or perspective of those being studied and those who are studying them? Hammersley suggests we must supplement a respondent's perspective with a more scientific or rigorous account on the context of study; applying a theoretical understanding will build and develop the participant's own 'thick description'.

In an effort to follow Hammersley's position, the following chapters will provide a two-layered presentation of research findings. The initial layer will discuss the respondents' trajectories and influences. Illustrated by direct quotes from interviews, respondents provide their own 'thick description' of their trajectories. The subsequent layer is a theoretical consideration of the role of social class – habitus and capital – on their pathways. Respondents were placed into conceptual groups and, then, into categories based on their current graduate employment status. This empirical discussion begins with an analysis of respondents stratified by graduate employment categories before moving on to provide a wide-angle discussion.

The strategic middle class

The first of the conceptual groups that fall under the 'graduate employed' banner is the strategic middle class. This category was one of two conceptual groups populated by middle-class respondents. All members of this group displayed relational levels of capital – economic, social and cultural – that suggested they operated within the dominant levels of social space. Each respondent was also deemed to be in a graduate job at the time of their initial interview.

The strategic middle class group members were employed in a number of different occupations, including: engineering, lecturing, human resource management and television production. The group was comprised of seven respondents; there was a mixture of gender, ethno-national identity, institution where their first degree was read, degree classification and time since graduation.

Aspirations/expectations

Respondents within this conceptual group displayed high levels of aspirations and expectations toward their educational trajectories. A commonality between members was a clear sense of confidence in their own abilities and appearing quite relaxed when discussing their educational trajectories. These high levels of confidence were evident from an early age. Respondents were all educated under the previous 11+ transfer system; all sat the optional exam and were very confident in their ability to do well. During a follow-up interview with Annie, it was clear that, for her, there was no consideration of a path other than to attend grammar school:

> *I thought – I didn't know you didn't have to do it [11+]. I thought it was just something you did at the end [. . .] all I wanted to do was go to King's.*

For Annie and her strategic middle class counterparts, sitting the 11+ was seen as natural and part of the primary school curriculum, despite it being an optional exam. Furthermore, her goal was to attend 'King's', a leading grammar school in Northern Ireland. Annie did not entertain the idea of attending a secondary school; she aspired and expected to be accepted by 'King's'. This high level of educational expectation was also present in other periods of respondents' lives. As entry into leading grammar schools was seen as a certainty, so, too, was entry into higher education. There was little to no hesitation from respondents that, once they had successfully finished their time at grammar school, they would begin the next, natural step in their educational trajectories. Annie demonstrated the clear and linear educational trajectory that this group expected:

> *Yeah, it was a – I wasn't ever not going to go to uni, and I wanted to go.*

As might be expected from previous levels of educational expectation, members of this group expressed very similar levels of confidence toward post-graduate study. A significant number of respondents had carried out some form of post-graduate study, including taught master's degrees and doctoral degrees. Matthew demonstrates a similar perspective to his master's degree and PhD as previous respondents' attitudes to the transition from grammar school to university:

> *I was pretty confident that I was going to do well in the masters [. . .] that meant that I could go on and start the PhD.*

A common theme of confidence and high levels of expectation, initially located at age 10 in relation to the 11+ exam, has followed the strategic middle class group throughout their time in education, whether it is secondary, higher or post-graduate studies. Importantly, these high levels of aspiration have clearly followed members of this group through the transition from education to work. Respondents presume that they will either enter suitably high-status positions within their company/institution or that they will eventually, although still relatively quickly, reach these offices. As such, members from this group had constructed a clear boundary on an acceptable form of employment. For example, in Matthew's interview, he feels that he has reached a point in his life where he can expect a certain level of employment. His level of employment expectation has steadily increased over the years, and, like many of the strategic middle class graduates, he would not be prepared to settle for a lower-status, non-graduate, job:

> *There's certain things that I really wouldn't be willing to do now. I have a certain level of snootiness. I have a sense that I have skills that can be applied and are useful to people in certain jobs – skills not applicable to work in a [mini-market] – and I've done that and it's annoying. It's just not interesting to me in any way.*

In order to critically examine the habitus' directive role of practice, it needs to be empirically located following Bourdieu's (1986/1987) comments that an individual's beliefs and behaviours that are constantly repeated point to their habitus. Respondents from within this conceptual group displayed a longevity of high levels of aspirations and expectations. They could be quite clearly observed from attitudes in primary school to and including graduate employment. Their attitudes toward the 11+ and the natural progression into grammar school is reminiscent of an inversion of Connolly and Healy's (2004a) comments on the influence the habitus had over working-class primary students from Belfast; they were more likely to opt out of the 11+, seeing themselves as being academically incapable and unsuitable for a grammar school. For the strategic middle class group, the idea of sitting and passing the exam was taken for granted – or pre-reflexive – to the point that Annie did not know it was possible to opt out. Even from this young age, their expectations had become pre-reflexive. The longevity or durability of their high levels of aspiration can be seen through tracing similar attitudes to university, once again, seeing it as natural and the next step, and post-graduate study. Respondents demonstrate clear parallels between their own educational aspirations and the middle-class respondents in previous studies from Reay *et al.* (2005) and Bradley *et al.* (2013).

Importantly, the level and form of expectations did not alter when the field changed. When respondents graduated and entered the labour market, they held equally high levels of expectations and aspirations. There are clear parallels between levels and longevity of aspirations and expectations respondents displayed and previous research (Reay *et al.*, 2001, 2005), pointing to a general middle-class/dominant mindset directed by a middle-class/dominant habitus. Respondents' field of the possibles led them to see higher education and graduate employment as 'for the likes of them' (Bourdieu, 1979/1984: 110).

Within Bourdieu's theory of practice (1972/1977), the family is a central figure in the establishment and reproduction of the habitus. For the strategic middle class group, the influence of the family was quite apparent. All members of this group received constant encouragement and support from their families. Phil's parents took an active role in his education:

> *[. . .] because Dad worked at schools, he would always take a bit more of interest in my teachers and would take a more active role in like helping me with homeworks in certain subjects at certain levels. Education is a collaborative process between school and parents. He was interested in that as much as possible.*

There was an observable level of reassurance from parents concerning their educational ability. Respondents received a constant level of backing that increased their own confidence and formed their expectations. Maeve demonstrates how the primary focus of the family was education and employment:

> *Some kind of parents bring their children up, you know, you know, marry a nice guy settle down with, you know, children or whatever. My Mum and Dad brought me up to believe I would go to uni.*

From their life histories, it is evident that these respondents' parents constantly reinforced a high level of educational aspiration, telling them from a young age that they *would* go to university. Before conscious memories, family members have instilled expectations, norms and values through inculcation to the point where they seem natural and pre-reflexive. The attitudes of the middle-class parents – essentially, confidence and high levels of expectations – have been reproduced within their children's attitudes, their habitus and level of capital. This position is apparent in Reay's (1998) comments on the familial habitus; the level of expectation her respondents displayed was directly related to those of their parents and the nature that it was expressed to them. As previously observed (Ball *et al.*, 1997), the middle-class parents played an active role in their children's education, with Phil understanding that school and family life was a 'collaborative process'. The family was central in the habitus formation, demonstrated in part through aspirations and expectations.

The extent of familial influence was reinforced by the contrastingly weak level of significance and importance respondents placed on their school. Respondents were often critical of the educational system. According to Katie, her school had no serious impact over her chosen career path:

> *[H]onestly, I don't think my school was overwhelming – the school careers advice and stuff like that. It was only several paths you went down: law, medicine or engineering [. . .] I wouldn't have seen my school as being a great influence on what I chose to do as a career.*

Respondents often measure the lack of influence from the educational system by the strong and central role of the family. When discussing attitudes toward attending higher education, Phil commented:

> *Phil: Well, I was always expected to.*
> *CB: From family or school?*
> *Phil: Oh, from family.*

This direct comparison from Phil further demonstrates the secondary importance the strategic middle class group placed on the educational system. Education is an important cog of social reproduction; it provides both practical and cultural education to reproduce the position of the dominant class (Bourdieu and Passeron, 1970/1990; Reay, 2013). As the education system is complementary to the dominant classes' norms or doxa, the norms and environment of the institution will appear as 'normal' to those privileged students; it will reinforce what is already there and will not stand out as being apparent or obvious. It is logical that the strategic middle class respondents would understand their families as more influential, as the education system is repeating or reinforcing what their parents and relatives have already formed. The educational system is contingent upon the family. These findings mirror Atkinson's (2010a) comments on the influence of class with regard to the relationship between a parent and a teacher. Atkinson reported that middle-class parents play a more forceful and controlling role in their children's schooling, so the education system is, essentially, an extension of their values. What is clear, through comments regarding the educational system and overt discussions concerning their parents' influence, the families of the strategic middle class group played a key role in the creation and reinforcement of their attitudes. The families' middle-class attitudes were reproduced in their children.

Strategies

The high levels of aspirations and expectations, synonymous with middle-class respondents in previous studies, within this conceptual group were met with an equally high level of strategy – an ability to play the game. Once again, starting from a very early age, respondents demonstrated a thorough understanding of the educational market and made conscious decisions on their own trajectories. In the case of Lindsey, during her final year in grammar school, she began to research different universities that offered the specific course she was interesting in reading, allowing her to make an informed decision:

> *[W]hen I started looking into it, there's only a few universities that do aero-engineering, so that was a strong reason for going to [Southern]. They're a good aero-engineering department [. . .]*

Strong levels of strategic action were observable throughout respondents' time in higher education, as well. Returning to Lindsey's life history, she explained that she was aware that an engineering degree is no longer adequate to secure a graduate position. During her time at university, she took a part-time position in a spin-off engineering company, essentially getting involved in an ECA that was directly related to her degree and future employment trajectory. In addition to objective measurements, such as taking part in ECAs, members of the strategic middle class group also displayed high levels of strategy through more subjective levels: their form of reflection. Symbolic mastery can be measured through adapting Noble and Watkins' (2003) position on ordinary reflection,[1] essentially seen as an understanding of why the individual acts in a certain way and possesses an outlook for future actions. Respondents offered *consequential* accounts of their actions; they were able to explain why they had done something, such as choosing a certain degree, and also were able to offer a practical plan for the future.

As was the case with aspirations and expectations, respondents' high levels of strategy demonstrated a clear durable character and followed them throughout their time in (higher) education and into the graduate labour market. Early labour market experiences, and early labour market strategies, appear to have laid the groundwork for future employment trajectories. Members from the group were often able to negotiate their 'foot in the door' at graduate-level positions that, importantly, had a promotional ladder. Alternately, respondents would take up non-graduate positions; however, all of the graduates who fell within this sub-group approached these jobs as short-term situations, which they would leave when the conditions were right. For example, Lindsey's first job after university was working in a local confectionery shop:

> *When after I left university, I worked in a [confectionery shop]. I think I was there 2 years; I can't remember. I had a problem at the time. I was buying a house and my husband is self-employed, and halfway through my* working *in the [confectionery shop], I had to stay there while the sale of the house and whatnot went through because one of us needed to be, well, not self-employed, for the mortgage, so I did stay there a little longer.*

Lindsey waited for the right conditions in her personal life and the engineering field to develop and, then, applied for a position. Importantly, she was successful in her first application to a graduate position. Central to either of these strategies was a clear understanding of the labour market or, in Bourdieusian terms, of the game. This understanding was, again, demonstrated via consequential accounts where respondents displayed an appreciation of the relations and requirements of a certain position and explained what they did in order to be successful within that context. Katie was able to provide a decidedly consequential account of her employment strategy:

> *I do know that having a degree and a masters when you're in the 'firm'[2] serves well for promotion . . . I suppose I've always had that in the back of my mind, I don't just wanna go in and stay at [entry] level . . . I mean people would initially assume, a [x][3] degree or a [y] degree. No, they want something a bit different. Mostly what you would have is psychology or business studies for promotion.*

Here, Katie shows an understanding of the field and strategy on two levels: the use of a master's degree for promotion and the type of less obvious subjects that the 'Firm' prefers. The level of reflection demonstrated through this conceptual group demonstrates that, while action can be pre-reflexive (such as Annie expecting to go to a prestigious grammar school and not being aware you could opt out of the 11+), action is also reflective, albeit in a mundane or ordinary sense. Their consequential accounts of practice demonstrate how reflection is influenced by the habitus, how it reinforces the habitus, and how it also has a subjective character within the habitus.

The form of work that Katie does is within a tightly regulated and bureaucratic institution; however, she also discussed the need for a particular strategy in order to advance and continue to do well in the 'Firm', explaining that, once her three-year probation is concluded, she will wait a few more years before she applies for a significant promotion:

> *Yeah, I don't want to be someone with a few years' [experience] telling someone with 9 or 10 years' [experience], who is good at their job, standing there telling them what to do, not saying they wouldn't respect me but at the same time, I want people to have respected what I've done you know, so I've earned it, and after 3 years – barely the tip of the iceberg you know. It wouldn't be bad to get a lot of experience. There are a number of different fields in my job I would like to try before I think about promoting. I mean it wouldn't be like I'd be promoting for monetary reasons. I'm on fairly good money at the minute, but more sort of keep myself occupied. You need to earn respect to be taken seriously.*

While places of work such as the 'Firm' operate in theory closer to Merton's (1957) concept of the 'bureaucratic personality', in practice, these institutions are becoming much more de-structured, mirroring previous studies on increased flexibility of labour structures (Bell, 1973; Brown and Hesketh, 2004; Tomlinson, 2013) or what Bourdieu and Boltanski call 'fuzzy' (1975/1981: 145). It was a common necessity for many of the strategic middle class group; however, there were a number of respondents who had to negotiate a far less structured labour market, one that does not attempt to preserve a sense of rules and regulations. Maeve, who is now a producer for a national television and radio company, provided an account of the complex and prolonged strategy that she needed to apply in order to successfully manoeuvre within the media. After working on a number of unpaid media projects, she registered with the television company, as all prospective staff are required to do, and employed her own follow-up strategy:

> *The guy on the panel who interviewed me – he is a production manager in the newsroom. He looks after all the staffing, all the budget, all that kinda stuff, makes sure the newsroom runs smoothly. I pretty much, since I got on the register, I emailed him, and, when I say I emailed him, I emailed him a lot, um, I built up like a, you know, email relationship with him.*

In the interim, she had managed to organize some shadowing work with a political correspondent for the same television company. When her shadowing came to end, the person she had been emailing wanted to discuss employment possibilities with her. After a few more emails (mostly from her end), she was invited to meet him in person:

> *I think it was a Friday afternoon or a Thursday afternoon. I went into the [company], went up to him, and he said 'Maeve, such and such and such are moving on'. I was like 'right' and he said, 'you know, here, we'll bring you in for a trial, these are dates you can come in', and I was like 'right'. It was as instantaneous as that.*

While, in effect, Maeve's successful entry into the media was anything but 'instantaneous', her life history does demonstrate the need for a strong strategy to fully negotiate the labour market. A common theme among all the strategic middle class graduates was an appreciation of the fragility of the labour market – the need to constantly move and become more and more integral to their place of work.

Members of this conceptual group appear to inhabit the middle-class habitus discussed in previous literature (Bourdieu and Passeron, 1964/1979; Reay *et al.*, 2001, 2005; Gilchrist *et al.*, 2003; Bathmaker *et al.*, 2013). The strategic middle class's habitus is characterized by strong or high levels of both aspirations and expectations. Members of this conceptual group have demonstrated a constantly high level, moving through various stages of education and into post-graduation employment. Clear influences from respondents' families have been observed in forming and reinforcing their habitus; parents and relatives are, in effect, reproducing their own norms, values and dispositions. To examine the role of habitus in strategies undertaken to find graduate employment, a consideration of whether the habitus influences the respondents' trajectories is required.

Previous research argues that the middle classes, directed by their habitus, enjoy a more successful and linear progression with regard to educational trajectories (Reay *et al.*, 2005; Bradley *et al.*, 2013). A similar linearity has been observed in middle-class graduate employment pathways (Brown and Scase, 1994; Furlong and Cartmel, 2005; Smetherham, 2006); however, the research on which this book is based, as a means of bridging these two areas of inquiry, provides a thorough and accountable examination of the role of habitus on these pathways. Mirroring previous research, elements of the strategic middle class's trajectories appeared to be quite 'natural'; especially within educational transitions, there did not appear to be a significant level of thought or reflexivity toward their progression, appreciated through the high levels of confidence demonstrated by both Annie and Matthew. This confidence could be accounted for with a one-sided reading of Bourdieu's 'feel for the game' through focusing on practical mastery – a classed pre-reflexive disposition influencing how an individual moves within the field(s). Atkinson (2010a) adds support to this position through the characterization of his dominant/middle-class conceptual group's progression through education and into employment as merely following their 'statistical odds', requiring no level of reflexivity. A common-sense or lay understanding of this idea could also be typified as inertia: middle-class students and subsequent graduates mindlessly 'going through the motions' without any desire or overt plan. Wacquant comments that the habitus is 'endowed with *built-in inertia*' (2005: 319, emphasis in original) in the sense that the practical mastery influencing action tends to reproduce the social structures that created them, and these structures and processes appear to be 'natural'.

In contrast to Atkinson's (2010a) position, members of the strategic middle class group displayed a certain level of reflection with regard to their trajectories. This reflection can be appreciated in the consequential accounts that respondents such as Katie and Lindsey, offered concerning their approach to the graduate labour market. From Lindsey's account, it is clear that she understood the engineering field. She was comfortable taking a non-graduate position and 'biding her time' knowing that she would be able to transition to a graduate position when the timing and circumstances were more appropriate. Her life history mirrored previous findings from Brooks and Everett (2009) reporting the tendency and ease in which middle-class graduates enter non-graduate positions until the conditions are right for them to make that move.

There is little evidence of this group suffering from prolonged hysteresis of habitus (Bourdieu, 1979). Graduates understood that the labour market had changed and that it has become much more complex, where educational capital is just one of many factors that are required to successfully enter the market. As such respondents were clearly creating and increasing their, as Tomlinson (2008: 52) puts it, *graduateness*. Reinforcing findings from previous work (Tomlinson, 2007, 2008; Bathmaker *et al.*, 2013), resources such as ECAs – in the case of Lindsey – or unpaid internships – in the case of both Phil and Maeve – were crucial for gaining the experience necessary to re-balance their devalued degree. Phil commented that unpaid internships were much more useful than training courses, as people should be adding things to their qualifications, rather than merely more qualifications. Members of this group were creating their own graduate identities and trying to build up a portfolio that would increase their employability in an increasingly de-structured market.

The strategic middle class's reflection on their trajectories could be understood as reflexivity (Beck and Beck-Gernsheim, 2002), or, more specifically, autonomous-reflexivity (Archer, 2007). Respondents demonstrated an ability to play the game as well as an understanding of why they acted in a certain way or followed a specific path. Their actions, however, are influenced or constrained by their habitus, their norms, values and dispositions, influenced by their parents, (middle-class) environmental experiences and capitals. Katie is able to negotiate the graduate market and craft a sustained graduate job for herself; the impetus or genesis of her actions can be traced to her family's encouragement and practical advice. She very clearly cites the importance of her family. With her parents and siblings also employed by the 'Firm', she sees herself very much as entering the family business:

> *[B]oth my parents were in the [firm], so I come from a [firm] background big time . . . I'd say it's sort of inevitable that I ended up in the career that I did. . . . when I was at uni, it was the [firm] I wanted to go into.*

The apparent fleeting level or experience of hysteresis of habitus can also be traced to the family. For Phil, the understanding of the changing market and the devaluation of educational capital came from his family:

> *My brother was around the house when I was growing up. He didn't just walk into a job. He did go away to get work. Now, he's got a doctorate, and now he's teaching at a university and stuff, so just observing that I guess shows that there's a lot of different ways of going about things.*

There was a set of rules or a field of the possibles – 'set' by the position in social space and articulated/reproduced via the family – within which the habitus moved; the journey to achieve it is much more reflective. In the context of degree devaluation, graduates must rely on *a priori* forms of capital to direct their strategic actions. In addition to family and ECAs, capitals played a central role in respondents' trajectories. Following Bourdieu's logic, capital does influence an individual's aspirations and expectation; however, it is also something that can be tangibly *used* and acts as a form of currency that can be transferred for position, status or a certain trajectory. An important form of capital that allowed respondents to take up unpaid internships or initially enter the market in a non-graduate position was access to economic capital via the family. In Maeve's case, her ability to work as an unpaid intern when first starting out was predicated on access to financial assistance from her parents. Social and cultural capital, too, played directive roles in respondent's trajectories, though in more subtle forms than financial support and access to free accommodation.

Katie's understanding of the specific market was influenced by her parents and the social capital afforded to her by her parents. She was able to use her high levels of social capital to aid in her employment trajectory:

> *I've always been told by the likes of my Dad, who was in the 'firm' until recently, and his friends – he has a lot of friends who went higher than him, his best friend is [General Manager] – he said 'listen, get your degree under you. If you can do it now, get it under you and have it there. It helps to have a degree, so you can promote while [*working*]'. He always said, if you want to promote and go places, get the degree under you now, and, you know, see how – keep it there. You'll have it; it'll save you later on.*

This advice is precisely the trajectory that Katie followed. Her consequential accounts of understanding the market and the strategies she employed were, in part, created from her social capital. Other respondents developed their social capital as they progressed. Maeve's rationale for working as an intern was to build up contacts that she would then utilize later in her career:

> *But with that, with the stuff I had done on shorts, you met people. You got to hear about other things, and it grew that way.*

In addition, cultural capital, or soft skills, played an important role in the final stage of constructing a graduate identity: the interview. According to Tomlinson (2007, 2008) and Brown (2013), a rising premium is placed on the performance an applicant can produce at the interview stage. The demonstration of soft skills or 'graduate qualities', such as communication and interpersonal skills, are increasingly important for an economy that has shifted from one based on manufacturing to service. Katie's first position after graduation was in a marketing role at a regional radio station. She explains that she did not have the required credentials but 'talked a good talk':

> *Straight after my masters, I just wound up in a really good job for [Radio Station] in marketing. It was a really good job. It was a graduate marketing thing. It was a really good job, really well paid . . . I talked my way into the job because I didn't have a marketing degree or a marketing background, but I gave a good interview, and I could talk a good game.*

Katie was able to employ high levels of cultural capital to foster the image of an employable graduate. The comfort that she felt in an interview situation points to a form of practical mastery. The ease and confidence she demonstrates is indicative of Brown and Scase's (1994) findings on middle-class transitions into the labour market.

The strategies undertaken by this conceptual group within their educational and graduate employment trajectories demonstrate the increased role of individual strategy within a post-industrial labour market. The source, however, of these strategies is far from individual; rather, it is clearly influenced by both habitus and capital and how these variables affect an individual's understanding of the field. The parallels between HE research (Reay *et al.*, 2005; Bathmaker *et al.*, 2013; Reay, 2013) and graduate employment research (Brown and Scase, 1994; Furlong and Cartmel, 2005; Smetherham, 2006) have been reinforced with findings from this research. As argued in Chapter 2, within much graduate employment research, Bourdieusian social theory is referenced rather than applied. The research on which this book is based, as a means of bridging these two areas of inquiry, provides a thorough and accountable examination of the role of habitus on these pathways, demonstrating that one is an extension of the other rather than merely complementary traditions.

High levels of ordinary reflection suggest there is a subjective and generative element of the habitus at work. Members of this conceptual group are strategic and not merely cultural dopes – albeit, privileged cultural dopes, as suggested by Atkinson (2010a). Their habitus has provided them with a level of practical mastery to enjoy a 'successful' life history; their high level of ordinary reflection demonstrates that members understand why and how they have met their subjective expectations and what they are still capable of achieving. To comment on the differing effects of the middle-class and working-class habitus, a discussion of my remaining conceptual groups is required. Strategic practice and social class is relational; to fully consider the influence of the habitus, we must be able to compare social groups.

The strategic working class

The second conceptual group within the graduate employed cohort of my research sample were the strategic working class. Respondents were deemed to be working class occupying the dominated spheres of social space based on their accumulation, or lack, of capitals. Although this group was few in number, housing only two respondents, they clearly question the social closure theory position as they were both in graduate employment: regional politician and national charity coordinator. Similar to the previous group, they were comprised of a mixture of gender, ethno-national identity, and time since graduating; however, they both read their degree in the same pre-1992 institution – Southern.

Aspirations/expectations

Members of this conceptual group demonstrated very low levels of aspirations and expectations. They displayed low to middling levels of confidence in their educational abilities and uncertainty toward educational success and progression, often settling for merely passing examinations. Their low levels of expectations, similar to the strategic middle class, were evident from a very young age and expressed through attitudes to the 11+ transfer exam. Niamh, in contrast to her middle-class counterparts, expressed a sense of ambivalence toward the academic transfer exam:

> *11+, um, I think it was okay. Eh, like, I passed. My two older sisters and my older brother had been through it, so it wasn't such a big deal in the house, either. Two of them passed and one didn't, so it wasn't like I had to pass or anything like that. I think maybe 20 per cent got 1s. All of them passed but maybe 20 per cent got 1s.*[4]

It is clear from this account that sitting, nor passing, the exam was a foregone conclusion in Niamh's trajectory or in the majority of her classmates', demonstrating a clear difference to that of the previous middle-class group. A telling comment is offered at the end of this quotation from Niamh; she says that all of her classmates passed the 11+, but 20 per cent received 1s or the top A-grade. This demarcation was often the required grade for entry to a grammar school. Niamh and her classmates' measurement of being successful in the exam was passing the exam but not gaining high enough marks to enter a grammar school, the primary function and intended outcome of the process. A similar low level of expectation, characterized by increased levels of uncertainty, was equally present in attitudes toward accessing higher education. When I asked Niamh if she was always going to go to university, she appeared to be uncertain and clearly not as confident as her strategic middle class counterparts in her ability to reach university:

> *[W]ell, yeah, probably.*

While for the strategic middle class, entry to higher education was a 'given' and understood as the natural next step, the assumption of a liner educational trajectory was absent from Niamh's account. Low levels of aspirations and expectations were observed to be quite durable, apparently pursuing members of this group throughout their time in education and into the labour market. As respondents were willing to settle for average marks in exams, so, too, were they resigned to settling for low-status and non-graduate jobs upon leaving university. Pete, the other member of this group, during his time at university was willing to take any form of employment he could find:

> *I had applied for [fast food restaurant], and, even then, it was seen as the lowest of the low jobs.*

He applied for a number of positions, eventually securing a sales position in a high-street shop. Having worked in the same shop throughout his degree, he took up a full-time position on graduating. Pete was adamant that he would not work for the same shop on a long-term basis:

> *I always said I wouldn't [take a full-time position] because I knew people who had degrees who had been working there for years, and I didn't want to become those people. I saw how miserable they were, how dissatisfied they were, um, and went 'I'm not going to do this'. So I went full-time, but that was my kick to look for another job. I said, 'I'm not going to get stuck here'.*

Pete did find another position; however, it was a similarly non-graduate position with even more limited promotional potential. While he did not want to work long-term in a non-graduate sales role, he quickly settled for a job at a similar 'level'. There was a clear reproduction of aspirations and expectations and a constant willingness to settle, whether educationally or professionally. Unique to the strategic working class group, there was a clear shift in occupational aspirations and expectations to a level comparable with the strategic middle class. Whereas both Niamh and Pete displayed quite low expectations for their future, settling for non-graduate jobs, in the second half of their graduate trajectory, they displayed strong levels of confidence in their abilities and their future pathways. Niamh, who had been very unsure of her future path, often limiting her options through a discourse of 'not for the likes of me', now works for a national charity and Pete for a regional political party. Niamh was offered a full-time non-graduate job at the same time as she started working for the charity:

> *They [non-graduate employer] did, you know, offer to make it permanent. I knew I didn't want to work in [organization]. I left, and they got someone permanent in.*

Rather than settling, she decided to enter the graduate labour market. Additionally, she carries clear designs to move up within the organization:

> *I hope my next job will be more international and not so focused on Northern Ireland. Hopefully, I can carry the campaigns stuff over.*

This attitude is a dramatic change from a trajectory characterized by hesitancy and unsure choices to a strong aspiration to rise through the ranks. Similar to the strategic middle class, neither Niamh nor Pete would entertain the positions that they had previously held. Both the upper and lower cap of what is possible for these respondents has certainly shifted 'upwards' within the field. The genesis of this shift, for both respondents, came in the form an experience removed from their normal everyday life, an out-of-environment experience. In the case of Niamh, her aspirations and expectations dramatically shifted through a chance encounter working abroad and, subsequently, led to her reading for a master's degree.

These out-of-environment experiences appear to have had a significant influence on levels of educational and employment aspirations and expectations. Before either member of this conceptual group had their encounter, they displayed of low levels of aspiration and expectation toward their educational trajectories, such as Niamh's uncertainty over her likely performance in the 11+ transfer exam or transitioning into higher education. These findings reflected previous research on the classed nature of attitudes toward the transition from primary school to secondary/grammar school (Connolly and Healy, 2004a), transitions to higher education (Leathwood and Hutchings, 2003; Reay *et al.*, 2005)[5] and graduate employment (Brown and Scase, 1994; Furlong and Cartmel, 2005; Smetherham, 2006). As discussed in reference to the strategic middle class, Bourdieu (1979/1984) comments that there will be a certain set of objective probabilities or field of the possibles available to an individual in relation to their position within social space. More dominant positions within the space enjoy a greater or higher level of possibilities, while lower positions, such as those inhabited by the working classes, 'enjoy' a limited amount of possibilities. Each set of possibles are limited, though the limits imposed on the lower classes are understood to be more violent. For example, one common limitation is the disposition to understand reading for a degree or graduate employment as 'not for the likes of them'.

As was the case with the strategic middle class, the family was a key influence upon members of this conceptual group; however, the content and extent of their influence was quite different to the previous conceptual group. Respondents' families (parents) encouraged their children to attend university, an aspiration in the guise of becoming socially mobile, in the case of Niamh's family:

> *[M]y parents didn't go. They didn't even finish school, so, I think, because of that, my mum – she wanted the best opportunities and the best education for us. We were always told that education is really important.*

Familial influence can be defined as encouragement, whereas, for the strategic middle class, the role of the family could be read much more as expectation. The strategic working class respondents were encouraged rather than expected to read for a degree at university. The influence of the family could be described as 'looser' than their middle-class counterparts. In addition, there was no evidence of familial influence on employment aspirations. It may be a consequence of the working-class families operating under the assumption of a meritocratic relationship between higher education and graduate employment. In addition to the family, and in contrast to the strategic middle class, the educational system did play an apparent role in forming respondent's aspirations and expectations, repeating the same meritocratic discourse previously observed in the family. The school system also provided a sense of approval, essentially legitimizing respondents' lives at that time. Pete recalled that, after he received his A-Level results, he was awarded a grade B in one subject. He did not apply for a re-mark though his teacher had already told him he should have received an A grade:

> *[Y]eah, well, there is something still where there are certain people I want to impress. If I respect them, I want them to equally respect me. Getting it from him, ultimately, that was – I had already chosen Philosophy, and I had the grades for the next step.*

Approval from the school and his teacher was more important to Pete than the actual credential. This attitude demonstrates Bourdieu and Passeron's (1964/1979) comment that scholastic capital is the capital open to the working class; the education system will be seen as the source of symbolic capital, rather than the family. The education system, similar to the family, encouraged respondents to attend university, but it was not expected nor did this encouragement venture onto life after university. Importantly, neither the family nor the education system appeared to have created high levels of aspirations and expectations – these levels were the work of out-of-environment experiences.

In Niamh's case, once she had graduated from university, she decided to travel to South East Asia, where she could pick up casual work and also have the opportunity to travel. While there, she had an encounter with someone who was outside of her typical social environment, leading to a break with her previous aspirations and expectations:

> *Well, in [South East Asia], I was thinking about what I wanted to do, what career I wanted to follow. I sort of knew a girl who had done the course in [English university], and I was chatting to her about it, where she studied and what she did. It sounded like a pretty good course . . . I thought, you can actually study this? And you can actually have it as a career? I never thought about that before, working in development as a career.*

There was a marked and clear difference in levels of aspirations, typical of the working-class habitus, fuelling both respondents' trajectories after their out-of-environment experiences. Bourdieu (1992b) proposes that the habitus is open to change through a changing environment, though this change is quite unlikely. The strategic working class habitus has changed, via its permeable nature (Reay, 2004b), through new life experiences. The fact that Niamh's out-of-environment experiences happened in South East Asia points to the unlikelihood of entering a habitus-altering environment.

Individuals do not necessarily have to travel across the globe to break from their social backgrounds. Pete's out-of-environment experience, which came in the form of an opportunity to work for a political party, was much closer to home. Niamh's comments on her time at *Southern*, however, point to the homogeneity of the Northern Irish working-class environment and the need for something quite significant to shake an individual out of such a pattern:

> *I think if you're from Belfast, [Southern] is hard to enjoy socially because you stay in your wee cliques from school or you know...*

Similar to previous studies, (Reay *et al.*, 2009a, 2009b; Redmond, 2010; Bathmaker *et al.*, 2013), Niamh did not find any life-changing or even attitudes-altering experiences at university. When class was over, she would return to her working-class environment, with norms and values that reproduce and reinforce her habitus.

Strategy

The two sides of respondents' field of the possibles, demonstrated through levels of aspirations and expectations and established by an out-of-environment experience, were also clearly evident in the educational and employment strategies used along their trajectories. With regard to education, members of this group displayed weak levels of strategy. Neither Pete nor Niamh appeared to understand the educational market and, therefore, were not able to manoeuvre quite so easily (compared to the strategic middle class) within it. This was characterized by a recurring theme of failed strategies. Pete wanted to study philosophy at university; however, he continually picked inappropriate or incompatible modules:

> *In my degree, I dropped out of a number of modules along the way... by the end, when I should have finished my degree, I dropped out of 4 modules. I hadn't failed any, but I had to do an extra semester.*

Pete's poor understanding of the game was further demonstrated by sequential accounts concerning his educational trajectory. When asked to expand on his choice of A-Level subjects, Pete's answer was:

> *I did Maths, Further Maths, Economics and English.*

This response is quite a contrast to the consequential accounts concerning strategies afforded to the strategic middle class. Similarly low levels of strategy were evident during respondents' early market experiences. For Niamh, when she graduated from university, there was no apparent plan or strategy put in place:

> *Well, I was finishing up in [Southern]. I didn't really know what I wanted to do as a career.*

As a result of low levels of strategy, Niamh travelled to South East Asia, where she had an out-of-environment experience; however, this meeting was purely by chance and does not demonstrate a strong level of practical mastery. Niamh's attitude during her time at university was very different to the strategic middle class. Whereas a respondent such as Lindsey took part in ECAs and built up her graduate identity, Niamh described herself as having merely '*floated along*' at university.

At this stage of their graduate lives, both respondents' life histories mirror previous findings on the classed nature of graduate employment (Brown and Scase, 1994; Furlong and Cartmel, 2005). Members of this group, directed by a habitus characterized by low levels of aspirations and limited practical mastery, evident in their failed educational and early employment strategies, were unable to enter the graduate labour market. Additionally, both Niamh and Pete displayed narrow levels of symbolic mastery. In contrast to the strategic middle class consequential accounts of educational trajectories, neither respondent was able, even when pushed, to account or explain a particular path, suggesting a lack of reflection – the narrative signifier for symbolic mastery. The norms and values of their habitus are incongruent with the dominant group's habitus, which largely forms and reinforces the rules and relations of the social system – the doxa. Armed with only scholastic capital, which has lost its value in the current labour market (Brown and Hesketh, 2004; Tomlinson, 2013), both respondents 'opted' for a non-graduate path.

In the context of an increasingly fractured market with ever-fuzzy rules and regulations coupled with the devaluation of educational credentials, *a priori* capital becomes an increasingly valuable commodity for entry into the graduate labour market (Bourdieu and Boltanski, 1975/1981). Both Niamh and Pete have very limited resources on which to call, other than their devalued scholastic capital. University is a time for building social contacts for later in life; the academic portion of a degree is only one element of the overall product. Niamh, similar to working-class students in previous studies (Reay *et al.*, 2009a; Bathmaker *et al.*, 2013), due to low levels of economic capital, worked in a part-time job during her degree, precluding opportunities to gain contacts. The social capital that she did amass was from her colleagues and not her classmates:

> *They [classmates] were nice enough, and we went for lunch every day after class, but, um, just not really – didn't really click with them, just quite different. We didn't get that close. I think the class in general was a bit cliquey and a bit unfriendly. I'm sure they weren't all, but, you know – I didn't make*

> *that close friends in there [. . .] but I love the subject that I was studying, then working in the union. I – that was a social life [. . .] – the friends I had made in school and are still my friends now are very similar to myself [. . .]*

Niamh had not created any social capital that she could not have formed without going to university. When she took a brief break from her studies, the only position she could get was working for her previous secondary school, as she had kept in touch with some of the teachers. Niamh's unease with classmates is reminiscent of previous studies (Reay *et al.*, 2009a) and points to a low level of cultural capital. Additionally, she demonstrated a real sense of frustration at not having buoyant social capital:

> *The likes of law – if your Daddy*[6] *is a solicitor, then you're in there, and that puts me off because I don't have any connections like that.*

At this particular point in their lives, their trajectories have demonstrated the process of social reproduction. They still occupy similar levels of social space; Pete has as limited scope and strategy for employment opportunities as he did before entering higher education. Niamh, in a sense, put the consequences of not having a strategy on hold, but, except for her chance encounter, the same problems would be there when she came home.

As has already been discussed, there are two sides to the strategic working class's trajectories. Looking at Niamh's life history, her educational and early market trajectories were typical of working-class students and graduates from previous studies. Stemming from a chance encounter in South East Asia, her levels of aspirations and strategies dramatically changed. On returning home, Niamh enrolled in a development master's programme at a leading UK university. After graduation, Niamh returned to South East Asia – although, this time, it was not in an effort to escape but more job-focused:

> *Second time, I worked in a public school; the first time, I worked in [South East Asia] it was a private school. This time was much more enjoyable and, then, better hours and more respect as a teacher. You were working with all locals so you got to understand the culture more. I learned the language, saw the countryside a lot more and the customs and stuff like that.*

Niamh returned from her travels and began to situate herself within the graduate labour market. Contrary to her attitudes and understanding of the labour market before her out-of-environment experience, she now demonstrated a strong employment strategy, pointing to a good understanding of the processes involved in entering her chosen profession:

> *I was looking for jobs in development or human rights, and, um, it's really hard to get jobs, so I saw the [Human Rights charity] job advertised. To get*

> *into the sector, you're going to have to do a lot of volunteering, and you have to do internships because you need experience before they give you a job. It was a part-time job – it wasn't a job because it was unpaid.*

At the same time as Niamh took up her unpaid internship, the 2008 financial crisis was beginning to be felt in both the UK and, certainly, the Republic of Ireland. As a consequence, the labour market became more difficult to enter; rather than foregoing her internship, Niamh created a system that would work for her in the short-term:

> *I'd planned to move down to Dublin full-time and get a job down there, but this was kinda when the recession was still at its worst. There were no jobs going, [. . .] so I was working in Belfast a few days a week and working in Dublin a few days. I was also working in the bar, as well. I was working in [local football stadium] just at matches and concerts and stuff, then I was working in another bar – so busy! (laughs) [. . .] It wasn't a great time, but I knew it was only 6 months, and it was good experience.*

Niamh and Pete now understood the rules of the game. This shift is demonstrated by their apparent ability to craft successful strategies to enter increasingly de-structured and difficult labour markets: Niamh into the charity sector during the height of the recession and Pete into regional politics, a constantly volatile and changing landscape. Both respondents had created a graduate identity (Tomlinson, 2007, 2008) and, with a number of different resources – including but certainly not limited to educational capital – had fashioned the requisite skills and experience to enter their chosen professions. It is only after their out-of-environment experience that their habitus and, with it, their trajectory has altered to set them on a course where they understand the rules of the game and are in a position to develop their skills. Additionally, the strategic working class members are now building their levels of social capital, which now more resemble those of the strategic middle class.

The out-of-environment experience is significant not only in that it provides an example of the permeable habitus 'in action', but it also points to the types of interactions and experiences that are necessary to counter social reproduction. The previous levels of aspirations and expectations and subsequent strategies were highly influenced by the family and the educational system. I have previously described the influence of the strategic working class's family as 'loose', encouraging but not expecting their children to go to university, in contrast to the tight control the parents of the strategic middle class had on their children's educational pathways. Another key difference between the two class groups is the form of advice from family and school. The middle-class group received 'instructional' encouragement from their family and, in a lesser form, from their school; however, the working-class group received 'supportive' encouragement from their family and school. Working-class parents were unable to provide practical advice to their children. In the case of Niamh, she had been interested in reading for a degree in social work, but her parents were reluctant to discuss her path or offer advice for life after university:

> *I thought about social work, and I applied to a few social work courses, and, then, my parents – it's a very focused course. If you change your mind and don't want to be a social worker, you've got a course, but there's nothing you can do with it.*

They advised her to read for a more general degree, to keep her options open. Their advice appeared to be born out of fear or a lack of understanding of the graduate market rather than mastery, as a degree in social work provides a student with a more focused route but also with the transferable skills present within any humanities/liberal arts degree.

This lack of understanding is in direct contrast to the practical advice offered by the strategic middle class's family on how to negotiate the increasingly de-structured market. Bourdieu and Boltanski (1973/1978) comment that the education system replacing direct inheritance to offer the sense of equality by reproducing the same relations – in the context of mass education and degree devaluation, tacit knowledge of the game and access to resources via the family – is what reproduces the dominant and dominated social groups. The lack of practical advice from the parents points to their own low levels of strategy and the subsequent reproduction of these levels in their children's habitus. As previous studies have demonstrated (Reay *et al.*, 2005; Atkinson, 2010a), there are classed levels of parental involvement in both education and understanding. The parents' and schools' belief in the meritocratic system and the socially mobilizing effects of higher education point to a poor understanding of the market and a prolonged and inherited hysteresis of habitus. If working-class parents did not fully understand their labour, it could be reproduced in their child's trajectory, as was the case of Niamh before her out-of-environment experience. In contrast, both respondents' out-of-environment experiences were quite 'instructional'; for example, Niamh was told which university offered the best master's degree and the type of job she could apply for once she graduated. It was this level of advice that was already present in the strategic middle class respondents such as Katie, whose family and social contacts helped to map out her pathway until she entered her chosen profession.

This conceptual group initially demonstrates attitudes and an employment trajectory that appears to support the human capital position (Becker, 1964): as high levels of strategy seem to transcend classed backgrounds through increased levels of education. The members of this conceptual group, however, have demonstrated quite a contrast of attitudes, expectations and subsequent strategies. As I previously suggested, this break or change in trajectory appeared to not be influenced by education, as proponents of human capital would argue, but, rather, through what could be understood as a chance encounter with an individual quite removed from their typical or 'previous' environment. Their chance in trajectory came not after graduation but after their chance encounters. Again at first glance, this conceptual group also appears to support the reflexive theses of Beck and Beck-Gernsheim (2002) and Archer (2013). This group could be described as two working-class individuals, who, through a combination of education and meetings with external individuals through the, albeit temporary, collapse of cultural and geographical borders, have become reflexive individuals who understand the shifting nature of late modernity – in this case, a de-structured labour market – and create their own identity to navigate its path. The out-of-environment experiences, however, did not break the habitus but altered it to a certain degree. Pete and Niamh demonstrate a greater level of employment strategy; through consequential accounts of their trajectories, they have displayed a higher level of ordinary reflection. They have not become reflexive agents, as they are still influenced by the 'genesis' of their altered habitus. This can be appreciated as, while they have become more strategic, the strategies undertaken and processes applied follow the exact advice given by the gatekeepers during the encounter. This does not suggest that they are any less strategic, though it again supports the position that strategy is framed within the habitus, offering something closer to Archer's (1996) goal of 'centrism', rather than the upward conflationism advocated by both Beck and Beck-Gernsheim (2002) and Archer (2013).

The converted working class

The final conceptual group within the graduate employed cohort of my study is also working class. From a first glance, similar to the strategic working class, they appeared to have become socially mobile on graduating from university; however, as I will discuss, the specifics of their trajectory into graduate employment and the extent to which they have become socially mobile is very different to their working-class counterparts. Respondents from this group, totalling five individuals, were all measured as being working class. Identical to the previous group, this classification was based on access to and relational levels of capitals, including economic, social and cultural. All members from this group were understood, at time of interview, to be in a graduate job, ranging from schoolteacher to solicitor and civil service staff officer. This group, as others, was comprised of a reasonable split in terms of institution where first degree was read, degree classification and time since graduation; a notable change is that the majority of respondents were female, with only one male respondent in this group.

Aspirations/expectations

Members of this conceptual group displayed low levels of educational expectations and aspirations. These levels were observable in their life histories from a young age, where members were apprehensive and unsure about their suitability for the 11+ transfer exam. Paula, like all members of the group, passed the exam, but there was no sense that it was a natural stage in her educational trajectory – unlike for the strategic middle class – nor did she expect to achieve particularly high marks:

> *Even just sitting the 11+ wasn't – it was alright, like, done and dusted. I got a C, so it was pretty good. I got a C, but I wasn't really expecting too much else.*

This low level of expectation followed respondents, despite continued success in examinations. Alice had passed her 11+ transfer exam, gained a place in a grammar school and proceeded to do very well in her General Certificate in Secondary Education (GCSE)[7] exams. She was still surprised that she had achieved equally high marks in her A-Level exams:

> *When the A-Level results came out, I was quite gobsmacked but happy because I thought, 'well, I'm actually going to do a degree'.*

From Alice's life history, and many others', the belief and realization that going to university was possible only became evident once they had received their university offers and met the grade requirements. This form of delayed expectations, which need to be legitimized by the educational system, clearly contrast with the understanding of going to university as 'natural' from the strategic middle class. The theme of expecting to fail and, having once passed, expecting to fail at the next hurdle, was evident through the life histories in this group. Alice applied for a graduate-level position in the Civil Service; there were a number of stages through which she had to go in order to get the position (which she did eventually secure). Similar to the educational stage of her biography, however, Alice expected to be turned down after each stage:

> *When I saw the letter come through the door, I laughed, thinking, 'Oh, it's going to tell me I didn't get it', but I actually did get through.*

The same processes are being reproduced. Alice, once again, expects to fail, and it is not until her efforts have been legitimized by an external body, in this case the Civil Service, that she then believes this trajectory is possible. Regardless of which external body validates her pathway, it is clear that her 'personal' expectations are still heavily capped five years after graduating from university. The converted working class respondents are all in graduate levels positions. The specific conditions for their trajectories will be discussed; interestingly, respondents demonstrate an equally low level of expectation and aspiration now they have entered the graduate labour market. Paula has managed to navigate her way into the charity sector; however, she does not see herself being able to move up within her institution:

> *I want to do youth work, but I haven't looked into it at all. I mean, I'll probably stay in this job for the next 30 years.*

Paula is willing to settle for her current position – albeit, a graduate position – rather than rising up through the ranks like in the life histories of the strategic middle class and the strategic working class (post out-of-environment experience).

The final conceptual group within the graduate employed cohort share a number of similarities with the strategic working class group before their out-of-environment experience. These similarities include the low levels of aspirations and expectations with regard to educational and employment trajectory, demonstrated through Alice's comments of being 'gobsmacked' at passing her A-Levels and the equal level of surprise at being shortlisted for a graduate position. I would suggest that my comments or explanations from Bourdieu (and his various colleagues) and contemporary researchers such as Reay *et al.* (2005), Bathmaker *et al.* (2013), Brown and Scase (1994) and Smetherham (2006) concerning the strategic working class are equally appropriate with regard to this conceptual group. The converted working class's field of the possibles was capped by their dominated position in social space characterized by low levels of expectations and aspirations reinforced by habitus. Respondents displayed a lack of self-confidence, despite success, and further demonstrated through a willingness to settle even after breaking through to the graduate labour market. They, too, did not think it was 'for the likes of them', pointing to the development of a classed pattern within the wider sample.

Similar to the strategic working class, and previous findings (Reay, 1998) supporting a general Bourdieusian model, the family and the education system were quite influential in the formation of the converted working class respondents' habitus and, subsequently, their levels of aspirations and expectations. The family, operating under the human capital theory assumption of 'access equals success', encouraged their children to become educated, as it offered an opportunity for a better life. For Alice's family, education was the answer to breaking the socially reproductive process her parents had experienced:

> *[M]y parents, especially my mother, always pushed us in the direction of education . . . because we – I suppose, struggled. When we were young, my family struggled with money and with security and stuff like that. My Mum and Dad never had secure jobs, never had well-paid jobs, so it was always really important to my Mum that me and my brother and sister got a really good – achieved our potential in – education and have a more better secure future than my Mum or Dad ever had.*

A similar narrative was evident from respondents' experiences of school. For Jim, there was a constant transmission of higher education will bring increased life chances:

> *[S]o it was kinda drilled into us from first year to seventh year*[8] *that university is your goal, so do whatever you can to get there [university].*

Both the family and the educational system encouraged respondents to progress into higher education. Similar to the strategic working class and in contrast to the strategic middle class, there was no expectation from either institution that they would read for a degree at university. For Alice, she was *'pushed'* toward higher education, and Jim and his classmates were told they should do *'whatever you can'* to reach university. It is clear that higher education was a goal, but it was often not seen as attainable until it had already been reached. The same levels of self-doubt and lack of confidence consumed respondents in the labour market; the family and educational system had not spent time trying to form occupational aspirations, as it was assumed the socially mobilizing effects of higher education would, in a sense, produce options to the children or their students upon graduating from university.

Strategy

As there were clear parallels between aspirations and expectations of the converted working class and strategic working class (pre out-of-environment experience), so, too, were there common levels of strategy and an ability to play the game. Members from this group displayed a poor understanding of the educational market, often presented as failed strategies and seeing poor educational choices as being 'natural'. A common issue that respondents faced was the increased level of independence expected at university level education. Paula, who was originally studying for her National Vocational Qualification in catering at a FE college and transferred to university for her final year, enjoyed the security of the structure FE provided:

> *I, eh, preferred the catering college a lot better. Catering college, I suppose was much closer to the school setting. You came in at 9, you went home at 5, [. . .] and it [university] was like, 'well, you can come in for an hour here and an hour there and you might get some work done in between that'.*

Paula was unable to successfully navigate the field of higher education which, compared to FE, was largely unstructured and based on individual actions. The poor understanding, leading to reduced strategy, was evident in the sequential accounts of education trajectories offered by members of this group. In a follow-up interview, I asked Jim to tell me more about his trajectory toward university; he offered only a very short and sequential response:

> *I did my best, and I came away from school and went straight to [Southern] university.*

This account is very different to the rationale and planning provided by the strategic middle class. The absence of reflection in Jim's account demonstrates the limits of his symbolic mastery. The low levels of strategy directing the educational phase of respondents' lives was, again, clearly evident within their employment trajectories. They demonstrated a poor understanding of the labour market measured through superficial knowledge and failed strategies, pointing to a reproduction of levels/limits of practical mastery in the educational system in the labour market. Following Paula's employment trajectory, there are a clear number of failed strategies and an inability to negotiate the labour market. After graduating from a degree in food production, she entered this profession and, within six weeks, decided she could no longer continue. She left her job:

> *[W]ell, food product development – that was my main objective, and, for one point in my life, I was really focused, and, as soon as I started to work in it, I realized that wasn't me at all.*

Initially, this appears to be a strong strategy, as she knew what she wanted to do and read the appropriate course to get there; however, it was a failed strategy. The outcome of a strategy is just as important as the planning. Upon leaving her position in food development, Paula began to move from job to job. Her early labour market experience was populated by a number of non-graduate jobs with no connection or theme to the previous position:

> *Um . . . nothing related to food. More care assistant jobs roles I was applying for and retail, as well, in shops where I had experience. I worked in [supermarket], bio testing lab and, then, as a playroom assistant.*

Paula, guided by a poor understanding of the market, had moved very quickly from a linear and planned trajectory to one of uncertainty and temporality. For Paula, once she had left her food production job, she was essentially lost:

> *I left [food production company] and was unemployed, and, then, from that, I applied for jobs anywhere and everywhere because, eh, I knew I needed to get money to survive really.*

It was this sense of needing to survive that directed Paula's employment trajectory for the next few years, rather than a long-term goal fuelled by an understanding of the market. Once again, the theoretical analysis offered for the strategic working class (pre out-of-environment experience) is largely applicable for this group. Respondents' practice, characterized by low levels of aspiration and expectation, coupled with a limited understanding of the labour market affected their educational and employment trajectories. There is a clear friction between the norms and values of their habitus and of the dominant group's habitus and, by extension, the general rules of the game. From this lack of practical and symbolic mastery, respondents are unable to negotiate an increasingly de-structured and fuzzy labour market or create an employable identity (Tomlinson, 2007, 2008); rather, they are playing out a trajectory evident in previous studies from at least the last 20 years (Brown and Scase, 1994; Furlong and Cartmel, 2005; Atkinson, 2010a). As a consequence of graduate inflation, respondents could not rely on educational capital being exchanged for a graduate position. They did not have extra resources such as ECAs or the required *a priori* capital Bourdieu and Boltanski (1978/1981) and, more recently, Bathmaker *et al.* (2013), argue is required to offset this deficit. Respondents did not have access to economic capital to ease their transition into the labour market, evident in the financial urgency surrounding finding the first possible job, irrespective of form or status. Members of this group demonstrated low levels of cultural capital. During her time at university, for example, Alice felt that she did not 'fit in':

> *I made friends quite quickly and really nice people and all, but not people I would have seen outside uni. They were very different you know, they didn't – I didn't – we all came from very different backgrounds.*

Cultural capital is linked to soft skills, suggesting that they may not be able to 'talk a good talk' in an interview like the strategic middle class respondent Katie, which as Tomlinson (2007, 2008) demonstrates, is increasingly important in the formation of 'graduateness'. In addition, Alice did not extend her social circle at university, instead reproducing similar low levels of social capital. One of the few examples of access to social capital, on a long-term basis, also came from Alice:

> *I left there [hotel previously employed] on pretty good terms, and I know them, so they're always happy to take me back.*

While these relationships are a form of social capital, it must also be measured on how it can be used. In the case of Alice, this social capital allowed her to re-visit a previous non-graduate position, reproducing her dominated position within social space. Quite like the strategic working class, the family and education system played a direct role in reproducing an inability to play the game. Both of these institutions, while providing encouragement – certainly, a sense of success comes from education – did not provide any practical advice on how respondents should approach the labour market. In the case of Jim, his parents were very clear on the benefits of higher education, but it did not translate into pronounced guidance toward employment:

> *Mum – she was very 'you're going to go to university and you're going to get a degree and you're going to, eh, eh'. Ultimately, there was no career drive. I*

mean, she didn't say, 'you were going to be a teacher, set that in stone', but she was adamant that a degree was going to help me get to whatever career you're going to do.

The school system equally provided encouragement for going to university, but there was no guidance for life after graduation. Looking at Jim's life history, his school's approach to careers advice was to point to the increased earning potential for graduates:

School – at the time, they used to give us these exercises. It asked us to write down our name and, for example, doctor, teacher, and the annual salary that these people would get.

While this group has very low levels of aspirations and expectations and a poor understanding of the market leading to limited strategic action, they are also all in graduate positions. Paula's employment trajectory shifted from arbitrarily moving from non-graduate job to non-graduate job to quite a successful strategy:

I got a job in [health related charity] as well, so – um – I was covering maternity leave for somebody and in the area of volunteer co-ordinator.

From this temporary position, Paula was able to then move elsewhere within the graduate market:

I applied to charity jobs and got the one where I am now, which is Volunteer Co-ordinator for [Charity A]. Well, it was [Charity A]; now it's [Charity B], which is a –um – mental health charity.

She displayed a stronger level of strategy, as she knew in what field she wanted to work and where to find these opportunities. The converted working class trajectory into graduate employment was formed through access to a very specific capital with a one-time exchange provision. For many members from this group, this form of capital came from a family member; for example, Jim had a relative who helped him get a position in the school where he now teaches. Paula's capital took the form of embodied cultural capital, specifically illness. She already had a relationship with the first charity for which she worked; however, this connection was formed because she suffered from the health issues the charity addressed. When the maternity cover position became available, it was the charity that approached her:

Um, well (clears throat), Jill went off on maternity leave, and she asked if I would do it. The office manager phoned me and said, 'We think you would be great for this. Will you apply for it?' and that was that.

The actual process after this phone call was very quick:

> *Yeah, within days they offered me the post. It was 6 months, and then it got extended another 3 months. She came back. I was helping Jill and helping the fundraising manager.*

Paula was able to use her very specific embodied cultural capital – illness – to secure a position within a charity aimed at tackling that illness. Having her illness led her to volunteer in that charity, which created an opportunity for exchange. This position is strengthened through the observation that Paula had made no attempt to enter this profession before she was offered the job, despite later commenting that working with young people had been a passion since her time in secondary school. In addition, Paula only entertained the idea of applying for the position on the insistence of the charity, who essentially guided her through the process. Her habitus is characterized by low aspiration and an inability to play the game; however, her specific form of capital momentarily transcends it. In the case of Paula, her specific capital did not supplement devalued educational capital. It was the driving force behind her employment trajectory. She is only now gaining the qualifications required for her graduate-level position:

> *With that [starting her current job], I have done quite a few courses, as well. I completed an Open College Network (OCN) in Management, first line management, so I've got my Level 4 Diploma in management and then an OCN whatever, level 3 or something in management, [. . .] so that's now some qualification related to actually what my job is.*

I have termed the form of capital the converted working class can transfer as a one-time exchange; the reason for this terminology is that the capital is so specific that it has a very limited range for application. Jim's relative who managed to secure his teaching post works in the same school and could not do the same for Jim in another educational setting. Similarly, there is only one charity in Northern Ireland connected to Paula's illness; as such, she would not have the same connections with other charities. In addition to the limited scope for use, this capital also carries a level of temporality. After the initial use of specific capital, respondents demonstrated an increased level of strategy, suggesting a split with previous trajectories and, indeed, with their habitus; however, respondents have returned to similar levels of aspirations and strategies as before the capital exchange, in a sense, returning to their habitus. As has been previously discussed, Paula is not particularly happy in her current role, but she has no plans to move to a different job and expects to work there until she retires. Louise demonstrates a sense of being lost and is no more capable currently of navigating the market than before her capital exchange:

> *I have been looking for jobs at home for the past year, but I haven't even applied for one, and there's been no nothing – nothing's really come up. You know, you go to university. They say, 'get a degree, and you'll get a job'. You know, 'life will be a lot easier', but, you know, just the way the climate is going at the minute, the boom's ended. There's hardly any jobs.*

Louise is still a similar position to members from this group before their capital exchange. Once the initial benefits of their specific capital fades, their aspirations and strategies return to their previous state. There are parallels between the situation in which Louise currently finds herself and that of the strategic working class respondent Niamh. She, too, saw finding a job difficult in the midst of the recession, but, rather than, as Louise has done, suspend her job search and settle for her current position, Niamh created a strategy of unpaid internships and a collection of part-time jobs to make herself more employable and able to enter the graduate labour market. This level of strategy is absent from this conceptual group. On a superficial level, by any measurement in official statistics, such as HESA's Destination of Leavers Survey, this group appears to be socially mobile. A closer inspection shows that they have *converted* a specific form of capital into one particular graduate position. It is not the same as the strategic working class, who were given instructional advice; they have been given a graduate job not requiring a significantly high level of strategy. Two issues arise: first, none of the respondents appear able to rise up through the promotional system in their company/institution, as they lack both the expectation and the strategy. Second, the employment market is an increasingly de-structured and fast-paced system, often requiring individuals to have a number of jobs over their lifetime. As the age of a job for life is gone, the converted working class do not carry the necessary practical or symbolic mastery to move into a similar graduate position where their specific form of capital is not recognised.

Conclusion

This chapter has traced and analyzed the educational and employment trajectories of three very different groups of respondents. Their commonality, of course, is that – on paper at least – members from all three groups were in graduate employment. The etymology of the three groups' names is derived from the character in which they approach, and exist within, the labour market. The strategic middle class and strategic working class have both skilfully and strategically manoeuvred the increasingly de-structured labour market, whereas their colleagues – the converted working class – have, essentially, converted a form of capital – carrying both a temporal and one-off buying power – to enter the graduate labour market.

The strategic middle class illustrates the continuing reproduction of the dominant position within social space. Contrary to a meritocratic system of class becoming a 'zombie category' (Beck and Beck-Gernsheim, 2002), this conceptual group mirrors both recent work by authors such as Diane Reay (*et al.*, 2005) and, equally, the research by Tyler (1977) nearly 40 years ago. Established by the family and supported through the educational system, members from this group have an expansive field of the possibles. Their middle-class habitus and dominant position within social space has encouraged respondents to expect successful educational and employment trajectories. In addition to high levels of aspirations and expectations, their habitus, complementary to the doxa, is able to navigate *le champ* – the battlefield – in question. In the context of graduate inflation and the reduced buying power of a degree, or scholastic capital, members of this group have shown the renewed importance of *a priori* capital, demonstrating how economic, social and cultural capital are a great benefit when trying to negotiate the graduate labour market.

The strategic working class's early life histories – certainly, the educational and early labour market experiences – further reinforce the reproduction of dominant and dominated positions within social space. In contrast to their middle-class counterparts, also deemed strategic, respondents displayed a habitus characterized by low levels of aspirations and expectations – again, fostered by the family and reinforced by the educational system –leading to members from this group settling for non-graduate jobs upon leaving university. Equally illustrative, during these periods of their life histories, is the clear deficit and lack of opportunity individuals experience when they carry low levels of *a priori* capital and rely on the now devalued scholastic capital. Non-legitimate forms of capital and a habitus incongruent to the doxa resulted in an inability to 'play the game', leading to failed strategies. In contradiction to the critiques against Bourdieu and, by extension, Bourdieusian informed scholarship from a range of commentators, (Archer, 1996, 2007; Jenkins, 2002) the strategic working class detail the type of process required for a shift/change in an individual's habitus. Following Bourdieu's own comments (1992b), a total change in environment can lead to an altered habitus and the resources to navigate the field; however, an altered habitus is not synonymous with a break from habitus, and respondents still followed the norms, values and dispositions of the habitus – albeit, new ones. It is quite telling that the working-class conceptual group who have been the most successful in negotiating the graduate labour market and breaking away from the reproduction of domination is also the smallest group, housing only two respondents, pointing to the unlikelihood of a large enough change in environment leading to an altered habitus becoming commonplace.

The early life histories of the final conceptual group, the converted working class, in similar fashion to the previous working-class cohort, suggested a process of reproduction of position – in this case, a dominated position. Their habitus and position within social space had seemingly capped their aspirations and expectations, resulting in respondents expecting failure regardless of how many times they were, in fact, successful. In addition to their habitus and forms of capital limiting their field of the possibles, they were also at odds with the dominant norms and values, leading to an ability to strategically move through particular fields. Similar to the strategic working class, members of this group illustrated the limited opportunities for mobility when relying on an outdated understanding of scholastic capital's buying power. While respondents' inability to adopt an equally strategic trajectory as other graduate employment respondents, which was directed by habitus and capital, it was also a particular or *niche* form of capital that allowed respondents to enter the graduate labour market. The converted working class held a particular form of capital that, when used in the right context/situation, had a one-time exchange value. In addition to quite strict terms and conditions, this capital was also temporal in nature; once it was used, it could not be used again, and its effects on respondents would fade. Initially, when respondents used their capital, it led to increased strategic ability; however, this boosted ability soon returned to its previous low level. While respondents were in graduate employment, the temporality of their capital and regression of their strategic practice suggests that, in the increasingly likely event of having to change jobs or roles within a company, respondents would be unable to enter a comparable position.

Notes

1 I choose to use the term 'reflective' rather than 'reflexive' to counter or balance the Bourdieusian position concerning the pre-reflexive element of agency. As I have argued in Chapter 1, reflexivity suggests an ability to remove oneself from the social phenomena in which one is personally involved to observe and appreciate the combination of processes/relations currently at play. Reflection is an understanding of what and why one has done something and what one is able to do in the future; however, it is tied to the habitus. As the empirical findings demonstrate, while individuals are thinking beings, they are also bound to the habitus, and, as such, 'reflective' appears a more appropriate term to adopt.
2 Katie requested that her specific job not be discussed. As such, I refer to her place of work as the 'Firm'. Her current position is a graduate job; there is a significant opportunity for advancement.
3 Naming these degrees suggests quite clearly what her job is, so I have removed them. Regardless, the names of the degrees do not carry any weight; it is her comments on these degrees that are significant.
4 Equivalent to an A grade.
5 The working-class respondents within my study have expressed higher aspirations and stronger levels of strategy than the working-class respondents from Reay *et al.*'s (2005) study. They should be understood as, perhaps, upper working class; however, the class patterns still exist. As Brooks (2006) comments, regarding researching working-class graduates, while they are more 'successful' than a typical working-class cohort, the class influences on aspiration and subsequent strategy are still evident.
6 Underlining a word or a phrase in the transcript signified emphasis.
7 GCSE exams are taken at the end of a student's compulsory time in education. Acceptance onto A-Level courses are often based on gaining high grades at GCSE level.

8 If a student continues and completes their A-Level course in a school, they will typically spend seven years in the same school. When Jim says 'first year to seventh year' he means his entire time in secondary level education.

Chapter 4

Non-graduate employed

The entitled middle class

The second conceptual group housing middle-class respondents was the entitled middle class. This group was much smaller than the larger strategic middle class, containing two respondents. Like the other middle-class respondents, members of this group displayed relational levels of capital, which pointed to a dominant position within social space; however, respondents were classed as currently being in non-graduate employment: working in sales or office administration. Within the group, there was a mixture of gender, though both respondents read for their first degree at the same institution, *Southern*, and graduated only two years apart from one another.

Aspirations/expectations

There are a number of clear overlaps between the two middle-class conceptual groups, especially during the early portion of their life history; the two groups only part ways after graduation. As such, respondents from the entitled middle class presented high levels of aspirations and expectations toward their educational abilities. Both Hannah and Jonny expected to do well in their 11+ transfer exam and progress, quite seamlessly, from primary school into the grammar school system. While it was an optional exam, there was no question of Hannah not sitting the exam:

> *Hannah:* *It was absolutely the norm to do it. There was always, um, a lot of focus put on your 11+.*
> *CB:* *Was there ever any talk of not doing the 11+?*
> *Hannah:* *No, unless you had a learning difficulty, you did the 11+.*

For Hannah, sitting the exam was seen as the normal thing to do. Unlike many of the strategic middle class respondents, she was aware that students could opt out of the exam, though this action was apparently met with contempt. The progression from primary school to grammar school was quite normal and expected, as, too, was the transition from secondary level education to higher education. Once again, Hannah understood this trajectory as a foregone conclusion:

> *It was important that I went to university because I saw it as the closing of a chapter [. . .] I saw university as 'that's your education: you go to primary school, you go to grammar school or secondary school and then you go to university and then you go off into the world'.*

A general middle-class understanding of a linear education progression, culminating in higher education, as a natural trajectory had emerged from the overall findings. In addition, members of the entitled middle class would not consider reading for a degree in a post-1992 university. While Katie (strategic middle class) read for her degree in *Northern* because it made the best strategic sense, Hannah and Jonny would only entertain attending *Southern*, understanding that they belonged in a prestigious, more academically focused, institution. Their high levels of aspiration and expectation were also evident in attitudes to future employment prospects on leaving higher education. Respondents had markedly higher levels of specific employment expectations than the previous middle-class conceptual group. Regardless of criticism or contradictory advice, they expected to enter specialised fields. For Jonny, the aspiration to become a writer – specifically, a fiction writer – was significantly stronger and more directive than advice he received from his school careers department:

> *I think, initially, I thought, 'Oh, I can write. Maybe I'll become like a journalist'. In our school, he was one of those careers advisers. No matter it seemed what anyone came in with, he was just like, 'No, no that's not going to happen'. I can't remember what else he suggested [. . .] I'd say an English teacher. It was probably that, actually. I was like 'No, no, not doing that'.*

During a follow-up interview, he qualified this comment:

> *It sounds weird saying that I thought I was good enough to do it, but, at that age, you don't have any knowledge of what it takes to go and do that, but, at the time, you think, 'I can do that. I don't care what you say'. I didn't really bother much with the careers thing.*

Jonny had such high levels of expectations that they were the primary drive in his attitude and subsequent trajectory. While both middle-class conceptual groups presented high levels of aspirations and expectations, Hannah and Jonny's appeared impervious to critique or comment. The repetition of such attitudes points to a habitus that is characterized by high levels of self-confidence and increased expectations. The overlap between this portion of the habitus for both middle-class conceptual groups extends to the comments I provided concerning the strategic middle class. As such, there is no need to provide an extended repetition of similar observations. The entitled middle class, too, demonstrate a similar middle-class habitus, previously discussed by Reay *et al.*, (2005) and originally sketched and developed by Bourdieu (1972/1977).

There are, however, two major differences between the two middle-class groups: the level of independence from the educational system and the strength of their expectations. A central influence in the, albeit narrow, split between the two middle-class groups was the family. According to Bourdieu (1972/1977), the family and the education system, in that order, are the two key directive influences on habitus formation and the limits to the field of the possibles. As previously commented in relation to the first middle-class conceptual group, the educational system will be understood as playing a secondary role in their life histories. For Bourdieu, the educational system complements the dominant habitus; as such, it will be seen as reinforcing the norm and will largely go unnoticed. It is clear, however, that the educational system had very little to do with the formation of their future plans. For Jonny, the genesis of his ambitions to be a writer and to read English at *Southern* did not lie within the educational system. Rather, he understood both his teachers and his school as not being particularly supportive or helpful:

> *Yeah . . . I don't think – I don't think the other teachers had any, 'Oh, you're good at this, you know, either. You should keep it on'. I don't think there was any kinda specific, 'Oh, you should do this as a job'. It was more me saying, 'I'm thinking of going to [Southern] for creative writing', and then they were like, 'Yeah, yeah, that's a good idea' rather than them saying, 'Oh, do you know about this?'*

In addition to the understood general lack of advice or guidance from the educational system, when Jonny was offered careers advice, he refused to accept their words of caution and suggestions of alternative career paths. As is evident from his comments, he had already set on the aspiration of becoming a writer, independent of the education system, and would not consider its opinion of his chosen trajectory. This disposition to question the educational system, a purveyor of symbolic capital, can be traced back to the family. For Hannah, education began in the family home and formed her attitudes to the formal school system:

> *I enjoyed listening to my Mum and Dad, conversing with them, and I enjoyed reading and such, like, so when it came to be educated in school, I was never scared to put my hand up and go 'I don't like that' (laughs).*

Hannah provided an example from her time as an A-Level drama student to illustrate her point:

I wanted to do a play, and our teacher said, 'No, it's a man's play'. At no point did it specify gender roles. It could have been done, but our teacher would never think that it could be done. That was frustrating for me because I knew the world was bigger.

The entitled middle class's families, who also played an active role in their children's school lives, encouraged their children to approach the educational system from a critical perspective. Similar levels of parental engagement with the educational system were observed in the strategic middle class's families and in previous studies (Reay, 1998; Reay *et al.*, 2005; Atkinson, 2010a); however, encouraging their children to approach the school with a critical gaze was specific to the entitled middle-class's families. In addition, the nature of support from the family was central in forming this conceptual group's high levels of aspirations and expectations. Both Hannah and Jonny's family, in comparison to the other middle-class respondents' families, were much more supportive of their ambitions while still expecting success from their children, reinforcing and legitimizing their aspirations. It was a combination of their critical dispositions and hyper-aspiration that led to a sense of entitlement. Respondents had significant levels of self-belief and constantly questioned the objective relations within a field, often unwilling to accept these relations or re-assess aspirations to provide a better fit between the two.

Strategies

Similar to their middle-class colleagues and in line with findings from previous studies, the entitled middle class's high levels of aspirations and expectations were equalled by a clear ability to play the game and strategically navigate the field. Respondents presented a strong understanding of the educational system and appeared to be in control as they progressed through their education. The application of their middle-class habitus can be seen through Jonny's rationale for choosing his degree:

But then, by the time I came to leave school and choose university, I thought, 'Writing might be something I can do', so, when I was looking – when I was looking at university courses, I was looking for creative writing courses, which, um – at the time [. . .] none of the universities here had an undergraduate creative writing course. So I decided to go to [Southern] because I thought, 'I'll do English undergrad' and then I knew [Southern] offered a masters in creative writing, so I thought, the aim was do English then do the masters and then see what happens from there. So that's what I did.

Jonny's consequential account highlights his understanding of the market and the process of strategy formation. Additionally, his educational strategy was very much based on subsequent employment. Indeed, respondents' ability to play the game was also evident in their graduate lives. Jonny's early market strategies demonstrated an understanding of the market and the beginning of a promising trajectory:

> *Um, 2004/2005, I wrote that and sent it to this publisher in England because I had one of those big books of all the publishers. I flicked through that and sent it to this, um, publishers, a small one on London called the [Z Press]. It was a bit of it – I thought, at the time – a gamble because they mostly dealt with black interest fiction. I suppose, weirdly, I thought – the main character in mine I thought was kind of really into hip-hop and stuff. I thought they might be interested [. . .] I thought 'worth a go', and, actually, they got it. They liked it, and they were, like – I signed a contract to publish it, but then it ended up falling through because I think they went out of business because they were such a small publishing company.*

Jonny's decision to initially publish through a small publisher to build a reputation illustrates Tomlinson's (2007, 2008) argument that 'graduateness' is an identity that is formed through increasingly reflexive graduates. In the context of devalued education, members from this group were collecting other resources to prepare their entry to the graduate labour market. While the final result of Jonny's strategy failed, it still demonstrates a very real example of practical and symbolic mastery. Similar to the strategic middle class, the entitled middle class habitus, its norms and dispositions, complement the rules of the game, doxa, and they are, therefore, able to successfully navigate particular fields. Their educational trajectories and early market strategies point to a classed ability to play the game in an increasingly de-structured labour market, as discussed in previous research (Brown and Scase, 1994; Brown and Hesketh, 2004; Reay *et al.*, 2005; Atkinson, 2010a; Bradley *et al.*, 2013; Reay, 2013). In addition, their consequential accounts point to an increased level of reflection; respondents are able to account for their actions and plan into the future.

Despite early market experiences mirroring those of the strategic middle class, pointing to the case for a single middle-class conceptual group, soon after graduating from university, the entitled middle class's trajectories and, in particular, their strategies, broke from their previous course. This break set them apart from the larger middle-class group into quite unsuccessful strategies, stalled trajectories and increasingly sequential accounts fuelled by hyper-aspiration. Initially, similar to the other middle-class respondents, both Hannah and Jonny took a non-graduate position to build on their graduate identity formation and wait for more favourable conditions within the field. In the case of Jonny, he kept on his non-graduate job from when he was reading for his degree:

> *I applied for a job at a market research company [. . .] this would have been, now – this would have been maybe my 2nd year of uni [. . .] So I got that job,*

> *I did about four hours a day for a few years and even into my masters. I just stayed there. It was flexible. It was fine. I kinda enjoyed it. It had nothing to do with what I wanted to do career-wise, but it wasn't interfering. I guess it was just money.*

This strategy, again, reflects strategic middle class respondents such as Lindsey and findings from Brooks and Everett's (2009) study that the middle classes are increasingly comfortable taking non-graduate positions on leaving university, as they have access to economic capital to supplement low wages and, through an understanding of the market, they know that their current position is temporary and they will be able to enter the graduate labour market. Hannah and Jonny's strategies, however, are now directed by their hyper-aspiration, meaning that they will not leave their non-graduate positions until their specific intended jobs become attainable, nor will they entertain a different profession than the one they aspire to enter. The previous need to re-balance their devalued degree has been removed by increased levels of expectation. The resilience evident in Jonny's attitudes to his careers teacher is still present and directing his, now stalled, trajectory. When Jonny's market research job reduced his hours two years after graduation, rather than moving jobs, he took on a second, non-graduate, part-time job to supplement income as he worked on becoming a writer.

Reflecting on the entitled middle class's early strategies, in the context of their current trajectory, the role of hyper-aspirations and a sense of entitlement do appear to have laid the foundations for their future break with the larger middle-class group. Hannah has aspired to be an actress for most of her life, but she read for a degree in English and film after turning down a degree place in drama from a university with stronger links to the acting community:

> *I had an unconditional offer[1] to go to [Northern] to do drama, which, you know – I want to be an actress. I <u>am</u> an actress, but probably, if I had done drama in [Northern], getting into more roles would have been slightly more straightforward, I suppose, but the course I wanted to do in [Southern] was so perfect for me and such who I am.*

Hannah's habitus, characterized by a critical attitude and an independent stance, directed her to forego a linear route to her preferred job. This strategy was facilitated and softened by hyper-aspiration, essentially meaning that, regardless of which degree she read, she expected to become an actress and, therefore, did not have to adopt the typical/traditional route to reach her goal. She does stress '*I <u>am</u> an actress*' in this passage, pointing to increased levels of frustration toward her unexpected and extended stay in non-graduate employment.

Respondents appeared to adopt pseudo-graduate positions; both Hannah and Jonny made tenuous links between the position to which they aspire and their current non-graduate jobs. Hannah, who has spent most of her graduate career working in sales or hospitality, rationalized that her various roles will help her as an actress:

> *I learned so much being a waitress [. . .] that has assisted my acting because I know how to serve and please and organize people, and it does help if you can organize when you're acting, and you can do something to please someone [. . .] it's almost like drama school.*

Through respondents' prolonged stays in non-graduate employment, rationalized as pseudo-graduate jobs, both Hannah and Jonny appear to be quite stuck, constantly waiting to enter a field they have been trying to enter for four and six years, respectively. Their hyper-aspiration-driven trajectories appear to be quite damaging and stressful, as Jonny comments:

> *I don't want to try something else. I want to be a writer. (laughs) I don't want an office job that isn't writing. Anything that isn't writing is a failure. The fear of failure is a looming thought. I need to hope that something happens.*

The entitled middle class members are continuing to wait until the environment is 'right' for their entry into a very specific corner of the graduate labour market. Neither member of this group will take a promotion in their current jobs or apply for an alternate position, as their labour market experience thus far is still understood as a stop-gap measure. The entitled middle-class's more recent trajectories and current labour market position is closer to the graduate employed working-class conceptual groups – before their respective breaks or bumps in their habitus. Their current location in social space, however, is not the product of low aspirations or an inability to play the game but, rather, of increased levels of aspirations that have clouded their practical and symbolic mastery. The process of hyper-aspiration transcending strategic practice appears to be the consequence of inverted symbolic violence (Burke, 2015).

Symbolic violence, in its 'traditional' sense (Bourdieu and Passeron, 1970/1990), is the process of reinforcing caps on the dominated group's field of possibles. Through the inculcation of particular dominant/symbolic norms and values, the educational system and the family, in a secondary capacity, form attitudes of what is for the likes of certain classed groups. It is the exclusionary function of symbolic violence that explains the classed drop-out rate of the 11+ (Connolly and Healy, 2004a) and the classed nature of higher education, both in terms of attendance and institution attended (Reay *et al.*, 2005). Symbolic violence can and does affect both the dominated and the dominant. In reference to Virginia Woolf's *To the Lighthouse*, Bourdieu (1992b) comments that the common patriarchal system can too be violent toward men. Through masculine norms, men are unable to show weakness or emotion, requiring them to suffer upset and discomfort in silence. Similar to Connolly and Healy's or Reay *et al.*'s respondents seeing grammar school or a particular university as 'not for them', so, too, do men often see expressing their emotions or asking for help as unsuitable for themselves.

In the context of the entitled middle class, they are subject to inverted symbolic violence, as their field of the possibles has also been capped; however, it is the lower level that has been reinforced through the inculcation of dispositions such as increased aspirations. As such, their habitus is informed and directed by hyper-aspiration. When they encounter a field, such as the graduate labour market, which requires an increased malleability in expectations, they are unable to negotiate the space and, essentially, wait for the field to fit around them. The practical and symbolic mastery that characterized their educational life and the very early portion of their labour market experiences has been overshadowed by hyper-aspiration. It is not the case that their practical and symbolic mastery has been removed; via inverted symbolic violence, they understand their current course as a highly strategic approach to enter their chosen profession.

In a sense, when their inverted symbolically violent habitus meets an objective reality, such as the graduate labour market, hysteresis of habitus (Bourdieu, 1972/1977) occurs. There is a prolonged, perhaps permanent, gap between the changing field and the habitus. The hysteresis of habitus is exacerbated by the entitled middle class's success during their education phase at school, partly due to the educational environment rewarding and encouraging aspirations. As Hannah comments:

> *I think I expected it to be slightly more straightforward because everything was so straightforward in my life.*

Strategies, practical mastery, required to make up the distance between field and habitus are replaced by vague pseudo-middle-class strategies. Both Hannah and Jonny, in a bid to placate their frustrations, have found non-graduate positions in middle-class institutions/establishments. Hannah has typically worked in renowned restaurants or artisanal shops, whereas Jonny's second part-time job is in a university. None of these jobs are graduate level, but they appear to use the associated capital from working in these various places to substitute their stalled trajectory.

For all respondents within this study, the habitus, informed by (inverted) symbolic violence or not, has been significantly influenced by the family. As such, one source of the inverted symbolic violence can be found in the family. The same increased support that led to the high levels of aspirations and expectations has also fostered the process of inverted symbolic violence. As previously discussed, there were subtle differences in familial attitudes and support between the two middle-class groups. The strategic middle class's families, in addition to their expectations of success, provided their children with practical advice about degree subject and life after graduation, including the need to move with the market. In contrast, the entitled middle-class's families, in addition to support, encouraged them to question objective relations, fostering increased aspirations, and provided financial assistance during their prolonged period in a non-graduate position.

Hannah and Jonny appeared unwilling or unable to exchange levels of capital for entry into the labour market. Both respondents self-identified as being middle class and presented examples of relationally high levels of cultural capital. Hannah clearly understood that she came from a very 'cultured' background:

> *I was brought up in a very educated and very cultured household. I got to travel a lot. I had my first solid food in Sweden, uh, at the age of 9 months [. . .] I'm lucky that my parents experienced the world a lot more and the fact that I knew different names of pasta. I liked pâté. I knew how to behave in restaurants – that sort of thing. I knew who Shakespeare was before I went to secondary school. I knew lines from Hamlet when I was 8 years old, and that came from my father being so educated.*

In an increasingly service-based economy, soft skills, cultural capital, are becoming more important to carry out employment tasks and to do well at the interview stage (Tomlinson, 2007, 2008). One would expect that Hannah and Jonny could exchange these soft skills for a graduate position. Their inability to do so could be, at least partly, explained by their increased aspirations. They understood themselves to be self-sufficient and able to realize their goals unaided. The only occasion where cultural capital appeared to play a role was to their detriment. Hannah had started a part-time job in a largely working-class environment and was unable to fit in with her colleagues:

> *When I worked at the [theatre box office], it was a sort of call centre-y [sic] type thing. I didn't fit in there.*

Additionally, they clearly appreciated the need and value of social capital. Jonny provided a comprehensive list of the benefits of social contacts:

> *Yeah, it's important to know people just for advice because, yeah, sometimes – I mean, it depends. If you know people, then maybe they are more likely to think of you if they need something written. That could get you work and getting feedback on scripts and stories or whatever – it's not like cold calling them and asking them for help.*

Despite these comments, there was little evidence that either respondent had amassed a series of contacts that could be used in order to further their careers. This situation, again, may be partly explained through the increased level of self-belief and an attitude that they can reach their goals without anyone's assistance. The early support for Tomlinson's (2007, 2008) position that graduates create a graduate identity through a plethora of recourse appears to be firmly absent from later periods of their life histories. Rather than creating a level of 'graduateness', respondents are largely waiting for employment to find them.

Via the process of inverted symbolic violence, both Hannah and Jonny have presented stalled trajectories. The overshadowing of practical and symbolic mastery through hyper-aspiration and a willingness to circumvent capital has led to their employment pathways floundering for four and six years; however, their convictions and self-belief appear to be reinforced rather than retreating pointing to a new durable set of dispositions. In an increasingly de-structured market with a fluid relationship between staff and products, a successful entry into the labour market requires pace, agility, patience and a willingness to meet market demands, none of which members from this group appear to recognise.

Static working class

The final conceptual group and the third collection of working-class respondents was the static working class. This category has the largest conceptual group, consisting of 11 respondents. Similar to the other working-class groups, each member presented levels of capitals indicating a dominated position within social space. Each respondent was deemed to be in a non-graduate job, often involving the service industry or retail. There was a mixture of identifiers including gender, time since graduation, degree classification, university attended and degree classification.

Aspirations/expectations

Members of this group displayed substantially low levels of aspirations and expectations. As was the case with previous groups, the character of educational aspirations and confidence was presented at a very young age through attitudes to the 11+ transfer exam. A number of respondents passed their entrance exam and went on to grammar school; however, the process was characterized by uncertainty. In contrast to the middle-class respondents, Nikki commented that the experience was quite stressful and not merely the natural progression in her educational trajectory:

> *Yeah, [I] did the 11+, passed it. [I] was very scared about that whole experience.*

Additionally, one member of the static working class opted out of the exam due to the apprehension toward attending a grammar school. Caoimhe's rationale for this decision was that she did not belong in a grammar school:

I never had any want to go to [local grammar school] or anything like that. I wouldn't have got on there, like.

From these comments, it is apparent that, regardless of the end result, members of this group had very low expectations regarding their educational ability. Following Caoimhe's attitudes throughout education, it was clear that this low level of expectation was a constant disposition. Quite like her approach to the 11+, she, too, opted out of her A-Level examinations, again due to lack of confidence:

I dropped out because I knew I wasn't going to pass them.

Through tracing Caoimhe's life history, we can see that, over an observable period of time – in this case, seven years – low levels of aspiration have been a constant feature. Respondents like Caoimhe presented a high level of uncertainty regarding the transition from primary level education to secondary/ grammar and, subsequently, to higher education. At no stage was there a sense of comfort or choice; they continually expected to be unsuccessful until proved otherwise. In the case of Rose, it was only through achieving high grades that she thought academic success was a possibility:

I realized I had a bit of potential in me, and that was when I started to take myself seriously as an academic.

As was the general trend with previous conceptual groups, levels of educational expectations appeared to be reproduced regarding attitudes to graduate employment. The static working class demonstrated their low levels of employment expectations through a constant and un-critical willingness to settle for low-status and non-graduate positions. Caoimhe has had what could be described as a lateral employment trajectory since graduating from university. She has moved from one low-level administrative role to another for a number of years. Discussing this trajectory, she presented a clear willingness to settle for positions in which she was generally unhappy and did not enjoy:

It's not [that] I ever want to do it or I enjoy it, or really want to be there, but it gets me my money to go out and get my holidays.

Caoimhe expects to be in similar jobs for the foreseeable future, she has no intention of climbing the corporate ladder or being promoted. One explanation of these types of attitudes is respondents' apprehension regarding the labour market. Michael illustrated this point when discussing his employment chances:

[It's a] lottery, really, really because, like, with so many people going for jobs, you don't know who's going for what – you don't know what type of person is going for what job.

Most members of this group count themselves as lucky to currently have a job. As a result, they see any attempted move within the labour market as a gamble, further demonstrating their prolonged levels of low confidence and accounting for the lateral trajectories.

There are a number of similarities between the static working class, the strategic working class (pre out-of-environment experience) and the converted working class (pre-temporal exchange of capital and once this capital had been 'spent'). As such, most of the theoretical observations and discussion provided for these groups is equally applicable here. The static working class's dominated position within social space affects their field of the possibles; they often have limited/capped levels of expectations and see activities, such as reading for a degree, as not for the likes of them (Bourdieu, 1979/1984). They, too, mirror levels of working-class aspirations present in previous research (Furlong and Cartmel, 2005; Reay *et al.*, 2005; Reay, 2012; Bradley *et al.*, 2013).

What this conceptual group perhaps best illustrates, from a Bourdieusian position, is the durability and character of the working-class habitus when individuals do not have an out-of-environment experience or possess a context-specific capital that can be exchanged for a certain level of social mobility. Bourdieu (1992b) and Hodkinson (1998) argue that, more often than not, the habitus will be reinforced by environments similar to those in which it was formed. The life histories of the static working class could be suggested as a more typical attitude and trajectory for working-class graduates.

While there are overlaps between the three working-class conceptual groups, there are some specific or nuanced patterns pertaining to the static working class that merit consideration. Members from this particular group offered quite fatalistic attitudes to their educational and employment prospects; lack of self-confidence was considerably more pronounced within this group. A reason for these attitudes, I would suggest, is that their static position has been constant. Their labour market experiences have had a cumulative effect, influencing a much lower level of attitude or confidence. Similarly low educational expectations were displayed by Caoimhe, the only respondent in this group who opted out of the 11+ transfer exam. Respondents approached the exam with quite low expectations, but she was the only one who removed herself completely from the exam. Caoimhe demonstrates the 'not for the likes of me' dispositions that Connolly and Healy (2004a) discuss in working-class children who opt out of the 11+, believing it to be too difficult or not appropriate for them. These relationally lower levels of educational expectations will only have added to the cumulative impact of a sustained level of graduate underemployment.

As has been the case with successive groups, the family appeared to play a significant role in respondents' aspirations and expectations. The majority of families encouraged their children to apply to university, often understanding that reading for a degree will create opportunities for social mobility. For Sarah's family, higher education was seen as the beginning of a better life:

> *I think my Dad's – well, he's not very academic, but he's very intelligent and the same with my Mum – so they wanted better things for us, to get a really good education, and then go on.*

In line with previous comparisons between middle-class and working-class families, the encouragement the static working class received did not translate into expectation of entering higher education. Academic success was something to work toward but not something to expect, leading to a habitus comprised of dispositions such as low levels of expectation. Similar to previous working-class groups, the family did not bestow clear employment aspirations. One account for this attitude is that the working-class families assumed that entry into higher education would provide employment opportunities; encouraging education, by proxy, encouraged employment. The educational system, once again, reproduced and reinforced the character of influence from the family. Respondents were encouraged to work toward reading for a degree, but it was not something to expect. In addition, the educational system provided no comment for graduate life, as they, too, assumed encouraging education was encouraging graduate employment. Michael's careers classes while at school appeared to be primarily focused on inculcating these meritocratic assumptions:

> *I remember being given this document. On the first page, possibly, it was written, 'Why do I need to go to university?' It was a document that said, 'You want to go to university so that you can get a degree and, thus, get a well-paid job that will keep you in a life to which you are comfortable and the people around you can have whatever'.*

The family formed and the school reinforced a disposition within their habitus that did not expect academic success but understood that academic success brought about increased life chances. The inclusion of this disposition within the habitus is permissible, as it was a durable attitude. Specific only to the static working class, however, there were some families that did not encourage their children to go to university – rather, their working-class families expected them to enter a similar trade or form of employment as they had. For example, Kyle comes from a traditional Protestant working-class background; the most common professions were working in the Harland and Wolff shipyard or in Shorts, an aeronautical engineering company. His family expected him to follow a similar path:

> *Well, my father worked in aircraft. He was trying to get me to go down his path, and my younger brother did that, you know. So, it was kinda like family thing. My grandfather worked in the shipyard. The kind of job – you go into work, that's it. You know, come home, forget about it.*

While Kyle actively did not follow in his father and brother's employment trajectory, his family's dispositions, the familial habitus, can be seen in his own life history. Kyle settled for a low-status position in a university reprographics department and, nine years later, is still working there, following his family's attitude that a job is for life.

> *I've been there ever since, which brings us up to modern day which probably would be about nine years I'd be there in full-time employment.*

It is quite a traditional working-class attitude to employment to stay in one job until retirement. It is reminiscent of attitudes from employees who would have worked at Belfast's shipyard like Kyle's grandfather. In a somewhat protracted way, the familial habitus has been reproduced within Kyle's own habitus, directing his aspirations and expectations.

Strategies

The static working class, as with the previous working-class groups, presented quite weak educational strategies. These presentations were often expressed by failed strategies through a lack of understanding the educational system. Paddy had registered to study a diverse range of subjects at A-Level; however, he did not understand why he chose those subjects, resulting in a particularly damaging failed strategy. Paddy was forced to withdraw from studying physics due to poor grades. As such, he had to take on other classes to fulfil his quota, meaning that he had to extend his time in grammar school:

> *I dropped that [physics] in 6th year and picked up politics, um, and, um, politics was just boring but a chance of learning something, so, because of that, I had 2 A-Levels and 2 halves. Because I didn't have 3,[2] I didn't get into uni in the first year, so I had to stick around just doing politics. So, got that and then went up to uni.*

Similar failed strategies were apparent in the transition to university. On first attending university, Mark realized that he had chosen a degree to which he was quite ill-suited; he had to suspend his studies for one year and return the following year:

> *[I] moved up to Belfast, and, at first, the plan was to do Architecture. [I] got into that and moved up. I did that for all of about 6 weeks. That didn't really work out, so I basically dropped out and bummed about for a year, and, uh, I decided I was going to do film studies. [I] did that, went back for 3 years and graduated. [I] got a 2.2.[3]*

On returning, Mark conceded that he still did not fully understand the new degree that he had registered to read. He was under the assumption that this particular degree would not be taxing and getting a high degree classification would require little effort. He achieved a 2.2, a degree classification he was disappointed to have received.

A poor understanding of the market was reinforced through a general trend of sequential accounts concerning educational trajectories. Similar to many of the previous working-class respondents, there was very little discussion of why or how they did something. Sarah displayed a lack of planning or thought in her approach to choosing a degree pathway, essentially arbitrarily deciding to read drama at *Southern*:

> *I think one day randomly – I'd seen [Southern] did a drama course, and I thought, well, might as well do that, so I did.*

It is the lack of thought or consideration that points to the low strategy within this quite important educational progression. I pushed Sarah on this point again, asking her to tell me more about applying. She, again, responded:

> *I think I was watching The Simpsons and going on the Internet and just seeing the prospectus for [Southern] and just applied. I'd seen they did drama – went down the D list and then just hit drama. I thought I could do that. [It'd] be great craic.*[4]

Again, there was no rationale or explanation of her reading drama in *Southern*. I pushed the topic one last time in the follow-up interview; I asked her if she had known anything about the degree pathway or the university:

> *Sarah:* *No, just that it was in Belfast.*
> *CB:* *Did you go to the Open Day?*
> *Sarah:* *I did, but all I can remember from it is walking from the bus to across the road.*

I exhausted this issue with Sarah; her initial remark, explaining that she randomly choose *Southern*, appeared to be the only process or influence on her trajectory, pointing to a low level of reflection – symbolic mastery.

Unlike the previous working-class groups, failed strategies have followed and stayed with the static working class, as they have attempted to enter the (graduate) labour market. Respondents' early market trajectories often set the course of their future employment pathways. Mark has stayed in the same non-graduate position as a barman since graduating from university:

> *I got a job in the [nightclub] part-time, then I graduated. I got a full-time job in a bar, and I've been doing that ever since.*

Mark read for a degree in film studies and drama. He had enjoyed the vocational aspects of his degree; however, on graduating, he decided to go full-time in the position he had as an undergraduate rather than pursue a career associated with his degree. A number of respondents had been primarily involved in quite unstable casual employment. Many of these jobs were minimum wage and carried no benefits or security. Paddy found his first job after graduation purely by chance:

> *I was going to the bus station to go home for the weekend [. . .] I called into [the bar] to say hi, and he offered me a job and a spare room.*

Respondents appear to be quite stuck in these positions. When they do move jobs, it is a lateral trajectory, demonstrating a static position within social space. I asked Paddy about the various jobs that he has had since graduating; he explained that they were all quite similar:

> *I don't try to apply for too many jobs. Every time I update my CV, it's the same stuff.*

A key influence in these static trajectories is a poor understanding of the game. Similar to their educational trajectories, respondents displayed a lack of understanding on how the graduate labour market works. Nikki was aware of the difficulties of entering the market, but she also expected a position to organically create itself:

> *I always just thought something will present itself. I thought I'd meet somebody who will know somebody who needs somebody to start working for them, but I didn't really have any clear idea, you know.*

Additionally, a number of respondents, following the meritocratic discourses bestowed by both family and the educational system, assumed that their degree would, quite quickly, translate into a graduate position. Sarah expressed a great deal of frustration in the non-linear transition from education to employment:

> *When I came out, I thought, 'Right, I have a Bachelor's in drama with an entrepreneurship certificate.' Lots of people were telling me I could get a graduate job where they train you up to do something, um, when I came out. There's not that many things for Belfast and jobs I thought I could do.*

Sarah did not understand the mechanisms or processes of the graduate market, assuming she would be offered a high-status job on the strength of her degree. She expanded more on this idea in sub-session 2 of her interview:

> *I thought I could go into marketing and PR because I did part of that in the last year of uni in a couple of productions, and I really, really enjoyed it. Um, they were asking for two years' experience. I was like, I'm only out of university, and no one's giving me a break, it was just like . . .*

I pushed Sarah a little further on this thought (sub-session 3) and asked her where she got this information:

> *I don't really have – I basically have that to go on. They said – it was basically just word of mouth, really.*

She appeared to have nothing on which to base this assumption; she simply expected that it would be the case as she is a graduate. This demonstrates a clear inability to understand the employment market. The tone of her voice was quite agitated, which again points to her firm belief that she should have walked into a graduate position.

As was the case for aspirations and expectations, the parallels between the strategies employed by previous working-class conceptual groups and the static working class lends itself to a similar theoretical account of such strategies. Again, this conceptual group could be understood as presenting a typical working-class graduate employment trajectory, as discussed in previous literature (Furlong and Cartmel, 2005; Smetherham, 2006). Their quite static and socially immobile trajectories are the consequences of not having an out-of-environment experience or specific temporal capital exchange, i.e. a more 'normal' working-class experience. The static working class's habitus was incongruent with the rules of the game, the doxa, formed by the dominant group. As such, they were unable to successfully navigate the labour market. Respondents demonstrated low levels of both practical mastery, in their failed strategies, and symbolic mastery through sequential accounts of their actions. A number of respondents expressed feelings of regret for not understanding what they needed to do when at university to make an easier transition to work and now see their time in higher education as a wasted opportunity. Sarah appeared quite frustrated in her lack of additional resources/experiences caused, as she understood it, through lack of advice:

> *If someone had explained to me, 'It would be quite good for you to have a part-time job, and do this, and go out to places, and travel, and use your student loan', or 'Don't get a student loan because student loans are too high in interest rates, so don't get them'...*

The static working class's lack of practical mastery – in particular, lack of symbolic mastery – further questions Beck and Beck-Gernsheim's (2002) reflexive modernization and Archer's (2013) morphogenesis thesis. Members of this group have progressed within social space formed through Western welfare policies and have access to higher level education. They have not been able to reflexively craft their pathway; rather, they appear directed by their class habitus. Sarah commented that, at this stage of her life, she would have benefited from someone telling her how things work and what she needed to do in order to manoeuvre within the market. This desire to be told how to do things, this need to discuss plans with others before making them, could be understood as a form of communicative reflexivity (Archer, 2007), though I would argue that it is not the case. Archer understands communicative reflexives to be socially static; in other words, they do not wish for social mobility. Sarah laments over not being given advice or an opportunity to discuss her trajectories to become socially mobile. Additionally, Archer argues that her three forms of reflexives are not classed, though the only possible examples of communicative reflexives within my sample are from the working-class cohort of graduates. Sarah is not a communicative reflexive. Her frustration and need to be guided points to a classed understanding of the field, an inability to play the game or weak practical/symbolic mastery.

In the context of an increasingly de-structured and vague labour market paired with the decreased buying power of educational capital, members of this group are unable to enter the graduate labour market solely on their credentials. Members of this group did not possess sufficiently solvent levels of capitals to exchange for entry into the graduate market. As was the case with previous working-class respondents, the immediate need for economic capital drove members of this group toward the first possible position, regardless of status, etc. I asked Paddy, 'what was important in a job?', to which he quite aggressively responded:

> *What? I didn't have the luxury of thinking about that – food, really, food and rent, because I worked nights, I wasn't able to search for jobs.*

The uncharacteristic hostility present in this comment – especially the use of the word 'luxury' – suggests that he thought my question was unreasonable. The need for money clearly transcended all else. Respondents did use social contacts in order to find and secure employment; however, social capital is measured not only on its use but also on the end results. In other words, if respondents could only use their social capital to continually find low-status positions, then it demonstrated low levels of social capital. Mark often found temporary positions in bars through these social contacts:

> *Well, I hear things. I know a lot of people. I hear things of where someone's looking.*

He is limited in his use of social capital, as his contacts provide a static trajectory. Through the emergence of post-industrialization, the importance of soft skills, cultural capital, has grown significantly. The economy is increasingly based on service, pointing to the need for soft skills. Additionally, as Tomlinson (2007) recently argues, cultural capital in the form of interview skills is required for an applicant to stand out from a cohort of similarly qualified applicants. In direct contrast to many of the middle-class respondents who could 'talk a good talk' in an interview, Paddy often feels uncomfortable and struggles in this crucial aspect of the employment process:

> *I don't know. I just try and rely on natural charm. (laughs) Interviews aren't my strong suit.*

The static working class group did not have the required or symbolic levels of *a priori* capital to re-balance the devaluation of their scholastic capital. The assumption that this re-balancing was unnecessary and educational capital would be sufficient for entry into the labour market was most pronounced in this group. The frustration in Sarah's account of what she expected would happen upon graduation or Nikki's assumption that a graduate job would essentially materialize point to the most 'traditional' form of hysteresis of habitus (Bourdieu, 1972/1977, 1979/1984). The lag between the shift in the field – in this case, devaluation of degrees – and an individual/group appreciating the shift and altering their strategy is directed by habitus. The working class, dominated habitus, illustrated in practice through low levels of practical mastery, will experience a much longer lag than the middle class. As has been demonstrated in previous studies (Reay *et al.*, 2009a; Redmond, 2010; Bathmaker *et al.*, 2013) the static working class focused on their degrees and did not build up any other resources required for a graduate position. The trust put in the socially mobilizing properties of education are evident in Rose's reaction when she received high marks in school:

> *[W]hen I actually got those results, it was like there's a possibility I could escape this crap, basically, rather than just sit and listen to this and have no future prospects. I think I saw it as a glimmer of light that there may be something more for me.*

Once again, the family and the educational system were quite influential regarding the strategies that respondents undertook in both the field of education and employment. As previously discussed regarding aspirations and expectations, the family generally provided support but did not necessarily expect success from their children. In addition, the family did not provide any practical advice concerning higher education or the graduate labour market. This attitude, I suggest, is a consequence of their own limited practical and symbolic mastery characterized by their working-class habitus and faith in the meritocratic processes within the higher education system. For Sarah, her family rarely offered any active discussions on life after graduation:

> *[Speaking as her father]: 'If this [degree] is what makes you happy, if you get a career at the end of it, fair enough. I'm not going to put pressure on you.'*

Some of the families' negative attitudes toward education, as in the case of Kyle, can be seen to direct their employment trajectories. I previously commented that Kyle's working-class family have, in part, formed the dispositions within this habitus, leading him to settle for the same low-level job for the past ten years, staying in the first job he found upon graduating from university. In addition, Kyle's most recent strategies can be traced back to his family's attitudes of 'safe', 9–5, working-class jobs:

> *I can't keep doing this here forever. It's just – there's too many people doing it. Kids coming out of college, multimedia-based [. . .] Seeing my dad and brother come in, get the dinner on, forget about their day's work. (laughs) Looking back at it, I'm thinking I really should have done that.*

The education system played a central role in the strategies respondents employed. Kyle's higher educational strategy was entirely based on advice he had received from his school:

> *I remember going to the careers counsellor or the adviser, sorry. Um, I remember sitting down with her, saying, 'Here's my results.' She was like 'Right, what do you want to do?', and I was going, 'Well, what can I do?' She said, 'Okay, well, you've an A in art. You seem to be good at art, so why don't you look into some sort of path? Go to art college, see if you like it.'*

This advice, then, formed his employment trajectory. Similar to the family, the educational system encouraged respondents to read for a degree but did not provide any practical advice about life in university or graduate life. The educational system was quite important to respondents; Sarah saw it as the main site of social mobility, and she understood her static trajectory to be caused by the lack of direction from the educational system:

> *I guess that's why I have fallen into my job because I wasn't really guided. It was just more like a sort of random thing. An advert appealed to me, and now I've been there like 31/2 years, so, yeah, I'm always keeping my eye out still.*

The educational system did not provide practical advice or practical mastery, as a result, the respondents' working-class habitus was reproduced. Without an out-of-environment-experience or an unlikely temporal exchange of capital, these respondents remain in a static condition within the (graduate) labour market.

Conclusion

This chapter, similar to its predecessor, has traced and analyzed the life histories of two contrasting cohorts of graduates. One of the few common themes of these groups is their status of not being in graduate employment. Once again, the conceptual groups' names are drawn from a central characteristic of the labour market experience. In this case, the entitled middle class group have opted for a stationary position within the labour market, choosing for the labour market to almost come to them via a sense of entitlement. In contrast, the static working class group have not opted for a stationary position but have, all the same, occupied a static trajectory since graduating from university.

The entitled middle class's education period of their life histories demonstrates high levels of aspirations and expectations and a comprehensive, successful strategy, pointing to a strong level of practical and symbolic mastery akin to their middle-class habitus. As such, their educational trajectories point to a single middle-class conceptual group reflecting previous studies, highlighting the general reproduction of the dominant group. Upon graduation, however, respondents' once successful strategies began to diverge from their previous path. Driven by increased levels of aspirations and expectations, respondents have created a very narrow employment trajectory they have wished and expected to follow. Through the process of inverted symbolic violence – facilitated, in part, by the family and, to a much lesser extent, the education system – their understanding of what is for the likes of them is narrowly fixed and ultimately damaging, as respondents have opted for a lateral trajectory, taking on non-graduate positions until they enter their preferred form of employment.

In the concluding comments of the previous chapter, I suggested that the early periods of the other working-class conceptual groups pointed to a classic depiction of social reproduction; however, this group shows exactly this concept in action. Through the influence of habitus and capital, fostered by the family and the education system, respondents had very low levels of aspirations and expectations, often settling for non-graduate employment and expecting to remain in these forms of work for the foreseeable future. The employment trajectories of members from this group most clearly question the human capital meritocratic narrative. Without high levels of *a priori* capitals, an out-of-environment experience or a niche form of capital, respondents were unable to exchange their devalued scholastic capital for entry into the graduate labour market and, therefore, appeared stuck in their current level of employment.

Notes

1 Applicants to UK higher education apply for undergraduate degree courses via the Universities and Colleges Admissions Service (UCAS). If successful, they are given either a conditional offer – which can only be taken up if the applicant achieves particular grades in exams they are currently taking – or an unconditional offer, where the applicant has already met the academic requirements for the course.

2 At the time, students progressing to university via the A-Level route were expected to hold suitable qualifications in three subjects at A-Level.

3 UK degrees are measured on a scale in ascending order of first class honours (1st), upper second class honours (2.1), lower second class honours (2.2), third class honours (3rd) and ordinary.

4 The term 'craic' is Irish for fun or entertaining.

Chapter 5

Theoretical discussion

A wide-angle approach

During the previous two chapters, I have discussed the subtle processes and influence habitus has had over my five conceptual groups. Combined with forms of capital in the specific fields of education and graduate employment, I considered the impact or effect it has had upon the strategies undertaken when looking for graduate employment. While there are specifics or nuances appropriate to each group, general classed themes were beginning to emerge. In this third and final empirically based chapter, I will offer a 'wide angle' discussion, commenting on the more general classed themes within my empirical results.

The habitus – essentially understood as dispositions, attitudes, aspirations and expectations of an individual – can be, as Nash (1999) succinctly explains, extended or generalised to cover a group of individuals, typically one drawn on classed lines. Within this chapter, I intend to discuss the collective classed character of the habitus as it pertains to my working-class and middle-class respondents. The influence of the habitus will be considered through a discussion on the classed forms of both practical and symbolic mastery, culminating with a comparative examination of the strategies undertaken to find and secure graduate employment or the failure to do so. I will conclude by discussing variables that were present within my sampling quota or would, from previous literature, be expected to be present or influential but were not – gender, institutional capital and ethno-national identity.

Working-class habitus

The static working class, the most 'traditional' working-class group with regard to the social closure theorists (Bourdieu and Passeron, 1970/1990; Bowles and Gintis, 1976) and contemporary applications of Bourdieusian social theory (Reay *et al.*, 2005), demonstrate working-class graduates' strategies when nothing out of the ordinary occurred, with no out-of-environment experience (strategic working class) or context-specific exchange of capital (converted working class). Rather than creating an upper and lower working-class group, however, I am comfortable discussing a collective working-class group. While the three working-class conceptual groups have experienced different and, at times, contrasting life histories, their point of origin is the same. The static working class provides the greatest thematic overlap with the other two working-class conceptual groups before their specific influences and encounters forged different paths. Additionally, the converted working class respondents, while being in graduate positions, were examined on more than their current position, taking into consideration their knowledge of the field, their ability for further promotion and whether they would still be mobile if they had to leave their job. Members of this group appear to be quite stuck in their current position, demonstrating an almost re-joining with the static working class. As such, the largest working-class group appears to be an appropriate place to start when discussing a collective or general working-class group.

Attitudes and dispositions displaying low levels of aspiration, expectation and confidence were apparent from the working-class sample, demonstrating Bourdieu's often quoted 'not for the likes of me' attitude. Educationally and occupationally, all the working-class respondents, in at least one phase of their life histories, demonstrated these outlooks. The general recurring theme within my working-class sample of low aspirations, expectations and levels of confidence illustrates a collective working-class habitus. The presence of these attitudes, in both early (educational) and late (occupational/advanced educational) phases of their life history interviews, demonstrates the durability of these working-class dispositions within the working-class habitus. This position is reinforced when one considers Bourdieu's (1992b) comments on the rarity of an out-of-environment experience altering the habitus and the subsequent likelihood of a durable habitus, regardless of the position within the social space; indeed, only two working-class respondents (from a sub-sample of 18) appeared to have their habitus altered by such an experience.

The familial and educational influence on the habitus was relatively constant within the working-class sample. This point is of central significance as Bourdieu (1972/1977) understood the family to be a crucial facet within the formation of the habitus. With the exception of a small number of static working class respondents, the family was quite supportive of their children attending university. Respondents were told, often from a young age, that education would provide access to social mobility; they would have a 'better' life than their parents. The influence of the family more often took the form of encouragement than advice. Working-class parents were unable to offer any practical mastery advice to their children, especially about what to do once in university and in their post-graduation life. They were concerned about getting their child into university, but they did not appear to understand the issues or processes beyond this point, demonstrating, as I have previously commented, a prolonged process of hysteresis of habitus.

A similar form of encouragement from the educational system could be seen for all working-class students. The educational system was quite influential over the life histories of the working-class respondents, presumably due to the level of importance and socially mobilizing abilities the family understood it to possess. Like the family, the educational system encouraged the working-class respondents to attend university through the discourse that access equals success; it argued that higher education would provide them with increased life chances and more security. As with the working-class families, the educational system's influence was more about encouragement than advice. It was more concerned with getting the students to university rather than equipping them with the knowledge of what to do once they got there or what came next.

The working-class respondents displayed a generally low level of capital (economic, social and cultural). While the converted working class did use social or cultural capital to find graduate employment, once this capital had been 'spent', it could not be used again. Bourdieu (1983/2004) argues that forms of capital, especially social, should be judged not only on their level and application but also on the opportunity to repeatedly use it. The temporality and context-specific nature of their capital points to a general low level of capital. Additionally, the strategic working class (post-encounter) did not display levels of capital comparable to the middle-class respondents; any increase they did have would have been in the form of social capital.

Middle-class habitus

With regard to the middle-class respondents, I am equally comfortable discussing a collective middle-class group. While there appears to be a lower and upper middle class, the strategic middle class and entitled middle class respectively, there are clear parallels between the life histories of members from each group. Before entering the post-graduation phase of their lives, both Hannah and Jonny (entitled middle class) demonstrated very similar life histories to the other middle-class respondents. While their life histories diverge, the strategic middle class provide a good place to start when discussing a collective or general middle-class group. Strong aspirations and high levels of expectations were common among the middle classes compared to the working classes, demonstrating a sense of 'this *is* for the likes of us'. While the entitled middle class display a much higher level of aspiration and expectation, extending to a dangerous level fostered by, as I suggest, a process of inverted symbolic violence, it was still a general theme throughout the entire middle-class sample. The longevity or durability of these middle-class dispositions – their middle-class habitus – can be appreciated through their constant presence during both the educational and occupational/advanced educational phases of their life histories, leading me to consider these to be permanent dispositions within the general middle-class group.

The role and influence of the family was quite evident from their biographical interviews. Middle-class families, similar to those of the working-class respondents, were quite encouraging and supportive toward their children going to university; however, the support available went beyond the encouragement provided by the working classes. Their families were able to offer practical advice about life post-graduation. In addition, and in contrast to the working-class respondents, the influence of the educational system (primary and secondary/grammar) was much weaker over the middle classes. As students, they did not only feel the school was ineffectual, but they overtly challenged the educational system, illustrating a general middle-class understanding of the school as a somewhat impotent institution. This result is not surprising, as the educational system transmits and normalises, via inculcation and pedagogic authority (Bourdieu and Passeron, 1970/1990), the middle-class norms or doxa. To the middle-class graduates, the environment the educational system is attempting to produce and the norms they are attempting to reproduce already appear as 'normal' and would, therefore, have little effect on them.

Middle-class respondents displayed a constantly high level of capital. As I have previously commented, the entitled middle class could be understood as upper middle class. This distinction is shown through a demonstration of possessing some of the highest levels of economic and cultural capital within my entire research sample. There remains, however, a general middle-class theme of high levels of capital in relation to the working-class respondents. These levels were presented through describing feelings of belonging and comfort in 'cultural' environments. Additionally, the middle classes, in general, had high levels of social capital in that they were able to use social contacts to reproduce, or move up to, a position of power/status within social space.

Occupational strategy: practical mastery

A central task of this research was to examine the strategies graduates undertake when looking for graduate employment. The 'common-sense' definition of strategy is understood as the plans they made and their ability to successfully complete or reach these goals. From the previous two chapters, it is clear that the level or form of strategy undertaken is repeated, to varying degrees, within each classed group. This suggests that there is a general classed model of strategy evident within my empirical results influenced by the collective class habitus.

While the various working-class groups have experienced different trajectories, due to different influences or the lack thereof, at one time, they all demonstrated quite weak educational and employment strategies. A common working-class theme was the presence of a high level of faith in or, simply, the expectation of education and its intrinsic ability to secure you a 'good' graduate position. The trust placed in HE was often presented through frustration when this assumed relationship did not materialize. Michael (static working class) expressed both agitation and surprise at experiencing such difficulty in entering the graduate labour market:

> *When I started third level education, it was 'You need a degree. Everyone needs a degree to get a job', and, then, when I came out of uni, it was suddenly 'No,*

> *we want work experience. We want 3–4 years' experience of* working, *which you obviously don't have'.*

As with previous respondents, this experience is a form of hysteresis of habitus, and the changing field is graduate employment. Working-class graduates assume the previous relationship between credentials and opportunities, i.e. a more linear system, is still valid, so they approach the current market with an outdated and ineffective attitude/understanding. The continued effects of hysteresis of habitus are demonstrated through the durable faith in the mobilizing effects of (higher) education. When discussing employment options with Steve (static working class), I asked him how one stands out if many more people have increased qualifications. He answered:

> *Well, that's the thing. Everyone's got a degree now, so the applications now are like 'You must have a masters or a PhD'. I don't know what that means for – is everyone – in the future, people will be told 'You go to school, then university, then a masters and then you get a job'. Is that how it's going to be? I don't know.*

Despite being in a situation of graduate inflation, Steve's only strategy was to gain more qualifications, further demonstrating the hysteresis of habitus. Additionally, Steve's comment about gaining more education points to the lack of other, *a priori* capital that the working classes can use to enter the graduate labour market. The general working-class sample often took up the first job they could get, as paid employment was their only access to economic capital. They did not possess high levels of cultural capital, soft skills that they could use to make themselves stand out in an interview. While many respondents relied on social contacts for employment, their social capital reproduced their dominated position within social space.

Hysteresis of habitus continued to produce negative results for the working-class graduates. For many of my working-class respondents, once they had entered low-level positions, they found it difficult – if not impossible – to leave them. Fergal (static working class), upon graduating from university, began working in retail. He appeared unable to make the transition into graduate employment, and, as he continued to have little success in finding a graduate-level job, he began to settle for his low-status positions:

> *I suppose – I suppose, at the minute, I've been thinking a lot about the future, where I'll be in 5 years' time, and it's hard to – any job I do get will be fairly low-level and something quite low paid, probably in, um, a big chain again, maybe in retail or the service industry.*

Fergal had hoped to eventually enter a graduate-level job. When it did not transpire, he settled for a lower-status job and, consequently, limited his level of aspiration, negatively affecting his employment strategy. The working-class respondents lacked both the understanding or practical mastery and resources (capital) to negotiate the field. By misrecognising the labour market, their subjective expectations or field of the possibles waned, limiting their strategy. As previously discussed, Brown and Scase (1994) report that their working-class respondents did not understand how the labour market operated. They expected to be handed a good job upon leaving university, and, when that did not materialize, they settled for whatever job they could find, essentially capping the level that they could reach.

This discourse of settling was also apparent within the strategic working class (pre-encounter). Pete explains that he took a low-level job within the civil service (operating a car park security barrier) as his family encouraged him to and because he had very few options; therefore, he was forced to settle. Settling was equally apparent within the converted working class. For Catherine, if she could not use her law degree to become a solicitor, then she would settle for working in a restaurant. In other words, if her degree did not provide a linear progression, the type of progression that Bourdieu (1979) demonstrates the working classes expect, she would be unable to formulate a plan or negotiate the labour market and would, therefore, settle for a low-status job. The absence of a strategic approach to the labour market outside of the direct application of scholastic capital again demonstrates that a combination of low levels of – increasingly required – capital and a working-class habitus reproduce working-class graduates' social backgrounds rather than providing social mobility.

Middle-class graduates also presented a general shared level of strategy. Hannah (entitled middle class) presented a clear understanding of the market, specifically the composition of her chosen profession and the challenges that she would meet:

> *I knew that my own personal job market was going to be very cut-throat and very difficult and – very much – I would have to do stuff for free before I could get paid.*

Hannah's comments, representative of the larger middle-class sub-sample, display an understanding of the field and, therefore, of the game. The ability to the play the game is based on an understanding of the rules. A stronger position within the field of graduate employment is synonymous with a higher or more privileged position within social space. As Reay *et al.* (2005) demonstrate with school leavers, and Smetherham (2006) with university graduates, the middle classes possess a greater understanding of the game and are, thus, in a better position to successfully negotiate the field. Phil, who had worked mostly in media, argued that his degree in film studies did not prepare or qualify him to work on a film set. He had to rely on more than his qualifications to secure employment, which he was more than willing and able to do:

When you're doing film studies, you're not looking at production design that much. It's directing, maybe cinematography, maybe performance, but not much beyond, not design. It was like, even though I had a degree in film, it was like I was going in fresh. That was really, really interesting [. . .] it's about getting to know people and making sure they know your name [. . .] even if I had done a single honours film degree, I wouldn't have learned half of the first day on the film shoot and that energy as well – that kinda – there's a real buzz to it.

The middle-class respondents, through a better understanding of the field and the current value of a degree, were able to form appropriate strategies. As was the case in Tomlinson's research (2007, 2008), they were able to piece together different resources and capitals to make themselves more employable. A common, almost universal, theme within my research was that of taking a low-level position upon graduating from university. The ability to understand the graduate market was key to how long respondents remained in these low-level positions and decided when, how and if they should leave them based on relations within the field. Brooks and Everett (2009) discuss this recurring theme from their empirical research of middle-class graduates entering low-status employment until the time is right to move onto higher status/graduate positions. This shift can be illustrated from the life histories of my middle-class respondents such as Katie (strategic middle class). Through familial influence, Katie always expected to enter the 'Firm'; however, she worked in a lower-status job until it was the right time:

Ach, well, yeah, you know – I was always going to go into it. It was always at the back of my mind, but I didn't want to go into it straight after uni. I wanted to get my masters, and then, after that even, I took some time working. Like, I got a good job working for [radio station], really enjoyed it there. It started to get to me. I knew [the Firm] were getting ready to hire again. It was a good time for me to do it, you know.

She was able to make these decisions because of her feel for the game or practical mastery. This classed theme supports Bourdieu's (1979) position that, in the context of hysteresis of habitus in the graduate labour market, the middle class, equipped with their feel for the game, will be in a better position to know the right moment to pull out of low-status jobs and enter a higher ranking profession.[1] The ability to wait until the lag, hysteresis, closes between individuals and field is supported by capital. Many respondents used social contacts in order to know when certain areas of the labour market were ready for entry. Katie's social capital, extended from her family, allowed her to plan out when to apply for the 'Firm' and what she should do in the interim to make her application stronger. The middle-class respondents were generally more flexible in their employment strategies. They often had reserve plans or had set out a timeline to successfully enter a profession; if they had not, then they would reformulate their strategy to avoid a static occupation of social space.

The level of understanding and the successful negotiation of the labour market are highly classed among my sample. Respondents' aspirations and expectations, coupled with the influence of institutions such as the family and educational system, are central in directing their life histories. There is a clear connection between the character of the habitus and the form and level of practical mastery. The constant working-class habitus of the static working class and the constant middle-class habitus of the strategic middle class produce a consistently low or high level of strategy, respectively. While the other working-class and middle-class sub-groups diverge, due to niche situations and influences, they further illustrate the habitus' influence.

Ordinary reflections – symbolic mastery

Alongside practical mastery, or the feel for the game, lies reflection. In Chapter 1, I offered my own position on the role or presence of reflexivity within a Bourdieusian model. There is a conscious or reflective element of the habitus; however, it is also bound to the habitus and, therefore, the symbolic mastery it generates will be influenced by the habitus in the same way that practical mastery or the feel for the game is understood to be. Noble and Watkins (2003: 531) argue that ordinary or mundane reflection is not a critical understanding of the field or societal power struggles, but, rather, an account of what an individual has done and is capable of doing in their everyday ordinary or mundane life. It is this form of ordinary reflection that I observed as being generally classed within my empirical results. In an effort to measure or gauge reflection, I discuss levels of reflection as consequential and sequential accounts of action and trajectory – essentially, the level at which an individual is able to provide a reflective account of what they have done and what they are capable of doing in the future. I seek to observe whether they can discuss the consequences of their actions or if they tend to provide a sequential account of their trajectory with a low level of reflection on what they have done or are able to do in the future. I was able to follow this line of inquiry due to the staggered approach of the BNIM interview (Schütze, 1992, 2008; Rosenthal, 2003, 2005). Conducting two out of three sub-sessions where the interviewer is provided little opportunity to ask questions creates an opportunity for an individual's level of reflection (high or low) to become apparent, unaided by questions, providing a more honest representation of their levels of reflection.

As was the case with practical mastery, the general working-class sample displayed a low level of reflection or symbolic mastery, suggesting a broad working-class form of ordinary reflection. Working-class respondents were able to offer, at best, a limited account of their educational and occupational trajectories. For example, Paddy (static working class) offered a very short and sequential account of his occupational trajectory, during his initial narration:

> *So I did that [went to university] and, um, joined the public sector in sales, selling beer and coffee, um, for, what is it? 4 years – wait, that's a bit quick, isn't it?*

Paddy did realize that this response was quite short and extended his answer. He offered more specifics relating to the types of positions, where they were and what he did. Despite adding length, he added no real depth to his answer, providing no discernible consequential account.

A similarly low level of reflection was evident among the converted working class. This observation adds weight to my suggestion that, while this conceptual group has found itself within graduate employment, they support the inclusion of a discussion pertaining to a general working-class group. Additionally, while the strategic working class demonstrated a high level of reflection, it is in direct contrast to their level of reflection before their out-of-environment experience.

Within the general middle-class sample, there was a common theme of high levels of ordinary reflection or symbolic mastery, complementing their high levels of practical mastery. Middle-class respondents provided quite consequential and reflective comments with regard to both their educational and occupational trajectories. When discussing practical mastery, Phil (strategic middle class) presented a strong understanding of his particular field – media and teaching; however, he further demonstrated a strong level of symbolic mastery when accounting for why he took a position he did not really want or in which he did not have any long-term interest:

> *They [the production team] already had their art department in place, so I just came on as a production runner, making coffee, lifting things, but I would always help out the art department in my own time, you know, keeping my hand in on the sets, doing props, like.*

Phil is able to provide a reflective statement explaining his actions and subsequent occupational trajectory. As is the case with practical mastery, the entitled middle class respondents do not follow or demonstrate the same high level of reflection as the other middle-class graduates in relation to the labour market; however, during earlier periods of their life histories, they, too, presented high levels of symbolic mastery. When discussing his rationale for choosing his degree, Jonny (entitled middle-class) demonstrated an understanding of why he had done certain things and a plan for future strategies.

While there are nuances and contrasting levels and forms of reflection within each classed group, as is the case with their specific conceptual group habitus, there is a general classed character to ordinary reflection or symbolic mastery,[2] with a higher level of reflection being understood as more common, but not exclusive, within my general middle-class sample. Reflection is bound to the habitus, as is clear from both Katie (strategic middle class) and Niamh's (strategic working class) life history interviews. Katie's extended family worked for the 'Firm'. While she provides a number of examples of reflection, her dispositions, influenced by family, have still led her to seek a form of graduate employment that equates with 'joining the family business'. Her level of symbolic mastery was also tied to capital. It was through having strong levels of social capital that she fully understood the field and was able to present such a mastery over it. In the case of Niamh, when her habitus was altered, so, too, was her practical and symbolic mastery; however, the nature of focus of this mastery was aligned to her particular out-of-environment experience.

'Paired graduates'

It could be suggested that the difference in both understanding and success stems from the forms of graduate employment to which respondents either aspire or within which they are currently involved. As such, I will offer a discussion of 'paired graduates': comparing working-class and middle-class respondents who are attempting to enter or are currently employed in similar professions in order to consider any differences in understanding and success the respondents have had.

Managing human resources: Annie and Sarah

Understanding the rules of the game is central to a successful strategy; knowing how the pieces move on the board or where out-of-bounds begins is elementary for winning. Annie (strategic middle class) and Sarah (static working class) were both at a similar stage in the process of being fully qualified to work in the managerial side of human resources. The professional qualification for this career track is the Chartered Institute for Personnel and Development certificate (CIPD). The level of understanding of what the qualification is and how to best use it once attained was very different between these two graduates. On request, Annie was able to explain the CIPD in quite a lot of detail:

> *Yeah, basically, it's the charter that you need to get a job in HR. Basically, you'll be going into business policies and learning how to handle certain situations, um. With employee relations, it would be how to handle conflict, how you work in your best business practice, things like that, basically, and you'd be learning about recruitment and all the rules and regulations for things like that. The CIPD teaches you the best business practice, um, policies and things like that that are across any business [. . .] it's three years, but, if you have previous experience, it could be two years or one year. So, you would go in for an interview. They would gauge on your – on your – experience, how many years you would need to do.*

Additionally, she knew the most conducive avenues to go down with this qualification, citing the health profession as the best place to work for human resources:

Well, what I want to do is work for a HR department in the health sector because they offer way more benefits than the private sector. (she laughs)

In stark contrast, Sarah knew very little about the CIPD, which was the central element of a masters she was currently reading. Answering a direct question from me to explain the process, she explained:

The CIPD is the human resource qualification you need to practise human resource management.

Additionally, in terms of what to do after she had this qualification, she had little intention to, or plan of how to, use her new qualification, commenting:

I kinda got the next two years of my life sorted, and, after that, I don't really care.[3]

There is quite a contrast in the level of understanding between these two graduates. Importantly, the level of understanding is not based on degree qualification – Annie received a 3rd class honours degree while Sarah received a 2.1 – nor on time since graduation – Annie graduated four years ago, and Sarah graduated three years ago. Similarly, it is not based on supposed institutional status, as Annie read for her undergraduate degree at *Northern* while Sarah read for her undergraduate degree at *Southern*. The variable that does suggest itself is class; there is a general classed level of understanding within my sample, seen most clearly between two graduates both attempting to gain the same professional qualification. To further this point, I will compare the strategies applied by a pair of graduates who are trying to 'make it' in similar employment areas.

The self-reliance of 'DIY' occupations: John and Finbar

A successful occupational trajectory requires an understanding of the field. This point is even more significant in relation to less formal occupations, as these positions rely on self-motivation and creating a position for oneself rather than following structured procedures such as applying for a job, giving an interview, etc. In this comparison, I will discuss the occupational strategies and levels of occupational success of John (strategic middle class) and Finbar (static working class). John is a commissioned and active artist; however, the relatively low income he generates from painting requires him to supplement it with another job:

I think I did two years of basically just working here [studio], and working in Tesco as a driver, delivering shopping, you know and just trying to get in

> *here and painting all the time. [. . .] I got a job as technician in [FE College], which is up in Westpoint, an art and design technician, and did that for about 6 months, got to know some of the staff there, and then, basically, the next year they brought me back as a lecturer.*

Through a strong or high level of occupational strategy, John has managed to foster and create a middle-class position comprised of an art lectureship in a FE College while being an active artist:

> *[A]nd I think the most important thing is I can come in every day and try and do a little bit of work and doing various bits of teaching.*

What is particularly interesting in John's case is that his knowledge of the market is supplemented by his MA thesis, which focused on the issues of being an artist within Northern Ireland:

> *The pragmatic element of the thesis affected me a lot because a lot of things you think are possible as an art student aren't possible. Like, you can go and make art and, um, people are just going to like it. You have to make it in conditions that it will be liked. That's part of your job as an artist.*

I asked John if he can tailor his work for the middle-class art buyer, and he responded:

> *[Y]eah, of course, you have to. To be a working living artist, you need to do what they want.*

John essentially studied the specific market and was able to put his knowledge into practice and manoeuvre within it.

The case is very different for Finbar (static working class). On leaving university, he attempted to become a performing artist; however, unlike John, Finbar has only been able to supplement his income with low-status/temporary positions. He commented about the increasing difficulty to do this effectively:

> *It was becoming harder and harder to get office jobs, and I found a job – probably the job I disliked the most – counting money for a security company. That was truly grim. I did that for about five weeks, so I had enough money to work while I was doing my show. [. . .] Then it was after that, and I still couldn't. I think I realized I had a lucky run with the office work, and I had done a few temping one-offs around that time. I knew I wasn't up to standard. I was thinking, 'I'm better with people', you know. I was doing gigs and various things, so I ended up getting a cleaning job.*

Frustrated by his lack of success, Finbar has become a full-time, self-employed performing artist; however, he admits that he is not very well suited to this type of position:

> *I'm not a businessman, exactly, and I don't want to be caught up in all the organizational side, but I want to help get the organization together so that I don't have to . . .*

Since taking up performing as a full-time profession, Finbar has enjoyed quite limited success. He explained that, on average, he makes £30 a day, with little or no assurance of how many days a week he can expect to work. On further questioning, it appears that Finbar knows very little about the field he has decided to enter:

> *I don't know how they [other entertainers] did it. How do you make a living out of it? Can you do this all the time? How do you do it? I hope I'm starting to learn. I don't think I've got it sussed [. . .] touch wood, it's not the most secure thing to be in (he laughs).*

The occupational strategies John and Finbar undertook when attempting to enter the informal world of the arts were quite contrasting. John was able to fashion a middle-class/graduate-level position through combining being a relatively successful and commissioned artist and a lecturer in an FE College. He is able to enjoy the status of being an active member of the Northern Irish art community while creating a comfortable living. In contrast, Finbar has been unable to create a graduate-level position; through a weak or low level of occupational strategy, he appeared able to only supplement his art with low-status positions that were generally temporary. More recently, Finbar has decided to become a full-time artist. Again, he has enjoyed relatively little success and admits he has very little understanding of the field in play. Similar to Annie and Sarah, the contrast between John and Finbar cannot be accounted for through degree classification, as John received a 2.1 classification and Finbar a 2.2, both respondents graduated university at the same time and the more successful of the two graduates read for their undergraduate degree in the post-1992 institution, *Northern*. As with my previous 'paired graduates', I would suggest that class is the dominant variable that influences their occupational trajectories. The most significant factor in class is the differing levels of cultural capital; however, both social capital and economic capital are playing a key role in the graduates' trajectories.

Gender

One central variable within my research sample that did not appear to demonstrate a great level of influence was gender. When designing my sample,

I purposely ensured the sample was balanced by gender. My intention was to create a radical doubt within my own research question by providing gender with an opportunity to demonstrate its influence over graduate trajectories. Previous literature has discussed the continuing influence of gender; Reay *et al.* (2005) remind us that educational decisions, such as subject choice and attendance, are heavily influenced by gender and ethnicity. Gender, however, did not appear to have a significant influence over my respondents' educational trajectories.

The inequality of women or the gendered character of the labour market has been well documented. Grint (2005) discusses the historical development of women within the labour market, specifically the gender pay gap. While the gender pay gap has narrowed to 10 per cent in the UK (ONS, 2013a), the persistent differentiation of wages based on gender shows the durable gendered nature of the labour market. In the context of the 2008 financial crisis, it was women's wages that were most affected, leading to an increase in the gender pay gap (Fawcett Society, 2013). Previously, authors such as Hartmann (1982) and Walby (1986) have discussed the patriarchal composition of the labour market, arguing that it is quite difficult for women to enter such a field. It is very much still an issue within Northern Ireland. Miller (2004: 54–55) reported that the leading influences on men's current occupations were the same on women's: educational qualifications and status of first job; however, Miller adds that men have a greater chance of enjoying a higher employment status irrespective of labour market entry or level of educational credentials, as initial entry to the market is gendered. Women who enter the same employment level as men with similar educational levels will not do as well; this fact, Miller suggests, points to gender discrimination within the Northern Irish workplace. The most recent figures pertaining to the Northern Irish labour market (Rodgers, 2013) support Miller's observations. In 2013, the employed population in Northern Ireland was slightly male dominated, 53 per cent male to 47 per cent female; however, when looking at gendered levels of part-time work, women represented 80 per cent of this population, pointing to the continued gendered nature of work and earnings.

While there is still gender inequality within the workplace, the emergence and development of post-industrialization (Bell, 1973), characterized by a focus on soft skills and services and based on a human capital discourse of the most qualified being the most successful, it could be assumed that women's position within this new market will be significantly enhanced. Crompton (1999) comments that, as the twentieth century drew to a close, so did a number of the barriers within Western society to women. This effect was most clearly observed through the educational expansion of women and their increasing representation within the labour market, coupled with a shift from a predominantly manual-based industry to a service industry. There have also been observable changes in the level of women's aspirations and expectations. Shu and Marini (1998) report that younger women in their research were much less likely to aspire to 'traditionally female roles' than older women, pointing to a generational shift, via societal and legislative changes, with regard to 'what is for the likes of them'. Importantly, Shu and Marini found that this generational shift to a more empowered or strategic woman was more common among the higher and middle classes, suggesting the importance of class alongside gender when understanding occupational attitudes and subsequent trajectories.

Vallas *et al.* (2010) remind us that, while the gender pay gap has narrowed, life course events such as parenthood do pose a serious threat to the durability of this emerging equality. There is what is known as the 'motherhood pay gap'; Budig and England (2001) found that, while women still earn less than men, women who are at a time in their lives where having a family is a possibility also earn, on average, 7 per cent less than women who are no longer at that period in their lives. Crompton and Harris (1999) discuss the continuing expectation of (working) women to carry out household/domestic responsibilities. The increase of women in the workforce has not been met with an equal increase in the sharing of domestic roles within the household, resulting in women being required to 'work a second shift'. While they welcome an egalitarian division of labour, Crompton and Harris appear cautious to celebrate the apparent reduction in gender-segregated roles, both within the home and the labour market. As Hochschild remarks, women appear to be living through a 'stalled revolution' (1990).

Within the specific context of graduate under-employment, it could be suggested that women will be disproportionately affected. Women have enjoyed more success with educational expansion, so it is logical that they would suffer the most from the increasing graduate inflation and the decreasing value of a degree. Brynin (2002), however, suggests that it may not be the case. First, he argues that, quite simply, occupational inequalities are beginning to wane; women who do not take time off from work to have a family will enjoy similar levels of success and status as men. Second, women are still seen as 'new' graduates, and they stand out in an interview; as such, they enjoy more long-term jobs than men. The most recent findings from *Futuretrack* (Purcell *et al.*, 2013) question this position. The report found that, while female graduates tend to do better than their male counterparts in terms of degree classification, there were clear gendered employment trajectories, which could only in part be explained by different subject choices. While the emergence of post-industrialization has affected traditionally male industries and questioned their role in the greater market, men have been seen to be repositioning themselves within the market (Henson and Krasas Rodgers, 2001, Cognard-Black, 2004). This research has highlighted the strategies employed by men to re-balance authority within an increasingly feminized market. In addition, recent research has pointed to the re-emergence of the male breadwinner model (Berghammer, 2014). In this research, women – particularly those women with higher level education – who have young children opted for a male breadwinner model over dual breadwinner, taking up the role of primary caregiver to their children.

This particular strategy was understood as a consequence between limited availability of childcare places and cultural expectations on the role of mothers. The influence of prolonged gendered norms removing women from the labour market and the repositioning of men within a largely patriarchal system questions Hakim's (1996) position that women reflexively choose their educational and employment trajectories.

As I have previously commented, within my own research sample, gender did not appear to have had a great influence over respondent's trajectories. There was little evidence of gender segregation between the men and women I interviewed. There was one respondent, Lindsey, for whom gender appeared to be an influential factor. Lindsey, a member of the strategic middle class, is an aeronautical engineer; however, she has recently become a mother and, as a result, is unable to continue in her current profession. I asked Lindsey about the role of gender within her employment trajectory. She commented that she did not feel the influence of gender or the fact that she was a woman in a traditionally male industry was a factor until she became a mother:

> *Um, I'm not – it has affected it in the past, I suppose. I never found anything in [the company] at all being related. Well, I was the only woman as an engineer when I started there. There are more now. I never really found any problems. [. . .] Being a woman is affecting my engineering career because it's male dominated. There's no provision historically for flexible or part-time working the way there would be in other professions for new parents – the way there would be in other professions like nursing.*

This evidence supports the previous comments (Budig and England, 2001; Brynin, 2002) that parenthood, especially motherhood, will disrupt or alter an occupational trajectory, suggesting a continuing gender inequality within the labour market. Lindsey explained that she would have to take some time away from engineering. I asked her if she would ever go back to the industry. She fully expects to go back once her daughter is able to attend pre-school:

> *Absolutely. I'm looking for an engineering-related part-time job. There are no part-time engineer jobs, but I might get a part-time draftsperson job. That would keep my skills current. I'd definitely go back to engineering when I could.*

The use of the phrase 'when I could' is interesting, as there is little doubt in Lindsey's narrative that she will be eventually returning to her profession; however, the situation that removed her from her position is largely out of her current control. Until she is able, she has formulated a strategy to effectively negotiate the current situation. She demonstrates an understanding of her particular field, discussing which supplementary professions provide her with the time she wants to be a mother while also keeping her in the general engineering profession.

Her understanding of the field and the ability to effectively strategize within it are reminiscent of her general life history and that of the strategic middle class. Parenthood has affected her occupational trajectory and her life history in general; however, she is essentially able to 're-group' and formulate a new strategy for this phase of her life. I would suggest that this is another example of the strategic middle class members demonstrating their practical mastery within the field. I cannot be certain that Lindsey will eventually return to her current position. If she does, her career will not have progressed as much as her colleagues', demonstrating the continued gendered character of graduate employment. Lindsey was the only respondent who demonstrated this particular alteration in her trajectory. Without other middle-class respondents to strengthen this position and working-class respondents to offer as a comparison, I am limited to the extent that I can claim gendered issues – such as parenthood – while altering the life course, can be more effectively negotiated by the middle classes. It is certainly a weakness of having a small sample; however, the nature of my research question and my form of data collection required such a sample size.

Gender is an important issue within both educational and occupational attitudes and trajectories. Beck (1992) argues that 'permanent conflicts' such as gender and ethnicity have transcended classed issues. Proponents of the cultural turn in class analysis (Reay, 2000; Crompton and Scott, 2005) contend that both class and gender need to be appreciated together, not as independent variables but intertwined facets of identity when discussing educational trajectories (Reay *et al.*, 2005) and employment (Hebson, 2009). Gender has not always been included within class analysis. Crompton (1999) reminds us that Goldthorpe *et al.*'s (1980) class model measured women's social class by the occupational position of their husband or father. As Skeggs (1997) illustrates, the nuances of and the struggles between classed forms of gender need to be appreciated. Gender was not a prominent variable within my research; this fact, however, does not mean or support a position that gender is no longer an important factor on occupational trajectories and life histories. Brynin (2002) comments that occupational opportunities are essentially equal among men and women, provided that women do not take time off for motherhood – the traditional female role. From my sample, only two of my respondents were parents: Lindsey and Pete. Perhaps when more respondents, especially female respondents, become parents, the influence of gender will be more apparent.

Institutional capital

There is a wealth of research (Egerton and Halsey, 1993; Reay, 1998; Leathwood and Hutchings, 2003; Reay *et al.* 2005; Evans, 2009; Reay *et al.*, 2009a, 2009b; Sianou-Kyrgiou and Tsiplakides, 2010) discussing the classed stratification of educational institutions. The central observations are that working-class students, due to a low level of aspiration and expectation, are less likely to apply to a prestigious institution. The extent or presence of this classed division within higher education can be appreciated through studies such as Brown and Scase's (1994); the authors understood pre-1992 university and post-1992 university graduates to be synonyms for middle-class and working-class graduates. The danger or problem with the classed division of HEIs is, as Smetherham (2006) and Tomlinson (2008) argue, when other levels of capital, such as scholastic capital, are equal, the capital associated with the institution in which a graduate read for their degree can be exchanged for employment positions and status.

Within my empirical results, I did not find a prominent trend or theme to support this position. Graduates from *Southern* did not enjoy a more successful occupational trajectory, nor were they more likely to enter graduate employment than students from *Northern*.[4] The most discernible pattern or influence was one based on social class. A small number of working-class graduates did comment that the prestigious reputation of *Southern* led them to read for their degree there, particularly in order to use its reputation to help them find a good (graduate) job. When discussing her reasons behind choosing *Southern* over *Northern*, Catherine (converted working class) explained that it was due to reputation:

> *I put [Southern] down as first choice and [Northern] as second because everyone's first choice is Southern, because – I know it's snobbery, but it's [Southern], and [Northern] is still seen – it's the second university of Northern Ireland.*

This, again, is a failed strategy within Catherine's educational trajectory. Going to *Southern* over *Northern* did not appear to positively affect the working-class respondents' ability to enter the graduate labour market. In contrast, the middle-class graduates, when discussing why they chose one university over the other, explained that it was due to the specific course that they intended to read. On discussing university choices in Northern Ireland, I asked Lindsey (strategic middle class) why she chose *Southern* over *Northern*. She answered:

> *[T]heir [Northern's] engineering department isn't as good as [Southern], that's why.*

A number of middle-class graduates felt that they needed to defend their rationale for reading for a degree in *Northern*. Katie (strategic middle class) commented:

> *And I know there are so many people who slag it off and say things, but I had some absolutely awesome lecturers.*

The only instance of the middle-class graduates attending *Southern* due to its reputation was found within the entitled middle-class. When discussing choice of university, Hannah commented:

> *I really hadn't planned anything except to go to [Southern] . . . I hadn't planned on moving up to [Northern]. (she laughs)*

The reputation associated with *Southern*, while still understood to be quite high in contrast to *Northern*, is not as high as it once was and, therefore, cannot act as a benefit or an additional form of capital. A possible reason for this shift is the role that elite grammar schools play in Northern Ireland. These schools house the elite children of Northern Irish society. A common trend among these elite grammar schools is to push their students to read for degrees at elite universities such as Oxbridge, Bristol or Durham. As such, there are very few of the elite middle class/upper middle class reading degrees at *Southern* to reproduce its previous institutional capital. The middle-class respondents appreciate the devaluation of *Southern*'s institutional capital; thus, they read for their degree in the university that was most suitable for them, understanding that it outweighed the supposed institutional capital associated with *Southern*.

Some middle-class graduates who read for their degree in *Northern* felt the need to defend their trajectory, as there is still a residual effect from the previous binary relationship between *Southern* and *Northern*. The entitled middle class's insistence on attending *Southern* due to its prestige is another effect of hyper-aspiration fostered by inverted symbolic violence. The fact that Hannah laughed at the mere idea of reading for a degree in *Northern* demonstrates her attitude toward the institution and acts as an example of her poor understanding of the field. The working-class respondents, in line with the general working of hysteresis of habitus (Bourdieu, 1972/1977, 1979), did not understand this shift in the higher education field and assumed that an undergraduate degree from *Southern* carried its previous level of institutional capital.

Ethno-national identity

As I have previously commented, the influence of ethno-national identity has begun to wane within Northern Irish society. A number of authors (Horgan, 2007; Smyth and Cebulla, 2008) argue that the 'Troubles' within Northern Ireland, which marked over 30 years of civil violence, was a class conflict between working-class Catholics and working-class Protestants rather than a civil conflict involving all members of society. The continued class divide within each ethno-national 'group' can be appreciated in the composition or grass-roots support of the Northern Irish political parties; while parties represent each side of the divide, the parties within each divide are also split in terms of social class. The lack of influence of ethno-national identity within my empirical research serves to support comments by authors such as Coulter (1999). There was no observable pattern of Catholic or Protestant respondents following a particular trajectory or enjoying a certain level of success at the expense of the other 'group'. To add weight to this position, I posed the question of ethno-national identity during my follow-up interview or third sub-session of the BNIM.

The answers I received served to support the lack of any discernible patterns of ethno-national influence. Lindsey (strategic middle class, Catholic), on being asked about the influence of ethno-national identity, responded:

> *I never thought about it. It didn't occur to me until I started working as an engineer that I was the only Catholic there. It never occurred to me. It didn't really matter. (she laughs)*

Similarly, Paddy (static working class, Catholic) responded:

> *Only insofar as I've tried to completely ignore religion and all that shite as much as possible.*

The responses were quite similar from Protestant respondents; Jonny (entitled middle-class, Protestant) responded:

> *(He laughs) Um, no, not like – I wouldn't not go for a writing job or work with someone because I'm whatever, you know.*

Jonny added that, because he is middle-class, he would not necessarily think along ethno-national lines. It appeared that he understood that to be a working-class problem, as he commented:

> *I suppose, my upbringing being middle class, I haven't experienced discrimination or any hardship or anything like that. I'm sure that's because I'm middle class and don't really think about it . . .*

Each of these respondents and members of their conceptual groups did not entertain the influence of ethno-national identity; as there was no pattern associated with ethno-national identity, I tend to agree. The only respondent for which ethno-national identity appeared to be a factor was Kyle (static working class, Protestant). I suggested that his family's working-class Protestant habitus influenced him. It needs to be understood that a typical form of employment for working-class Protestants in Belfast was to work in the shipyard – traditionally, manual labour. When I suggested that he is influenced by the working-class Protestant habitus, I was referring to the type of employment Protestants in Belfast traditionally did; the fact that it was a Protestant form of employment is somewhat irrelevant as Kyle, too, understood ethno-national identity to have little influence over his occupational trajectories:

> *Um, none of that even entered my head. I just did what I liked. (he laughs)*

Miller (2004) comments on a comparison between data from the 1973/1974 'Irish Mobility Study' and from his 1996/1997 replication considering the continuing influence of ethno-national identity on social mobility or occupational trajectory; he reports, from the original Irish Mobility Study, that, when entry into labour market and educational credentials were taken into account, ethno-national identity had a significant, albeit weak, effect upon occupational status. Protestants within Northern Ireland were enjoying higher occupational levels in comparison to Catholics from equivalent backgrounds. The strength of this influence was appreciated through its durability in the light of additional variables such as educational credentials. In Miller's 1996/1997 replica survey, ethno-national identity was not a significant influence on occupational status.[5] Within this data set, the most important variables were educational qualifications and length of time spent in education – in other words, a university education and the status of first job. Attendance at a grammar school over a secondary school and a father with a high-status occupation will increase the levels of qualification, affecting occupational status. The academic transfer exam, which decides whether a student goes to a grammar school or not, is heavily classed (Smyth and Cebulla, 2008). Miller (2004) concludes that a further important influence on an individual's initial entry point into the labour market was social capital – again, something that is heavily classed. My empirical results support the position that the influence of ethno-national identity on Northern Irish society, and the labour market in particular, has been dramatically reduced.

Conclusion

Through this chapter, I have provided a wide-angle discussion of my empirical results. I have suggested that, despite specific processes and trajectories pertaining to each conceptual group, collective working-class and middle-class habitus can be observed within my research sample. As such, class habitus can be understood to have affected or influenced both the practical and symbolic mastery that directs an individual's trajectory – specifically, their occupational trajectory. The classed nature of occupational trajectory has been most clearly demonstrated through comparing respondents who are attempting to enter or have entered the same form of profession but who offer differing levels of understanding or experience of this profession. I have discussed the lack of influence that gender, institutional capital and ethno-national identity has had on the occupational trajectories of my sample, further supporting my position that class is a central variable influencing my respondents' life histories.

Notes

1 An obvious exception to the middle-class sample were members of the entitled middle class. They, too, took what they expected to be transitory positions until they moved into their chosen profession. The key difference is that these transitory positions must be found within middle-class institutions and the move from these positions into their chosen profession requires little strategy, as they believe they are 'meant' to enter their preferred occupational roles.

2 As with all Bourdieusian discussions of class, this level of reflection is understood or appreciated in relation to the other classes' level of reflection.
3 Two years is the length of time it would take to complete her masters.
4 For an account of graduate employment status by higher education institution, please see Appendix B.
5 It was only significant as an element of the father's position, i.e. as an artefact of the situation in the previous 1973/1974 generation.

Chapter 6

Social policy implications

Lessons to be learned

The UK higher education system has witnessed a number of significant and lasting developments. Beginning with the expansion of secondary level education, via the 1944 Education Act, and the increase in absolute mobility in post-war Britain (Devine and Li, 2013), higher education – a trajectory previously held for the social elite – became a possibility for the general population. As the academy's doors were opened to the public, these once reserved and distant institutions became a central focus of both private and public society. This chapter will provide a critical discussion of the developing narratives and policies within the higher education sector – in particular, the increasing role higher education now plays within larger social justice initiatives, the focus on skills provision within higher education and universities' increasing links with industry. The chapter will, then, provide a number of recommendations concerning the role that (higher) education, policy makers and business should take in order to foster social mobility.

Higher education and human capital theory: expansion, inclusion and marketization

Higher education and the graduate labour market, as many other spheres within a post-industrial society, have been driven and reinforced by a human capital or meritocratic narrative. As Wilton (2008) and Tomlinson (2013) note, the emergence and establishment of the knowledge economy has shifted the attention of both the market and policy firmly upon higher education. This focus has led successive governments, both conservative and liberal, to reify (higher) education as the central feature of social development and security providing working-class students an opportunity to become socially mobile or the reproduction of 'comfortable' life chances for the middle class. In other words, higher education has served the general march toward neo-liberalism where individuals are given the opportunity to invest in their education and, then, are responsible for subsequent trajectories and life chances. This sentiment can be clearly read in the Department for Business, Innovation and Skills (BIS) report *Higher Ambitions: The Future of Universities in a Knowledge Economy*, citing 'access to higher education is a question of basic social justice' (2009: 3).

Human capital theory has had a long-standing influence over the UK higher education system. The *Robbins Report* (1963), which provided recommendations on a number of aspects of higher education in the context of increasing demand for university places from non-traditional students, saw increased expansion or increased opportunity as a way of addressing the gendered and classed nature of higher education. An emphasis was placed on the need for increased funding outside the Oxbridge system. Education was seen as a continuous process, and the report recommended increased links with secondary level education, providing a holistic approach to access and participation. According to Mountford-Zimdars *et al.* (2013), the opening-up of HE through the *Robbins Report* was the first demonstration of the meritocratic discourse surrounding the Academy and a move away from established middle-class institutions. A clear principle from the *Robbins Report* was the provision of social justice/social mobility via participation in higher education.

In practice, very few of the report's recommendations were put in policy. Rather than expanding the higher education system, the incoming government amalgamated vocationally focused technical colleges into polytechnics. According to Ross (2003), Robbins, himself, presented a high level of apprehension toward the government's policy. He understood that, rather than creating a fairer and more meritocratic higher education system, it would entrench division in a permanent manner, establishing and reinforcing a two-tier system of institutional hierarchy where polytechnics were understood to hold working-class students and universities typically attracted middle-class applicants. While some polytechnics did gradually become universities, it was the White Paper *Higher Education: A New Framework* (DfE, 1991), leading to the 1992 *Higher Education Act*, which granted blanket university status. The restructuring, rather than dismantling, of the binary education system has been demonstrated and discussed by previous research (Connor *et al.*, 2001; Ross, 2003). The issue, according to Connor *et al.*, is that recently formed universities sit lower in the institutional hierarchy, often requiring lower grades for entry. These institutions invariably attract students from lower socio-economic groups, creating a new two-tier system and an assumed difference in the quality of a degree (Reay *et al.*, 2005), reproducing the university–polytechnic divide but under another name. The consequence has been a firmly placed institutional hierarchy – formed via the *Robbins Report* and re-structured by *Higher Education: A New Framework* – ultimately questioning the human capital project of 'access equals success'.

A similar theme of social mobility via participation achieved through widening participation continued to be a central element within (higher) educational policy in the UK under the New Labour government (1997–2010), commonly seen as the party of education. Access to further and higher education was understood to provide an opportunity to become socially mobile and increase life chances. New Labour's faith in education could be most clearly observed through their 2001 party manifesto pledge to achieve a 50 per cent participation rate for 18-year-olds in higher education within ten years. According to Heath *et al.* (2013), it is difficult to draw a line from a number of New Labour policies to increased participation in HE. They argue, however, a significant rise in university applicants was a consequence of the introduction of the educational maintenance allowance (EMA) – essentially, a small grant offered to students from low-income, working-class families to continue past compulsory education by subsidising income lost through continuing with their studies.

The coupling of social mobility via participation – essentially a human capital narrative – and the primacy of widening participation have enjoyed a sustained role in major higher educational policy within the UK. *The Future of Higher Education* (DfES, 2003), which led to the *2004 Higher Education Act*, recommended the establishment of access agreements to improve and support access from under-represented communities, including lower socio-economic background and ethnic minorities. In addition, these access agreements were to be monitored by an independent access regulator – The Office for Fair Access. The report articulates quite clearly that entry into higher education provides increased opportunities for social mobility; however, to ensure that these opportunities are realized, fair access must be provided and protected by legislation. The *Browne Report* (BIS, 2010a), which led to *Students at the Heart of the System* (BIS, 2011a), placed a greater emphasis on widening access arrangements by combining widening participation strategic assessments and access agreements into access commitments, to be reviewed annually.

Further demonstrations of the reification of higher education, within a human capital paradigm, can be seen in successive government policies and reports examining/addressing broader social inequality – in particular, social class – including: *Unleashing Aspiration: The Final Report of the Panel on Fair Access to the Professions* (Cabinet Office, 2009b); *Fair Access to Professional Careers* (Cabinet Office, 2012a); *New Opportunities: Fair Chances for the Future* (Cabinet Office, 2009a); and *Opening Doors, Breaking Barriers: A Strategy for Social Mobility* (Cabinet Office, 2011). According to these reports, the relationship between qualifications and mobility is based on acquiring skills that the economy requires, skills which can be obtained through further and higher education. A number of policies have focused on improving routes to higher education or training, therefore allowing diverse pathways. There is a clear pattern, however, among these policies that higher education is the preferred pathway; it is the choice that will provide greater opportunity for increased life chances. Many policies compare the earning power of a university graduate and an individual whose highest qualifications are A-Levels; there is no discussion of the earning power of an individual who has chosen a vocational route, and the focus on the economic benefits of higher education present this pathway as the optimal trajectory. Additionally, FE is often described as a pathway into higher education, reinforcing that higher education should be the end goal. Similar to the effectiveness of higher education widening participation policies, the central message of these policies that access to higher education will provide social mobility does not address the role of class, gender and ethnicity on higher education and (graduate) employment trajectories.

A clear consequence of human capital theory's influence on the higher education system, further demonstrating its centrality within the academy, was the introduction and systematic increase of university tuition fees. On the back of the *Dearing Report* – a government commissioned report that examined future higher education funding models in the context of an expanded university system – the 1998 *Teaching and Higher Education Act* introduced university tuition fees and substituted maintenance grants with student loans. As Hutchings (2003) explains, students had to pay, at point of entry, £1,000 per academic year. If they joined the fee loan system, graduates were required to pay a percentage of their loan once they began to earn more than £10,000 per year. A key rationale of both the *Dearing Report* and the subsequent *Teaching and Higher Education Act* was that, while higher education is beneficial to the larger society, the greatest beneficiary is the graduate. Education is an investment toward which the student was expected to make a significant contribution (Mountford-Zimdars *et al.*, 2013).

Policies concerned with the increase of tuition fees in the UK have followed a similar narrative. *The Future of Higher Education* (DfES, 2003) recommended an increase in the amount that students contribute to their tuition fees from £1,000 per year to a variable fee of between £0 and £3,000. Graduates were expected to begin repaying a percentage of their loan once they began to earn above £15,000 per year. The increase in the fees was based on the increased individual life chances graduates enjoy over those members of society who did not graduate from university.

The *Browne Report* (BIS, 2010a) and subsequent *Students at the Heart of the System* (BIS, 2011a) recommended a further increase of variable fees where higher education institutions could charge between £6,000 and £9,000 per year, once again essentially trebling university tuition. The rationale for this move echoed the reasons for the previous increase. The *Browne Report* argued that those who serve to benefit from higher education must take up the burden of payment. According to the *Browne Report*, because graduates can translate their educational capital into graduate employment and comfortable/increased life chances, earning over £100,000 more in their lifetimes than someone whose highest qualifications are A-Levels, they should pay increased tuition fees.

In addition to a long list of recommendations, the *Browne Report* also discussed proposals that were considered but not included in the final report; one concerned the idea that business should provide a contribution toward general university tuition fees. This concept was rejected, in part due to the position that the student is the main beneficiary of higher education and, therefore, is responsible for providing the capital for this investment. The consideration and rejection of this recommendation demonstrates the position that higher education is an individual investment in increased life chances. This position is further presented through the *Browne Report*'s recommendation that the income threshold, which triggers the repayment of the student loan, be raised from £15,000 per year to £21,000 per year.

In contrast to the apparent meritocratic principles informing educational policy, Brown (2013) comments, educational research has largely questioned how much these policies have addressed issues of class, gender and ethnicity on both educational and occupational trajectories. Findings from my own study have illustrated the strong classed influences on trajectories and the unlikely scenarios for these pathways to be broken. Additionally, Ross (2003) highlights that, while a number of working-class students have progressed to HE, the gap between social classes has remained at a steady distance, questioning the overall effect of these policies. The introduction and escalation of fees in UK higher education points to the reinforced social inequalities associated with higher education (Hutchings, 2003). There is a fundamental contradiction between having an assumed meritocratic system with access to this system that is grounded in an individual's current position within social space, in particular access to economic capital. As Moreau and Leathwood (2007) contend, the neo-liberal focus on individual responsibility within higher education, particularly employability narratives, turns a blind eye to social inequalities. The authors demonstrate a clear example of symbolic violence, via the narratives of individual responsibility, to where recent graduate respondents in their study did not consider the role of structural inequalities such as gender or ethnicity to have played any role in their trajectory, turning graduate underemployment into a trouble rather than an issue. It is clear from the rationale of the original expansion of the higher education sector, the most recent tuition fees policy and wider social justice programmes, that there is a human capital narrative that accessing higher education will foster social mobility. This narrative can be seen in the attitudes of this study's working-class sample, both in individual attitudes and family/school advice, that entry into higher education will provide increased life chances without the consideration of structural barriers such as social class.

Skills

A central recommendation and legacy from the *Dearing Report* (1997) was an impetus placed on transferable skills that all students should have on graduation to aid in their entry into the labour market: communication, numeracy, information technology and learning how to learn (Morrison, 2014) – in a sense, rebalancing unequal access to *a priori* capitals such as social and cultural capital. Since the publication of the *Dearing Report*, a growing body of research has questioned the effectiveness of employment provision within higher education (Hesketh, 2000; Tomlinson, 2007; Wolf, 2007; Archer and Davison, 2008; Mason *et al.*, 2009). According to Tomlinson (2012b), there are three assumed features of higher education's relationship to industry: higher education provides knowledge, which the economy requires; higher education legitimizes the knowledge a graduate has and provides a measuring stick for prospective employers; and higher education provides the 'right' kind of attitudes or cultural disposition for the graduate labour market. These assumptions, however, are now in question through increased participation and changes in the market. It was in this context of a changing market that the *Leitch Review of Skills*, a government commissioned report, argued that a re-working of the skills agenda was required to be more aligned with the requirements from industry and the wider economy (Keep, 2014).

A fundamental issue concerning skills provision is the apparent disparity between the transferable skills provided in the university and how these actually translate in the labour market. According to research from Wolf (2007) and Archer and Davison (2008), there is a mismatch between skills provided and skills required; there is too much emphasis placed on technical abilities and not enough on soft skills such as the ability to learn and, then, apply that knowledge. This issue has been highlighted in a British Chambers of Commerce (BCC, 2014) study, reporting that 88 per cent of firms believe school leavers are not prepared for work, while 54 per cent shared similar views of graduates. The uncertainty of graduates' compatibility with industry has led to a testing partnership (Cranmer, 2006).

In addition to issues concerning soft skills, Keep (2014) suggests there has not been enough provision for skills for the future. The UK higher education system's approach to innovation, according to Keep, is quite traditional and, unlike their European counterparts, does not adequately consider new forms of innovation such as employee-led policies or projects. This lacking is at odds with the Confederation of British Industry's (CBI) recommendation that 'businesses want graduates who not only add value but who have the skills to help transform their organization in the face of continuous and rapid economic and technological change' (2012, cited in Helyer and Lee, 2014: 351). For Keep (2014), the source of the disparity in skills provision comes from miscommunication at a departmental level specifying which government department, sharing responsibility for skills development with other departments, is responsible for particular roles. In addition to miscommunication, Tomlinson (2012b) suggests the apparent conflict between academia and industry has its roots in the 'short-termist' nature of policy makers. Skills need to be developed with the market. Alongside up-to-date skills, the temporal and uncertain character of a post-industrial market also requires graduates to continually up-skill and develop/renew their knowledge and abilities. In other words, the qualifications/abilities that secure a first job may not be enough to keep that position or guarantee suitability for future posts.

Boden and Nedeva (2010) comment that the emergence of the UK centre-right New Labour party in the mid-1990s saw a renewed and redefined relationship between higher education and employment. While the 1980s were characterized by laissez-faire policies, this new brand of politics meant that there was closer attention paid to the relationship between higher education and employment, leading to a greater centralization of policy. While skills provision differs between universities through the delegation of specific roles and responsibilities 'to the local level', the source of practices, and, therefore, the bearer of credit and critique, is government. Policy makers' reactions to issues within skills provision and approaches to address these problems can be seen in the recent *Supporting Graduate Employability* (BIS: 2011c). This report reiterates the government's commitment to increasing employment opportunities for university graduates. A central objective in meeting this aim is seen to be providing a greater focus on employability within the curriculum. The paper continues that academic staff and careers service staff need to 'teach' both hard and soft skills, including communication and presentation skills. In addition, extracurricular activities – in particular, those pursuits associated with employability skills – should be formalised into accredited activities. While it is encouraging and welcomed for greater focus on employability, the recommendation of particular attention being given to communication and presentation skills reinforces Keep's (2014) position that higher education skills provision in the UK does not lend itself to innovation and independent thinking – one of the *Dearing Report*'s key skills. In addition, while the BIS paper recognises that there are different issues concerning employment provision across disciplines – non-vocational subjects are seen as more problematic – the paper tends to largely gloss over the issue, commenting that it requires still further reflection.

The success of policy makers to forge an effective and 'profitable' relationship between higher education and employment can be demonstrated through the Quality Assurance Agency for Higher Education (QAA) 2014 review of engagement between higher education and industry. While the review did highlight examples of good practice, there were a number of areas that could be improved. Specifically, in relation to skills, the review argues that academic staff need to be kept up-to-date with applicable developments in industry. This concept is perhaps more pressing, as the BIS (2011c) paper appears to have named academic staff de facto careers advisers alongside staff from careers departments. This issue has been further highlighted by research from the HEA (Higher Education Academy). Tibby (2012) reported that issues raised at teaching and learning summits held by the HEA included a lack of resources and training for academic staff to offer employability advice and the need for a greater level of communication and collaboration between careers services and academics. In addition, in an evaluation of the HEA's flagship employability publication, *Pedagogy for Employability* (Pegg *et al*., 2012), Owens and Tibby (2013) report that a large proportion of academics interviewed after reading *Pedagogy for Employability* commented that it highlighted the issue of employability and provided practical approaches to embedding employability within the curriculum. While this focus is, of course, encouraging and points to the need for such publications, it also suggests that a significant portion of those interviewed had not considered employability or methods to embed it into their curriculums before 2012.

Outside of the policy sphere, there is increasing pressure on universities to provide adequate employment skills for students, a population who are increasingly adopting a consumer role within the higher education system. Higher education is seen as the central provider of social mobility, and students – increasingly becoming customers – demand value for money. This process can be most clearly seen through the introduction and gradual increase of university tuition fees in the UK; the financial responsibility has moved away from the state and onto the student. The *Browne Report*, leading to the most recent and largest increase in university fees, carried a clear narrative of consumer choice. It argued that there should be increased availability of information regarding degree courses to assistant students when making their choices of subject to read. According to the report, student choice will force the higher education sector to provide a better service; as the funding comes directly from students, there is an increased market relationship. Findings from the *Paired Peers Project* (Bradley *et al.*, 2013) support this argument, as students commented that the increase in fees to a maximum of £9,000 per year would require increased value for money – teaching and future life chances.

Higher education and industry

A key critique of employment provision within the higher education curriculum is that employability skills are best learned through doing – i.e. work-based learning and internships (Cranmer, 2006; CBI, 2009; Mason *et al.*, 2009; Keep and James, 2011; Andrews and Higson, 2014). The CBI (2009) comments that universities can and do implement various strategic policies in order to increase employability, including a university-wide employability strategy, encouraging the use of a personal development portfolio (PDP) to record students' activities, extra-curricular actives and bolt-on courses; however, universities need to do more with students in order to allow them to enhance skills. One action the CBI recommends is that the government needs to invest more to foster a relationship between business and academia. Mason *et al.* (2009) report that there are three key approaches used by UK universities to increase employability: teaching and assessment of employability skills by departments; engagement with employers during course design and delivery; and work experience via programmes such as sandwich courses. In their research, the authors found that work experience and employer engagement – particularly in course design and delivery – are important and add to the ability to get a job; however, the teaching and assessment of employability skills within departments was not as influential.

As has been discussed, research from Archer and Davison (2008) and Keep (2014) has argued that skills provision has not been able to deliver on the soft skills graduate employers require. According to Andrews and Higson (2014), soft skills are not developed within the curriculum but through work-based learning. The authors go further to suggest that work-based learning provides additional cultural capital, providing graduates a greater opportunity to 'play the game'. For Andrews and Higson, an 'employable habitus' – similar to Tomlinson's (2008) concept of 'graduateness' – can be formed through work-based learning, further addressing the classed disparity of access to *a priori* capitals. An issue with this particular argument is that, similar to government skills policy (BIS, 2011c), the authors focus on vocation-based subjects; there is little discussion on how to create this process across undergraduate degree courses. In the context of this research, Cranmer (2006) argues that limits to which employability can be 'taught' in the classroom points to a mismanagement of resources, which could be more effectively allocated in bringing industry into universities and facilitating work-based learning.

The higher education sector has moved increasingly closer to industry/business in order to meet increased demands upon universities to provide access to employment – a demand that is heard all the clearer through the new market relationship between students and higher education institutions. Beginning with the *Robbins Report* (1963), the relationship between universities and industry has been celebrated, protected and encouraged by successive major UK higher education policy. *The Future of Higher Education* (DfES) argued quite clearly that a central responsibility for HEIs was to 'meet rising skill needs', primarily through 'stronger links with business and economy' (2003: 4). The paper goes on to suggest that the government should play a role in pairing industry and the academy in order to facilitate this partnership and ensure that the economy is supplied with its necessary requirements. A core policy recommendation from *Higher Ambitions: The Future of Universities in a Knowledge Economy* (BIS, 2009) was for the Higher Education Funding Council for England (HEFCE) to create new funding incentives for programmes that were more in line with current market needs; the direction of universities should be market-driven. In addition, employers will be asked to work with universities in identifying any gaps in their provision in relation to their market needs. Similar attitudes were present within the *Browne Report* (BIS, 2010a); once again, the increased role of business/industry within HE was discussed in order, according to the report, to ensure a robust economy and a sustainable HE sector. Curiously, while the *Browne Report* called for a greater role of business, one of the rationales for not asking industry to contribute to higher education institutions was that it would increase the presence of business in the academy, something that it also supported.

A central development in this relationship, coming from both the *Browne Report* and the government's response (BIS, 2011b), was the commissioning of the *Wilson Review* (BIS, 2012a). This review was charged with considering effective mechanisms to increase the productive partnership between these two spheres. The review was very clear on the ongoing need for collaboration, arguing that 'strength and resilience in such a supply chain is derived from close collaboration and an understanding of each party's priorities and capabilities' (*ibid.*: 1). For the *Wilson Review*, it is the role of universities to fall in line with business and provide industry with its market requirements. A key aspect of this move is increased work experience through 'sandwich' degrees, internships and work-based programmes. Every student, the review recommended, should have the opportunity to participate in work-based learning. In a bid to encourage taking up such courses, the tuition fee for the year of a degree spent in industry should be reduced.

The *Wilson Review* discusses the benefits and need for a reduction in the red tape surrounding the relationship between business and academia – as long as this relationship is a proactive one. If a student's university place can be funded entirely by a company, this university place should not be included in the quota of places a university is permitted to offer, as set by HEFCE. In other words, businesses should be able to purchase extra places on a degree course outside of the spots otherwise available. The government response (BIS, 2012b) was a general acceptance of the recommendations, arguing that the *Wilson Review* and, before it, the *Robbins Report* had highlighted that universities must work with industry to create the necessary workers for the economy.

The effectiveness of these policies can be judged, in part, by returning to the QAA's (2014) review of higher education's engagement with industry. Again, while the review pointed to a number of good practices, there were a number of areas on which policy makers need to improve. The QAA recommended that a more strategic approach is required to engage with employers to create sustained partnerships. Currently, there is little evidence of a baseline or level toward which to work, as such greater consistency is needed. In addition, the QAA argues that there needs to be an 'equality of access to work-based and placement opportunities' (2014: 5). Equal access to work-based learning is an important point. For Wilson (BIS, 2012a) a main avenue to access work-based learning is internships; however previous research (Bathmaker *et al.*, 2013) has demonstrated that access to the top internships is influenced by social and cultural capital – class – and do not necessarily provide the increased life chances reports such as the *Wilson Review* would lead their readers to expect. There have been some developments on this point, as recent social mobility policies *Unleashing Aspirations* (Cabinet Office, 2009b) and *Opening Doors, Breaking Barriers* (Cabinet Office, 2011) have called for businesses to operate a fair and open system of internships on the basis that industry will benefit from a diverse labour force. To that effect, there has been the establishment of the *Business Compacts* (BIS, 2014), a contract of good faith that employers will practise 'socially ethical' recruitment policies. While this movement is an encouraging step, subsequent government research has found little improvement concerning fair access to internships and only limited uptake of outreach programmes to detail the benefits of internships to non-traditional students (Cabinet Office, 2012a, 2012b).

Policy recommendations: the need for an evidence-based discussion

Current developments in the Academy and the new status of HE as the main provider of social equality and social justice illustrate a number of flaws and dangers with this new relational system. Many of these issues are driven by the market and 'short-termist' policy initiatives/agenda; however, other problems are more deeply rooted and can be identified through social research. While the findings from this study are based on a limited number of respondents and therefore cannot claim generalizability, the life histories unpacked through this research and the analytical reading of respondents' trajectories can add weight to the critiques of this system but also provide lessons that must be learned for the future.

Pragmatic understanding of the market

The emergence and establishment of post-industrialization (Bell, 1973) brought with it a knowledge economy where the new social elite were those members with technical capabilities measured by qualification and not peerage. This shift in economy was also met with an increasingly de-structured social system, affecting identity, community and the market. University graduates are, thus, required to negotiate an increasingly fluid and changing labour market. Findings from this study demonstrate that there is a classed level of appreciating the new market demands and challenges facing graduates. A key difference was observed in attitudes toward the buying power of a degree. Middle-class graduates discussed at length the devaluation of the degree and the need to re-balance this deficit with various extra resources or *a priori* capital. In contrast, working-class graduates often expressed frustration at their inability to exchange educational capital for increased life chances. I have accounted for this classed difference through Bourdieu's concept of hysteresis of habitus (1972/1977). The gap between the change in the field – in this case, the labour market – and individuals' understanding the change and acting accordingly is prolonged by the prominence of human capital theory narratives in the social policies discussed. Middle-class students/graduates have access to other capitals and a habitus complementary to the field to appreciate this change much sooner. Recent work on graduate employability (Tomlinson, 2013), adopting a largely late modern approach, has characterized graduates as 'savvy customers' who are increasingly negotiating the market; findings from this study clearly counter this emerging tradition.

In order to provide increased opportunities for all graduates, the benefits of participation in HE and difficulties in entering the labour market must be equally articulated. This effort can be achieved in a positive manner by explaining the challenges that the new market presents but also discussing various activities students can do to tame the waves of the increasingly liquid system. A key element required to deliver this information is increased, up-to-date and robust employment provision throughout their degree. Respondents from this study, from both class backgrounds, very rarely made use of the resources provided by their university careers departments. Often, student engagement occurred at the end of their degree and was generally quite a negative experience. A similarly low level of interaction, across class lines, with the careers service was found in the Futuretrack study (Purcell *et al.*, 2013). The authors suggest that students often use other resources, such as family and friends, for information and guidance. This trend presents a problem; when working-class graduates turn to friends and family for advice, their similar habitus, characterized by an equal inability to negotiate the field, will more than likely reproduce their field of the possibles, limit their strategies and prolong a state of hysteresis. Careers advisers and policy makers need to appreciate the prevalence and influence of informal advice or 'hot knowledge' (Reay *et al.*, 2005) on both understanding and trajectories and ensure that, wherever students are sourcing their information, it is the most accurate and as up-to-date as possible.

This approach would be aided by forming links with careers provision at secondary level education. In this study, working-class respondents' peer groups were often formed before entering higher education. Providing employment provision at this stage leads to a more informed student but also creates an opportunity for more accurate information and advice to be accessed through peer networks. The role of the family and the classed level of practical advice have been well documented throughout this study. In addition to better informed peer groups, it is crucial that families are provided accurate and understandable information concerning the graduate labour market. This information could, perhaps, come in the form of dedicated careers sessions for parents/guardians to counter the social reproduction and static trajectory of working-class graduates, as demonstrated through this research.

While there are a number of resources for opportunities within university careers departments, employment provision needs to go beyond these centres. In order to ensure that students are provided with information and advice, a focus on careers needs to be embedded into the curriculum. There are debates surrounding what employability is and the practical use/presence of generic skills within a degree (Holmes, 2001, 2013) and whether resources in the curriculum should be reallocated to work-based learning (Cranmer, 2006). There is merit in placing a flexible and reflexive focus on employability within the set curriculum, including the material that is delivered and the various approaches to assessment within a degree course. As Pegg *et al.* (2012) have previously suggested, it needs to be done in an institutional environment that welcomes and values employment provision. There is, perhaps, some friction between the Academy's new responsibilities and academics who view such provision as a distraction from the course material. While skills such as communication and team-working are as necessary to understanding nineteenth-century epistemology as they are to appreciate quantum mechanics, these skills need to feature in both disciplines.

A middle ground between careers departments and the set curriculum can be found through top-up or bolt-on employment initiatives – essentially, additional or complementary employment courses provided in addition to the core curriculum. Helyer and Lee (2014) comment that, in relation to the increased demand for skills provision, there has been a significant shift toward providing bolt-on courses focusing on employability skills. Pegg *et al.* (2012) comment that there are over 50 employment programmes within UK universities, ranging from fully embedded in the curriculum to optional and generic courses/workshops. The continuing importance and position of such courses is demonstrated through the establishment of the Higher Education Record of Achievement (HEAR), endorsed by the *Wilson Review* (BIS, 2012a) and supported by the HEA. Students are encouraged to monitor, record and disseminate additional activities that demonstrate employability skills, often developed in bolt-on courses, in addition to their academic activities and achievements.

Apart from containing up-to-date and accurate information, these bolt-on courses require institutional support to efficiently function. In this vein, Bridgstock (2009) argues that the nature and involvement of the careers departments within employability initiatives is crucial to their implementation and effectiveness. In addition to requiring institutional support, bolt-on courses must also address the optional character of many of these initiatives. As this and previous research (Bathmaker *et al.*, 2013; Purcell *et al.*, 2013) has demonstrated, the action of opting in to various additional activities such as ECA is quite heavily classed. In order to address this issue, bolt-on courses need to: be aligned closer to the curriculum; articulate the function and purpose of these courses in order for students to understand why they should spend extra time in these courses, especially as time for working-class students may be more pressured due to the need for term-time employment; include employability initiatives as a mandatory course requirement.

Tomlinson argues that, in the contemporary labour market, graduates are required to 'decode employers' recruitment criteria' (2013: 197) and form an 'employability narrative' (2012a: 7). The central issue with a strategy as sophisticated as this one is that it requires resources and cultural competency; working-class graduates could find themselves in an autodidactic dilemma of having to operate in a social space in which they are both unfamiliar and ill-equipped to negotiate. Due to the nature of the market and the tacit qualities of capitals, it is inevitable that the dominant group will maintain its position. Through providing a pragmatic account and discussion of the market, working-class students/graduates will have a clearer understanding of the labour market – contrary to the human capital discourse present in policy – and appreciate the need to form an employable identity through resources such as ECAs and internships, while not forgetting the prerequisite of the degree.

Widening participation does not end at access

Widening participation has been a central element of both (higher) educational policy and general social mobility/social justice policy and reports. It has taken form in the establishment, and subsequent reforms, of access agreements and the Office for Fair Access. The primary function of widening participation policy and activities is to increase under-represented groups' participation in higher education and create opportunities for social mobility. Through a close analysis of the graduate trajectories of the working-class graduates in this study, the widening participation agenda appears to have largely failed. With the exception of the strategic working class, the general working-class sample are either stuck in non-graduate employment or are unable to leave or promote within their current graduate position in the event of restructuring or redundancy; in other words, we are still faced with a largely immobile and static cohort of working-class graduates.

One reason is that the support and attention working-class, or widening participation, students received when applying and upon entering higher education was not sustained during their time at university or upon graduation. There is a fundamental contradiction in that the rationale behind widening participation has been social mobility, but 'success' rates are not measured in trajectories after graduation – the very trajectories they are trying to influence. This discrepancy desperately needs to be resolved. This study demonstrates the need for consistency within widening participation provisions throughout the degree and upon entry into the labour market. This support could come in the form of a similar widening participation approach to internships. Previous research (BIS, 2012a; Bathmaker *et al.*, 2013) has demonstrated the increasing importance of internships in the contemporary labour market on both social and economic capital, as well as the continuing classed nature of internships.

There have been mixed governmental reactions and initiatives toward reducing the class barriers to internships. In response to the *Wilson Review*, the government (BIS, 2012b) argued that progress had been made through the uptake of the graduate talent pool website, an advertising site for employers to post internship vacancies. This website does not effectively begin to address the social and financial barriers in accessing internships. A more functional development was evident in the recommendation that degree courses that included a year in industry should only charge up to 15 per cent of the upper-capped tuition fee for the year outside of formal teaching. Additionally, the business compacts, as a result of recent social mobility policies, are a positive development of businesses creating increased opportunities for under-represented students and employees. These opportunities, however, are based largely on good will and the preferences of company boards and managers.

There are a number of high profile employers involved in these practices through the Business Compact and the Social Mobility Foundation (BIS, 2014), but it is still quite a piecemeal approach to tackling the issues surrounding widening participation beyond graduation. I am cautious that these recommendations are not reduced to a social justice 'wish list', but it seems clear that there will not be a broader attempt to increase access in the labour market without greater oversight and political will in the public sector and financial incentives in the private sector.

In addition to prolonged support during their time in higher education, working-class graduates require support once they have entered the graduate labour market. As was demonstrated by the converted working class, the composition of qualifications, resources and capitals that secure one graduate job may not be enough for a more senior position or a similar position in another company. Employers – in particular, HR managers – need to be aware of the support and encouragement employees may require in order to develop their roles and enhance their position within the particular line of work. This support will be beneficial to industry, as the resources/income that is needed to train a new member of staff will serve as a long-standing investment. The challenge to this particular point is to counter the common-sense position that, if someone can successfully enter the market, they can do it again with similar results.

Industry and academia

A strong relationship between industry and the Academy is required for an effective implementation of employment provisions. The *Wilson Review* (BIS, 2012a) and previous policies have lobbied for increased interaction between these two spheres. Indeed, the coming together of both sectors has steadily emerged, but the onus has been on academia to meet industry and business's needs. As Harvey (2000) points out, the government has placed increased pressure on HEIs to meet market demands. These market demands are temporal and more problematic because the policy initiatives suffer from short-termism. A more proactive and long-term strategy is a mutual relationship between the new spheres where the needs and support required for both industry and the Academy are discussed and enacted.

An active role for employers within employment provision, in whichever form it takes, would be helpful in the task of assisting students as they form their employability narrative (Tomlinson, 2012a). Employers working alongside academics and careers advisers can identify recurring issues graduates face and suggest actions that can be taken. Murphy and Gawthorpe (2013) discuss the friction between graduates' expectations and employers' expectations, leading to a frustrated workforce and poor retention. This issue could be addressed by students receiving first-hand advice from prospective employers before graduating, allowing them time to re-calculate expectations. In addition to advice to students, employers can also provide their industry experience to the design of employment provisions. An essential feature, it needs to be adopted by all degree courses – in particular, degree subjects without a traditional link with industry/business. Closer links with employers can address some of the friction between current skills and market needs, as reported by Wolf (2007) and Archer and Davison (2008), and provide links for knowledge transfers between spheres and future employment prospects for graduates.

Social class and public policy

The above recommendations are based on the prerequisite for a renewed focus toward social class, both in policy and popular debate. As previously discussed, projects such as the *GBCS*, in partnership with the BBC, have, to an extent, placed class back on the public agenda. The project team (Savage *et al.*, 2014) identify the increased discussion concerning class in the UK as being a significant achievement from their work, but there is an increasing issue surrounding the definition of social mobility with social policy. According to Payne (2012), recent social mobility policies have altered the definition of mobility, resulting in policy operating within its own dimension, detached from sociological understandings and definitions of what they ascribe to champion. Payne identified a three-stage process of what he terms the 'bowdlerisation of social mobility' (*ibid.*: 60). These stages are: inconsistent use of the term social mobility (typically at odds with academic understandings of the term); reporting academic findings concerning social mobility as if the definitions matched; and writing policies based on said double definitions. These policies often focus on disadvantaged families while ignoring the increasing gap between the dominated and dominant groups based on increased life chances for the latter. Mobility is generally measured as unspecific developments in life chances concerning the immediate future; for Payne, the existing account fails to appreciate the sociological understanding of mobility as moving through class barriers. Payne is quite blunt in his disappointment and frustration concerning these developments within policy narratives, arguing that 'the political discourse has been built around a series of definitions of mobility that are inaccurate, inconsistent, misleading and at considerable distance from those used in the body of conventional mobility analysis' (*ibid.*). As such, social mobility must be understood and considered within the context of social class.

The formulaic mobility narrative within social policy argues that widening participation increases access to higher education; through the investment and subsequent exchange of scholastic capital, graduates are able to enter a profession previously closed to them and their families before this point. The sociological understanding of mobility – one under which this study operates – is that, once again, widening participation increases access to higher education and can translate into entering the graduate labour market. Mobility is measured through a long-term ability to successfully negotiate social space and counter social reproduction. The durable nature of class makes a 'clean break' from one class group into another unlikely, and ultimately undesirable. A strategy that fosters a habitus and capitals that provide a level of mastery – both practical and symbolic – comparable to the dominant group is the beginning of real social mobility.

Without a sociological approach to social mobility, social policy will continue to offer short-sighted accounts and recommendations. It is quite frustrating, as some policy documents are closer to a sociological account but do not make that leap. Reading *Unleashing Aspiration* (Cabinet Office, 2009b), Milburn argues that barriers to social mobility include aspirations and access to (higher) education and employment – in particular, internships. On the surface, these comments are pointing to the role of class, or, more specifically, to the role of habitus. While many of the similarities may be surface deep, these parallels suggest that a theoretical – Bourdieusian – application of social class would be quite beneficial to the end goals of a large section of social policy by articulating the durable and directive nature of social class and the continuing role of social structures over trajectories. The challenges to realize this goal are significant, as Tooley and Darby's review of social theory from a policy perspective compared the work of educational researchers, applying conceptual tools such as habitus, to 'Nero fiddling while Rome burns' (1998: 76). If such a partnership is not created – if a joining up cannot be achieved – and current social policy continues to be applied with no critical gaze, policy will continue to operate in an inaccurate and ineffectual fashion due to their central ambition being misconstrued.

Conclusion

There have been massive changes both in higher education's composition and role since the *Robbins Report* (1963). A strong human capital theory narrative has directed the expansion of higher education under the guise of mobility via participation. This narrative has also rationalized the marketization of UK higher education demonstrated through the consistent increase in tuition fees. Students are seen to be the ones to get the greatest return through higher education participation, therefore they are increasingly required to make the largest contribution or investment. The linear presumption of access to university equating to access to the graduate labour market, supported by the emergence of post-industrialization and, with it, the knowledge economy, has placed a new responsibility upon universities – namely, employment provision. There have been developments within higher education to provide suitable skills for the market and to have a stronger relationship with business/industry. As the economy has developed the role of the university in providing employment, opportunities have changed from one avenue to the central site. This shift has been seen in the understanding of higher education as the solution to many of the issues discussed in general social mobility/social justice policies.

This chapter has identified a number of contradictions and limitations within policy narratives and presented a number of recommendations to how these can be addressed. I have said that these recommendations need not be seen as merely a 'wish list' but, rather, objectives that are achievable. In order to meet some of these goals, a closer relationship between social sciences and policy makers is required. The most high profile joining of sociology and academia was the relationship between Anthony Giddens and the New Labour Party; Giddens provided the theoretical narrative for the party's 'third way'. This partnership was certainly a positive start; however, a discipline such as sociology, comprised of competing perspectives, requires a broader and sustained discussion with policy makers. The above recommendations aspire to provide a route toward a holistic approach to employment, providing students/graduates with a clear understanding of the market and the access to resources required to successfully negotiate it and foster social mobility.

Conclusion

At the centre of this research was the question: *Are strategies that graduates use to secure employment influenced by social class?* In order to effectively answer this question, there were a number of sub-questions that needed to be addressed to offer an understanding of whether graduate employment strategies are classed and whether the habitus and capital are appropriate conceptual tools to examine and further understand these strategies.

Do graduates' expectations and aspirations of graduate employment differ by class, and, if so, can they be explained by the habitus and capital?

From the empirical results, there is a clear classed level of both aspiration and expectation present within the research sample. While there are nuances and specifics to each conceptual group, I have illustrated, via life history interviews, that there is a general working-class level of aspiration and expectation – demonstrating quite low levels – and there is a general middle-class level of aspiration and expectation – displaying a contrastingly high level.

Habitus and capital are understood to be a set of aspirations, expectations and dispositions. The level of aspirations and expectations – what is 'for the likes of you' – is bound to the individual's position within social space based on levels of capital, or more commonly understood as social class. The levels of capital create the 'field of the possibles' that works with the habitus to create practice. This process is evident from my sample: the classed aspirations, when 'put in play' with the dispositions associated with their collective class habitus, influenced their practice. The middle-class respondents' aspirations, when played alongside/through their habitus, have greatly influenced their successful graduate strategies. This success is particularly seen in contrast to the working-class respondents' low level of aspirations, when coupled with their habitus, negatively affecting their graduate trajectories. Aspirations and expectations are central to a successful trajectory, but the pre-reflexive 'field of the possibles' has formed a cap limiting what the working-class respondents understand themselves to be capable of achieving.

Do the strategies applied by graduates in the graduate employment field differ by social class, and, if so, can this be accounted for by the habitus?

Once again, there is a clear classed relationship between respondents and the occupational strategies they apply in the graduate labour market. While there are nuances and specifics to each conceptual group, there is a general working-class level and form of occupational strategy that can be understood as both weak and unsuccessful. The general middle-class level of strategy, in direct contrast, can be defined as both strong and successful. The question remains whether the habitus can account for this contrast in graduate trajectory.

The findings suggest that the strategies undertaken by respondents were influenced by habitus, illustrated by the direct influence of aspirations and expectations coupled with the influence of both the family and the educational system on strategies. According to Bourdieu (1986/1987), the habitus can be observed through repetition of practice and attitudes. Through the application of the BNIM, I have mapped or traced respondents' strategies, recording both practical and symbolic mastery. There is a constant relationship between habitus and strategy. When a respondent's habitus appears to be altered (through an out-of-environment experience), so, too, does the strategy or practical mastery demonstrated by the respondent. For respondents whose habitus remains similar for their life histories, their level of strategy appears constant or durable. There is a similar constant between habitus and the 'thinking element' of strategy, or symbolic mastery appreciated through ordinary reflection. Unlike a reflexive individual (Beck, 1992), a respondent's level of ordinary reflection is classed; as the habitus alters or remains constant, the level of ordinary reflection follows suit. The respondents' symbolic mastery was observed to be as equally influenced by the family and the educational system, as was their practical mastery. The durable demarcation of strategic practice – of playing the game – further points to the directive influence of habitus.

Are there differences in graduate strategies between graduates of a pre-1992 'old' university and a post-1992 'new' university?

In contrast to previous literature (Reay *et al.*, 2001; Leathwood and Hutchings, 2003; Mangan *et al.*, 2010), there did not appear to be an observable difference between the attitudes and strategies of respondents based on the type of institution they attended. There were a small number of working-class respondents who explained that they read for their undergraduate degree in *Southern* – a pre-1992 university – because of the reputation of the institution. Additionally, there were a number of middle-class graduates who felt they were required to explain their reasons for attending *Northern* – a post-1992 university; however, their choice of university was based on the course content and level of suitability. What I have suggested is that these findings point to a process of hysteresis of habitus within the field of higher education. *Southern* no longer carries the same level of reputation it previously did – or, at least, that it was previously understood to hold. Through the process of hysteresis, working-class students do not realize this change has occurred, and many are attending *Southern* with the understanding that its reputation will increase their chances of securing graduate employment. The middle-class graduates understand the situation and read for their degree based on the merits of the individual course; they appreciate it is that course that will increase their ability to find a graduate job, not the presumed institutional capital.

To what extent can other factors of identity, such as gender and ethno-national identity, account for trajectories?

Both gender and ethno-national identity were present as variables within the research sample. While gender remains a central issue within employment studies (Crompton, 1999; Budig and England, 2001; Brynin, 2002; Berghammer, 2014), it did not appear to have a strong influence over my respondents' occupational trajectories. The only occurrence where gender had a marked impact was the case of Lindsey (strategic middle class), an engineer who, during the interview process, was on maternity leave with her first child. She explained that, due to the nature of her job – which she described as masculine – she would not be able to return to work until her daughter was old enough to attend pre-school. Engineering firms, she continued, rarely offer part-time contracts to employees. Rather than being fatalistic toward or lost within her new circumstances, Lindsey – similar to her previous attitudes and strategies – reformulated her occupational strategy so she could remain within the engineering community until her daughter was old enough for her to return to her previous role, which she fully intended and, importantly, expected to do.

Without follow-up research, it is impossible to know whether she will be able to re-enter her previous position. As Lindsey is the only respondent that demonstrated this particular life history, it is difficult to generalise, even within my small sample. The symmetry between her previous attitudes and strategies and her new ones regarding her current situation suggest that her middle-class habitus is able to negotiate the graduate employment field in light of the gendered character of her particular profession.

The influence of ethno-national identity within Northern Irish society is understood to be decreasing (Horgan, 2007; Smyth and Cebulla, 2008). It is within this growing discourse of Northern Irish researchers that I find my own empirical results fitting. There was little to no observable influence of ethno-national identity on my respondents' attitudes or trajectories. There were no patterns or themes within their occupational trajectories that could be accounted for by ethno-national identity. When the subject was discussed in the final sub-session of my interviews, the questions regarding ethno-national identity were met with annoyance, laughter or a common theme of not having considered it until I mentioned it. With regard to both of these variables, social class appeared to transcend the influence they had over respondents.

Can the habitus and capital account for social reproduction?

Within the five conceptual groups, two groups demonstrated a constant life history, comprised of a durable habitus and a consistent position within social space, appreciated through an equally durable form of practical mastery and level of symbolic mastery. These groups were the strategic middle class and the static working class. The three remaining conceptual groups did not display a comparably linear life history.

The entitled middle class's occupational trajectory was quite contrasting with regard to the early phase of their life history – the educational phase. Through a process of inverted symbolic violence, members of the entitled middle class's habitus essentially fostered a form of hyper-aspiration that would eventually transcend the habitus, creating a strategy that could not negotiate the graduate employment field, as their subjective expectations went beyond the objective reality. Both habitus and capital are still relevant within their trajectory; it was 'they' who created their hyper-aspiration, and, as such, the hyper-aspiration has transcended their practical and symbolic mastery, negatively affecting their occupational trajectory.

The converted working class experienced a seemingly mobilizing shift in their occupational position, and, for a short period of time, their occupational aspirations and strategies became stronger. This temporal form of mobility was caused by a context-specific exchange of capital. Once they had 'spent' this capital, their previous low levels of aspiration, expectation and practical and symbolic mastery could be observed in their life histories. Habitus and capital are still both relevant within their occupational strategies. This conceptual group demonstrates the importance of appreciating both habitus and capital; once they had used their context-specific capital, they returned to their previous situation with their habitus returning to its previous 'form'. The influence of their habitus will, perhaps, be most felt in the future if they are required to apply for a promotion or find a new job, as all they have to rely on now is their working-class habitus.

The final conceptual group that demonstrated an unfixed life history was the strategic working class. This category was the only working-class group that displayed a durable level of social mobility. The overt contrast in both their attitudes and strategies between the previous stages of their life history and the present can be accounted for by an out-of-environment experience. Bourdieu (1992b) comments that the habitus can be affected by experiences outside of an individual's everyday environment, though this occurrence is quite rare. Both members of this group met what could be described as 'gatekeepers' who gave them practical instruction on how to find and secure a graduate position within a specific field – something missing from both their families' and schools' advice. On instruction, members were able to create a successful strategy to negotiate the graduate employment field. This practical advice did not transcend the habitus; rather, it altered it. An appreciation of this change is illustrated by the members of this group following the practical advice exactly as it was given, owing further support to Bourdieu's comment that '[habitus] is durable but not eternal!' (*ibid.*: 133).

Moving forward

According to Tomlinson (2013), the salience of class needs to be considered within the context of both changing class identities and the multi-faceted nature of class as discussed by Savage (2000). While the fractured nature of class can lead to multiple trajectories, the impact of social inequality provides a constant narrative of social reproduction, perhaps best illustrated in the recent double special edition of the *British Journal of Sociology of Education* focusing on social mobility. Tomlinson is quite right in his assertion that both the working class and middle class should be understood as plural and, therefore, open to different/contrasting experiences, influences and resources. When empirical research (Reay *et al.*, 2005; Bradley *et al.*, 2013; Purcell *et al.*, 2013), however, joins together various factions into working and middle-class groups, there are still clear examples of classed experience and trajectories.

From the answers to the questions posed above, it is clear that habitus and capital influenced the strategies that graduates undertook when looking for and trying to secure graduate employment. The classed nature of the strategies employed and the classed character of both aspirations and expectations and the influence from the family and educational system upon the graduates points to the continuing influence of the habitus. In the context of graduates increasingly being required to form 'employable identities', social class will continue to be a significant influence.

The symmetry between my findings and Bourdieusian discussion and that of research focusing on primary level education (Connolly and Healy, 2004a), secondary level education (Reay *et al.*, 2001) and higher level education (Reay *et al.*, 2005) points to the durable influence of the class habitus and the continuing importance of Bourdieu's conceptual tools within educational research. It also further strengthens my position that graduate employment research belongs within the sociology of education as the last phase of an individual's educational trajectory. Additionally, this research holds wider implications for the sociology of social mobility/reproduction. The enduring presence of the habitus model within my findings points to the continued relevance of Bourdieu within social mobility research. The conceptual tools the cultural class analysts (Skeggs, 1997; Reay, 2000; Savage, 2003; Crompton and Scott, 2005; Lawler, 2005) adopted to escape Goldthorpe *et al.*'s (1980) coupling of occupation and social class continue to provide a crucial understanding of class through combining the forms of capital (economic, social and cultural). Hebson (2009) and Atkinson (2009) comment that the cultural class analysts are hesitant to research occupational structures and trajectories, as occupations are seen to belong to a previous and outdated class model. What this research does is illustrate the importance of a Bourdieusian analysis of employment and demonstrates how this analysis can be placed within the cultural class narrative, i.e. appreciating different forms of capital along with gender and ethnicity.

The persisting issue obfuscating the prominence of social class is that, regardless of the research demonstrating the classed nature of access to higher education and the classed experience once there, through the assumed mobilizing effects of higher education, working-class students and their families expect a university degree to bring them success. Education is understood to be a mobilizing process, an opportunity to gain greater levels of capital, status and power – these levels of capital are earned through hard work and determination. Beck argues that it is access to education that allows us to become the 'producer of our own social biography' (1992: 93). As he clarifies, an increasingly diversified education system provides us with – and requires us to make – choices concerning our individual trajectory. Our subsequent entry into the graduate labour market requires us to become reflexive and individual in order to negotiate the market. Meritocracy fails to recognize the structural influences on graduates' ability to negotiate the labour market and, therefore, does not consider the limits that habitus and capital can create. Within this research, social class has played a more directive role than degree classification or time since graduation.

The danger of meritocracy is that human capital theory narratives found within the reflexive school are also present within official social policy discourses. A common theme within much social policy, pertaining to social mobility, is individual responsibility. For example, the government's response to Alan Milburn's *Unleashing Aspiration* (Cabinet Office, 2009b) articulated its commitment to social mobility as support for 'anyone with the ability and motivation [. . .] to get the best education and training' (BIS, 2010b: 4). This comment suggests that future life chances and trajectories are primarily the concern and responsibility of the individual rather than a partnership. Social mobility policy needs to approach the issue more holistically, considering inequalities between groups rather than seeing it as a working-class problem; as Payne (2012) comments, low social mobility should not be understood solely as the working class failing to enter the middle class but the middle class, effectively, keeping them out.

While rugged individualism is a central neo-liberal value, there is a contradiction between this laissez-faire approach to graduate employment and the current HE funding system within the UK. Since the introduction of deferred tuition fees, the solvency of the HE system has been based on graduates finding 'graduate' employment – a job with an above-average salary. As graduate underemployment increases, as has been demonstrated between the contrasting figures from Elias and Purcell (2004) and Purcell *et al.* (2013), then, presumably, the number of graduates eligible to repay their deferred tuition fees decreases, threatening the viability of the current system.

The belief or faith in meritocracy – the role of the individual – Conway (1997) argues, has been fuelled by a general understanding that class was an issue for a previous generation. A central element in both Beck and Beck-Gernsheim's (2002) *Individualization* thesis and Margaret Archer's (2013) morphogenetic society is access to higher education, through the provisions within a modern welfare state, addressing some fundamental classed inequalities characteristic of previous generations. The austerity culture, which swept across Western Europe and North America following the 2008 financial crisis, may lead to a resurgence in classed inequalities and frictions. Cuts in public services, including (higher) education and health, and increased privatization will reinforce classed barriers to the very resources Beck and Margaret Archer understand as transcending class.

One approach or contribution to addressing these issues is a theoretical examination of social inequality. Louise Archer (2003a) argues that, while many policy initiatives are atheoretical, the relations and processes they affect are not. In other words, a common-sense understanding of a situation creates a common-sense solution; these solutions may not be appropriate to the complex interchanges within this subject. As such, a greater partnership between critical social research and policy makers could provide an effective approach to social inequality.

A fundamental step in understanding and addressing social reproduction is to critically and effectively question the concept of meritocracy, both in policy and popular culture. The challenge, however, is that people do not take kindly to being told that structural barriers greater than themselves can prevent or influence their life histories and trajectories. Society seemingly requires the sense of individuality and freedom to choose one's own path; this choice is often seen to be fostered by education. Wacquant suggests that the rejection or unwillingness to accept the presence of structural barriers has fuelled a similar rejection of Bourdieu's work; he writes:

> Could the onerousness of reading Bourdieu stem from our uneasiness of seeing our social selves stripped bare, from a vital reluctance to embrace a mode of analysis that makes us squirm as it throws us 'back in the game' and cuts through the mist of our enchanted relation to the social world?
>
> (1993: 247)

The point of a Bourdieusian project is not to 'throw' people back into a classed game but to remind them that they still play one. In a situation of increasing graduate inflation and the subsequent decrease in educational capital, the responsibility of social researchers to highlight the prevailing influences of social structures – in this case, social class – becomes ever more pressing.

Appendix A: Respondent matrix

Name (pseudonym)	*Social class*	*Gender*	*Institution – primary degree*	*Degree classification*	*Years since graduating undergraduate*	*Employment description*
Alice	W/C	Female	Northern	2.1	5	Graduate employed: Civil Service staff office
Annie	M/C	Female	Northern	3rd	4	Graduate employed: HR department
Caoimhe	W/C	Female	Northern	2.2	4	Non-graduate employed: administrative assistant
Catherine	W/C	Female	Southern	2.2	3	Graduate employed: junior solicitor
Fergal	W/C	Male	Northern	2.2	4	Non-graduate employed: retail
Finbar	W/C	Male	Southern	2.2	7	Non-graduate employed: performing artist
Hannah	M/C	Female	Southern	2.1	4	Non-graduate employed: retail
James	W/C	Male	Southern	2.1	4	Graduate employed: substitute teacher
John	M/C	Male	Northern	2.1	7	Graduate employed: FE lecturer/artist
Jonny	M/C	Male	Southern	1st	6	Non-Graduate: administrative assistant
Katie	M/C	Female	Northern	2.1	5	Graduate employed: 'Firm'
Kyle	W/C	Male	Northern	2.1	10	Non-graduate: technical assistant

Lindsey	M/C	Female	Southern	2.2	7	Graduate employed: engineer/maternity leave
Louise	W/C	Female	Northern	2.1	4	Graduate employed: sports club co-ordinator
Maeve	M/C	Female	Northern	2.1	4	Graduate employed: production assistant
Mark	W/C	Male	Southern	2.2	3	Non-graduate employed: service industry
Matthew	M/C	Male	Southern	2.2	5	Graduate employed: proofreader/teaching fellow
Michael	W/C	Male	Northern	2.1	3	Non-graduate employed: service industry
Niamh	W/C	Female	Southern	2.1	5	Graduate employed: charity co-ordinator
Nikki	W/C	Female	Southern	2.1	4	Non-graduate employed: call centre
Paddy	W/C	Male	Southern	2.1	4	Non-graduate employed: service industry
Paula	W/C	Female	Northern	2.2	7	Graduate employed: charity co-ordinator
Pete	W/C	Male	Southern	2.1	8	Graduate employed: politician
Phil	M/C	Male	Southern	2.1	3	Graduate employed: production assistant/teacher
Rose	W/C	Female	Southern	2.1	2	Non-graduate employed: service industry
Sarah	W/C	Female	Southern	2.1	3	Non-graduate employed: call centre
Steve	W/C	Male	Southern	2.2	3	Non-graduate employed: hospitality industry

Appendix B: Graduate employment position by variable

Variable		*Graduate employed*	*Not graduate employed*	*N*
Gender	Male	5	8	13
	Female	9	5	14
Institution	Southern	7	9	16
	Northern	7	4	11
Degree classification	1st and 2.1	9	8	17
	2.2 and 3rd	5	5	10
Time since graduation	2–6 years	10	10	20
	6–10 years	4	3	7
Social class	Working	7	11	18
	Middle	7	2	9

Bibliography

Adams, M. (2003) 'The Reflexive Self and Culture: A Critique', *British Journal of Sociology*, *54* (2), 221–238.

Adams, M. (2006) 'Hybridising Habitus and Reflexivity', *Sociology*, *40* (3), 511–528.

Andrews, J. and Higson, H. (2014) 'Is Bologna Working? Employer and Graduate Reflections of the Quality, Value and Relevance of Business and Management Education in Four European Countries', *Higher Education Quarterly*, *68* (3), 267–287.

Archer, L. (2003a) 'Social Class and Higher Education', in: Archer, L., Hutchings, M. and Ross, A. (eds) *Higher Education and Social Class: Issues of Exclusion and Inclusion*. London: Routledge Falmer, pp. 5–21.

Archer, L. (2003b) 'The Value of Higher Education', in: Archer, L., Hutchings, M. and Ross, A. (eds) *Higher Education and Social Class: Issues of Exclusion and Inclusion*. London: Routledge Falmer, pp. 119–136.

Archer, M.S. (1970) 'Egalitarianism in English and French Educational Sociology', *European Journal of Sociology*, *XI* (1), 116–129.

Archer, M.S. (1996) *Culture and Agency: Revised Edition*. Cambridge: Cambridge University Press.

Archer, M.S. (2003) *Structure, Agency and the Internal Conversation*. Cambridge: Cambridge University Press.

Archer, M.S. (2007) *Making our Way through the World*. Cambridge: Cambridge University Press.

Archer, M.S. (2012) *The Reflexive Imperative in Late Modernity*. New York: Cambridge University Press.

Archer, M.S. (2013) 'Social Morphogenesis and the Prospects for Morphogenic Society', in: Archer, M.S. (ed.) *Social Morphogenesis*. London: Springer, pp. 1–25.

Archer, W. and Davison, J. (2008) *Graduate Employability: The View of Employers*, London: Council for Industry and Higher Education.

ARK (2007) 'Identity', (online). Available at www.ark.ac.uk/nilt/2007/Identity/ECADREL.html (retrieved 10 October 2014).

Atfield, A. and Purcell, K. (2014) 'Northern Ireland's Students: Key Findings from the Futuretrack Survey of Final Year Students on Three Year Courses', The Higher Education Careers Service Unit.

Atkinson, W. (2007a) 'Anthony Giddens as Adversary of Class Analysis', *Sociology*, *41* (3), 533–549.

Atkinson, W. (2007b) 'Beck, Individualisation and the Death of Class: A Critique', *The British Journal of Sociology, 58* (4), 349–366.

Atkinson, W. (2008) 'Not All that was Solid has Melted into Air (or Liquid): a Critique of Bauman on Individualisation and Class in Liquid Modernity', *The Sociological Review, 56* (1), 1–17.

Atkinson, W. (2009) 'Rethinking the Working Class Nexus: Theoretical Foundations for Recent Trends', *Sociology, 43* (5), 896–912.

Atkinson, W. (2010a) *Class, Individualisation and Late Modernity: In Search of the Reflexive Worker*. Hampshire: Palgrave Macmillan.

Atkinson, W. (2010b) 'Phenomenological Additions to the Bourdieusian Toolbox: Two Problems for Bourdieu, Two Solutions from Schutz', *Sociological Theory, 28* (1), 1–19.

Ball, S., Bowe, R. and Gewirtz, S. (1997) 'Circuits of Schooling: A Sociological Exploration of Parental Choice of School in Social-Class Contexts', in: Halsey, A.H., Lauder, H., Brown, P. and Wells, A.S. (eds) *Education: Culture, Economy, and Society*. Oxford: Oxford University Press, pp. 409–421.

Ball, S.J., Davies, J., David, M. and Reay, D. (2002) 'Classification and Judgement: Social Class and the Cognitive Structures of Choice of Higher Education', *British Journal of Sociology of Education, 23* (1), 51–72.

Ball, S.J., Maguire, M. and Macrae, S. (2000). *Choices, Pathways and Transitions Post-16: New Youth, New Economy in the Global City*. London: Routledge Falmer.

Barone, C. and Schizzerotto, A. (2011) 'Introduction: Career Mobility, Education, and Intergenerational Reproduction in Five European Societies', *European Societies, 13* (3), 331–346.

Bathmaker, A-M., Ingram, N. and Waller, R. (2013) 'Higher Education, Social Class and the Mobilisation of Capitals: Recognising and Playing the Game', *British Journal of Sociology of Education, 34* (5–6), 723–743.

Bauman, Z. (2000) *Liquid Modernity*. Cambridge: Polity Press.

Bauman, Z. (2001) *The Individualised Society*. Malden: Polity Press.

Beck, U. (1992) *Risk Society*. London: Sage Publications.

Beck, U. (1997) *The Reinvention of Politics: Rethinking Modernity in the Global Social Order*. Cambridge: Polity Press.

Beck, U. (2007) 'Beyond Class and Nation: Reframing Social Inequalities in a Globalising World', *The British Journal of Sociology, 58* (4), 679–705.

Beck, U. and Beck-Gernsheim, E. (2002) *Individualization*. London: Sage Publications.

Becker, G.S. (1964) *Human Capital: A Theoretical and Empirical Analysis, with Special Reference to Education*. New York: National Bureau of Economic Research.

Bell, D. (1973) *The Coming of Post-industrial Society: A Venture in Social Forecasting*. New York: Basic Books.

Berghammer, C. (2014) 'The Return of the Male Breadwinner Model? Educational Affects in Parents' Work Arrangements in Austria, 1980–2009', *Work, Employment and Society, 28* (4), 611–632.

Bernstein, B. (1971) 'On Classification and Framing of Educational Knowledge', in: Young, M.F.D. (ed.) *Knowledge and Control: New Directions for the Sociology of Education*. London: Collier Macmillan, pp. 47–69.

Bernstein, B. (1973) *Class, Codes, and Control. (vol. 2)*. London: Routledge and Kegan Press.

Blau, P.M. and Duncan, D.O. (1967) *The American Occupational Structure*. London: John Wiley and Sons.

Boden, R. and Nedeva, M. (2010) 'Employing Discourse: Universities and Graduate "Employability"', *Journal of Education Policy, 25* (1), 37–54.

Boudon, R. (1974) *Education, Opportunity and Social Inequality: Changing Prospects in Western Society*. London: John Wiley and Sons.

Bourdieu, P. (1966/1971a) 'Intellectual Field and Creative Project', in: Young, M.F.D. (ed.) *Knowledge and Control: New Directions for the Sociology of Education*. London: Collier Macmillan, pp. 161–188.

Bourdieu, P. (1967/1971b) 'Systems of Education and Systems of Thought', in: Young, M.F.D. (ed.) *Knowledge and Control: New Directions for the Sociology of Education*. London: Collier Macmillan, pp.1 89–209.

Bourdieu, P. (1972/1977) *Outline of a Theory of Practice*. Cambridge: Cambridge University Press

Bourdieu, P. (1973) 'Cultural Reproduction and Social Reproduction', in: Brown, R. (ed.) *Knowledge, Education, and Cultural Change: Papers in the Sociology of Education*. Birkenhead: Tavistock Publications Limited, pp. 71–112.

Bourdieu, P. (1978) 'Classement, déclassement, reclassement', *Actes de la recherché en sciences socials, 24*, 2–3.

Bourdieu, P. (1979) 'Epilogue', in: Bourdieu *The Inheritors: French Students and their Relation to Culture* (English Translation). Chicago, IL: The University of Chicago Press, pp. 80–90.

Bourdieu, P. (1979/1984) *Distinction: A Social Critique of the Judgement of Taste*. London: Routledge and Kegan Paul.

Bourdieu, P. (1980/1990) *The Logic of Practice*. Cambridge: Cambridge University Press.

Bourdieu, P. (1983/2004) 'The Forms of Capital' In: Ball, S.J. (ed.) *The Routledge Falmer Reader in Sociology of Education*. London: Routledge Falmer, pp. 15–29.

Bourdieu, P. (1985) 'The Genesis of the Concepts of Habitus and of Field', *Sociocriticism, 2* (2), 11–24.

Bourdieu, P. (1986/1987) 'The Biographical Illusion', Working *Papers and Proceedings of the Centre for Psychosocial Studies, vol. 14*, 1–7.

Bourdieu, P. (1989/1996) *The State Nobility*. Cornwall: Polity Press.

Bourdieu, P. (1992a) 'The Practice of Reflexive Sociology (The Paris Workshop)', in: Bourdieu, P. and Wacquant, L. (eds) *An Invitation to Reflexive Sociology*. Cambridge: Polity Press, pp. 217–253.

Bourdieu, P. (1992b) 'The Purpose of Reflexive Sociology (The Chicago Workshop)', in: Bourdieu, P. and Wacquant, L. (eds) *An Invitation to Reflexive Sociology*. Cambridge: Polity Press, pp. 61–217.

Bourdieu, P. (1997/2000) *Pascalian Meditations*. Cambridge: Polity Press.

Bourdieu, P. (2002) 'Habitus', in: Hiller, J. and Rooksby, E. (eds) *Habitus: A Sense of Place*. Aldershot: Ashgate Publishing Limited, pp. 27–34

Bourdieu, P. and Boltanski, L. (1973/1978) 'Changes in Social Structure and Changes in Demand for Education', in: Ginger, S. and Archer, M.S. (eds) *Contemporary Europe: Social Structures and Cultural Patterns*. London: Routledge and Kegan Paul, pp. 197– 227.

Bourdieu, P. and Boltanski, L. (1975/1981) 'The Educational system and the Economy: Titles and Jobs', in: Lemert (ed.) *French Sociology: Rupture and Renewal Since 1968*. New York: Columbia University Press, pp. 141–151.

Bourdieu, P. and Passeron, J-C. (1964/1979) *The Inheritors: French Students and their Relation to Culture*. Chicago, IL: The University of Chicago Press.

Bourdieu, P. and Passeron, J-C. (1970/1990) *Reproduction in Education Society and Culture. (2nd ed.)* London: Sage Publications.

Bourdieu, P. *et al.* (1993/1999) *The Weight of the World: Social Suffering in Contemporary Society*. Stanford, CA: Stanford Press.

Bourdieu, P., Chamboredon, J-C. and Passeron, J-C. (1968/1991) *The Craft of Sociology: Epistemological Preliminaries*. New York: Walter de Gruyter.

Bowles, S. and Gintis, H. (1976) *Schooling in Capitalist America: Educational Reform and the Contradictions of Economic Life*. New York: Basic Books.

Bradley, H. (2014) 'Class Descriptors or Class Relations? Thoughts Towards a Critique of Savage *et al.*', *Sociology*, *48* (3), 429–436.

Bradley, H. and Ingram, N. (2012) 'Banking on the Future: Choices, Aspirations and Economic Hardship in Working-Class Student Experience', in: Atkinson, W., Roberts, S. and Savage, M. (eds) *Class Inequality in Austerity Britain*. Basingstoke: Palgrave Macmillan, pp. 51–70

Bradley, H., Bathmaker, A-M., Waller, R. *et al.* (2013) 'The Paired Peers Project Year 3 Report', (online). Available at: www.bristol.ac.uk/spais/research/paired-peers/report (retrieved 5 September 2014).

Breen, R. and J.H. Goldthorpe (2001) 'Class, Mobility and Merit; the Experience of Two British Cohorts', *European Sociological Review*, *17* (2), 81–101.

Brennan, J., Williams, R. and Blaskó, Z. (2003) 'The English Degree and Graduate Careers', Centre for Higher Education Research and Information: The Open University.

Bridgstock, R. (2009) 'The Graduate Attributes we've Overlooked: Enhancing Graduate Employability Through Career Management Skills', *Higher Education Research and Development*, *28* (1), 31–44.

British Chambers of Commerce (BCC) (2014) 'BCC Workforce Survey', (online). Available at: www.britishchambers.org.uk/policy-maker/policy-reports-and-publications/workforce-survey-infogaphic.html (retrieved 20 October 2014).

Brooks, R. (2003) 'Young People's Higher Education Choices: The Role of Family and Friends', *British Journal of Sociology of Education*, *24* (3), 283–297.

Brooks, R. (2005) *Friendship and Educational Choice: Peer Influence and Planning for the Future*. Hampshire: Palgrave and Macmillan.

Brooks, R. (2006) 'Young Graduates and Lifelong Learning: The Impact of Institutional Stratification', *Sociology*, *vol. 40* (6), 1019–1037.

Brooks, R. and Everett, G. (2009) 'Post-Graduation Reflections on the Value of a Degree', *British Educational Research Journal*, *35* (3), 333–349.

Brown, P. (1997) 'Cultural Capital and Social Exclusion: Some Observations on Recent Trends in Education, Employment, and the Labour Market', in: Halsey, A.H., Lauder, H., Brown, P. and Wells, A.S. (eds) *Education: Culture, Economy, and Society*. Oxford: Oxford University Press, pp. 736–749.

Brown, P. (2003) 'The Opportunity Trap: Education and Employment in a Global Economy', *European Educational Research Journal*, *2* (1), 141–177.

Brown, P. (2006) 'The Opportunity Trap.' (Revised and Abridged), in: Lauder, H., Brown, P. and Dillabough, J.A. (eds) *Education, Globalization and Social Change*. Oxford: Oxford University Press.

Brown, P. (2013) 'Education, Opportunity and Prospects for Social Mobility', *British Journal of Sociology of Education*, *34* (5–6), 678–700.

Brown, P. and Hesketh, A. (2004) *The Mismanagement of Talent: Employability and Jobs in the Knowledge Economy*. Oxford: Oxford University Press.

Brown, P. and Scase, R. (1994) *Higher Education and Corporate Realities: Class, Culture and the Decline of Graduates Careers*. Kent: UCL Press.

Brown, P. and Tannock, S. (2009) 'Education, Meritocracy and the Global War for Talent', *Journal of Education Policy*, *24* (4), 377–392.

Brown, P., Hesketh, A. and Williams, S. (2003) 'Employability in a Knowledge-Driven Economy', *Journal of Education and Work*, *16* (2), 107–126.

Brown, P., Lauder, H. and Aston, D. (2008) 'Education, Globalisation and the Future of the Knowledge Economy', *European Educational Research Journal*, *7* (2), 131–156

Brown, P., Power, S., Tholen, G. and Allouch, A. (2014) 'Credentials, talent and cultural capital: a comparative study of educational elites in England and France', *British Journal of Sociology of Education*, *online first*. Available at: http://dx.doi.org/10.1080/01425692.2014.920247 (retrieved 15 January 2015).

Brynin, M. (2002) 'Graduate Density, Gender and Employment', *British Journal of Sociology*, *53* (3), 363–381.

Budig, M.J. and England, P. (2001) 'The Wage Penalty for Motherhood', *American Sociological Review*, *66*, 204–225.

Bukodi, E. and J.H. Goldthorpe (2011) 'Class Origins, Education and Occupational Attainment in Britain', *European Societies 13* (3), 347–375.

Burke, C. (2015) 'Graduate Blues: Considering the Effects of Inverted Symbolic Violence on Underemployed Middle Class Graduates', *Sociology (forthcoming)*.

Burke, C.T. (2011) 'The Biographical Illumination: A Bourdieusian Analysis of the Role of Theory in Educational Research', *Sociological Research Online*, *16* (2), www.socresonline.org.uk/16/2/9.html (retrieved 5 August 2014).

Burke, C.T., Emmerich, N. and Ingram, N. (2013) 'Well-Founded Social Fictions: a Defense of the Concepts of Institutional and Familial Habitus', *British Journal of Sociology of Education*, *34* (2), 165–182.

Cabinet Office (2009a) 'New Opportunities: Fair Chances for the Future', (online). Available at: https://www.gov.uk/government/publications/new-opportunities-fair-chances-for-the-future (retrieved 25 September 2014).

Cabinet Office (2009b) 'Unleashing Aspiration: The Final Report of the Panel on Fair Access to the Professions', (online). Available at: http://webarchive.nationalarchives.gov.uk/+/http:/www.cabinetoffice.gov.uk/media/227102/fair-access.pdf (retrieved 25 September 2014).

Cabinet Office (2011) 'Opening Doors, Breaking Barriers: A Strategy for Social Mobility', (online). Available at: https://www.gov.uk/government/publications/opening-doors-breaking-barriers-a-strategy-for-social-mobility (retrieved 25 September 2014).

Cabinet Office (2012a) 'Fair Access to Professional Careers: A Progress Report', (online). Available at: https://www.gov.uk/government/publications/fair-access-to-professional-careers-a-progress-report (retrieved 25 September 2014).

Cabinet Office (2012b) 'Opening Doors, Breaking Barriers: A Strategy for Social Mobility (Update on Progress Since April 2011)', (online). Available at: https://www.gov.uk/government/publications/opening-doors-breaking-barriers-a-strategy-for-social-mobility-update-on-progress-since-april-2011 (retrieved 25 September 2014).

Castells, M. (2000) *The Rise of Network Society*. Oxford: Blackwell.

Chowdry, H., Crawford, C., Dearden, L., Goodman, A. and Vignoles, A. (2008) 'Widening Participation in Higher Education: Analysis Using Linked Administrative Data', London: Institute for Fiscal Studies.

Cognard-Black, A.J. (2004) 'Will They Stay, or Will They Go? Sex-atypical Work Among Token Men Who Teach', *The Sociological Quarterly*, *45* (1), 113–139.

Collins, J. (1993) 'Determination and Contradiction: An Appreciation and Critiques of the Work of Pierre Bourdieu on Language and Education', in: Calhoun, C., LiPuma, E. and Postone, M. (eds) *Bourdieu: Critical Perspectives*. Oxford: Polity Press, pp. 116–138.

Collins, J. (2000) 'Bernstein, Bourdieu and the New Literacy Studies', *Linguistics and Education*. *11* (1), 65–78.

Collins, R. (1979) *The Credential Society: An Historical Sociology of Education and Stratification*. London: Academic Press.

Confederation of British Industry (CBI) (2009) 'Future Fit: Preparing Graduates for the World of Work', (online). Available at: www.cbi.org.uk/media/1121435/cbi_uuk_future_fit.pdf (retrieved 25 September 2014).

Connolly, P. and Healy, J. (2004a) 'Symbolic Violence, Locality and Social Class: the educational and career aspirations of 10–11-year-old boys in Belfast', *Peadagogy, Culture and Society*, *12* (1), 15–33.

Connolly, P. and Healy, J. (2004b) 'Symbolic Violence and the Neighbourhood: The Educational Aspirations of 7–8 Year Old Working-Class Girls', *The British Journal of Sociology*, *55* (4), 511–529.

Connor, H., Dewson, S. and Tyers, C. (2001) *Social Class and Higher Education: Issues Affecting the Decisions to Participate by Lower Class Students*. London: HMSO.

Conway, S. (1997) 'The Reproduction of Exclusion and Disadvantages: Symbolic Violence and Social Class Inequalities in "Parental Choice" of Secondary Education', *Sociological Research Online*, *2* (4), (online). Available at: www.socresonline.org.uk/socresonline/2/4/4.html (retrieved 5 August 2014).

Coulter, C. (1999) *Contemporary Northern Irish Society*. London: Pluto Press.

Cranmer, S. (2006) 'Enhancing Graduate Employability: Best Intentions and Mixed Outcomes', *Studies in Higher Education 31* (2), 169–184.

Crompton, R. (1999) 'The Decline of the Male Breadwinner: Explanations and Interpretations', in: Crompton, R. (ed.) *Restructuring Gender Relations and Employment: The Decline of the Male Breadwinner*. New York: Oxford University Press, pp. 1–25.

Crompton, R. and Harris, F. (1999) 'Attitudes, Women's Employment, and the Changing Domestic Division of Labour: A Cross National Analysis', in: Crompton, R. (ed.) *Restructuring Gender Relations and Employment: The Decline of the Male Breadwinner*. New York: Oxford University Press, pp. 105–127.

Crompton, R. and Scott, J. (2005) 'Class Analysis: Beyond the Cultural Turn', in: Devine, F., Savage, M., Scott, J. and Crompton, R. (eds) *Rethinking Social Class: Culture, Identities and Lifestyle*. Basingstoke: Palgrave Macmillan, pp. 186–203.

Crossley, N. (2008) 'Social Class', in: Grenfell, M. (ed.) *Pierre Bourdieu: Key Concepts*. Durham: Acumen, pp. 87–99.

Dearing, R. (1997) 'Higher Education in the Learning Society: The Report of the National Committee of Inquiry into Higher Education (The Dearing Report)', London, HMSO.

Deer, C. (2008) 'Reflexivity', in: Grenfell, M. (ed.) *Pierre Bourdieu: Key Concepts*. Durham: Acumen, pp. 199–212.

Department for Business, Innovation and Skills (BIS) (2009) 'Higher Ambitions: The Future of Universities in a Knowledge Economy', (online). Available at: http://webarchive.nationalarchives.gov.uk/+/http://web.bis.gov.uk/policies/higher-education/shape-and-structure/higher-ambitions (retrieved 25 September 2014).

Department for Business, Innovation and Skills (BIS) (2010a) 'Securing a sustainable future for higher education: An independent review of higher education funding and student finance [Browne Report]', (online). Available at: www.gov.uk/government/publications/the-browne-report-higher-education-funding-and-student-finance (retrieved 25 September 2014).

Department for Business, Innovation and Skills (BIS) (2010b) 'Unleashing Aspirations: The Government Response of the Panel on Fair Access to the Professions', (online). Available at: https://www.gov.uk/government/publications/government-response-to-the-final-report-of-the-panel-on-fair-access-to-the-professions (retrieved 25 September 2014).

Department for Business, Innovation and Skills (BIS) (2011a) 'Higher Education: Students at the Heart of the System (White Paper)', (online). Available at: https://www.gov.uk/government/publications/higher-education-students-at-the-heart-of-the-system--2 (retrieved 25 September 2014).

Department for Business, Innovation and Skills (BIS) (2011b) 'Higher Education: the Government's Response to Lord Browne's Review', (online). Available at: https://www.gov.uk/government/publications/higher-education-government-response-to-lord-brownes-review (retrieved 25 September 2014).

Department for Business, Innovation and Skills (BIS) (2011c) 'Supporting Graduate Employability: Practice in Other Countries', (online). Available at: https://www.gov.uk/government/publications/supporting-graduate-employability-practice-in-other-countries (retrieved 25 September 2014).

Department for Business, Innovation and Skills (BIS) (2012a) 'A Review of Business-University Collaboration: The Wilson Review', (online). Available at: https://www.gov.uk/government/publications/business-university-collaboration-the-wilson-review (retrieved 25 September 2014).

Department for Business, Innovation and Skills (BIS) (2012b) 'Following up the Wilson Review of Business-University Collaboration: Next Steps for Universities, Business and Government', (online). Available at: www.gov.uk/government/publications/business-university-collaboration-government-response-to-the-wilson-review (retrieved 25 September 2014).

Department for Business, Innovation and Skills (BIS) (2014) 'Social Mobility Business Compact', (online). Available at: https://www.gov.uk/government/uploads/system/uploads/attachment_data/file/325817/Social-mobility-business-compact-fact_sheet_july_2014_pdf.pdf (retrieved 25 September 2014).

Department for Education (DfE) (1991) 'Higher Education: A New Framework (White Paper)', Cm 1541, London: HMSO.

Department for Education and Employment (DfEE) (2000) 'Opportunity for All: Skills for the New Economy', London: HMSO.

Department for Education and Skills (DfES) (2003) 'The Future of Higher Education (White Paper)', Cm5735, London: HMSO.

Department of Enterprise, Trade and Investment (DETI) (2012a), 'Employment Statistics: Northern Ireland Employee Jobs – Seasonally Adjusted September 2011', (online). Available at: www.detini.gov.uk/deti-stats-index/stats-labour-market/stats-labour-market-employment.htm (retrieved 25 July 2014).

Department of Enterprise, Trade and Investment (DETI) (2012b) 'Unemployment Statistics: Seasonally Adjusted Unemployment', (online). Available at: www.detini.gov.uk/deti-stats-index/stats-labour-market/stats-labour-market-unemployment.htm (retrieved 25 September 2014).

Department of Finance and Personnel (DFP) (2011) 'Northern Ireland Annual Survey of Hours and Earnings 2011', Belfast: Department of Employment and Learning.

Devine, F. and Li, Y. (2013) 'The Changing Relationship Between Origins, Education and Destinations in the 1990s and 2000s', *British Journal of Sociology of Education, 34* (5–6), 766–791.

DiMaggio, P. (1979) 'Review: On Pierre Bourdieu', *American Journal of Sociology, 84* (6), 1460–1474.

Du Bois-Reymond, M. (1998) 'I Don't Want to commit Myself Yet: Young People's Life Concepts', *Journal of Youth Studies, 1* (1), 63–79.

Durkheim, E. (1893/1982) 'The Rules of Sociological Method' In: Lukes, S. (ed.) *The Rules of Sociological Method and Selected Texts on Sociology and its Method*, pp. *31–163.*

Egerton, M. and Halsey, A.H. (1993) 'Trends by Social Class and Gender in Access to Higher Education in Britain', *Oxford Review of Education, 19* (2), 183–196.

Elder-Vass, D. (2007) 'Reconciling Archer and Bourdieu in an Emergentist Theory of Action', *Sociological Theory, 25* (4), 325–346.

Elias, P. and Purcell, K. (2004) *Seven Years On: Graduate Careers in a Changing Labour Market.* London: The Higher Education Careers Service Unit.

Elias, P. and Purcell, K. (2011) 'Higher Education, Intergenerational Mobility and Earnings: the Case of the UK', (online). Available at: www2.warwick.ac.uk/fac/soc/ier/research/glmf/heeer (retrieved 15 June 2014).

Evans, K. (2007) 'Concepts of Bounded Agency in Education, Work and the Personal Lives of Young People', *International Journal of Psychology, 5* (3), 245–269.

Evans, S. (2009) 'In a Different Place: Working Class Girls and higher Education', *Sociology, 43* (2), 340–355.

Fawcett Society (2013) 'Pay Gap Widens as Women's Standing in Economy Further Undermined', (online). Available at: www.fawcettsociety.org.uk/latest/press-releases/gap-in-pay-between-women-and-men-widens-after-years-of-slow-steady-progress/ (retrieved 25 September 2014).

Fleetwood, S. (2008) 'Structure, institution, agency, habit, and reflexive deliberation', *Journal of Institutional Economics, 4* (2), 183–203.

Foster, P., Gomm, R. and Hammersley, M. (1996) *Constructing Educational Inequality: An Assessment of Research on School Processes.* London: Falmer Press.

Foucault, M. (1978) *Discipline and Punish: The Birth of the Prison.* London: Penguin Books.

Furlong, A. and Cartmel, F. (2005) 'Early Labour-Market Experiences of graduates from Disadvantaged Families', Joseph Rowntree Foundation.

Gábor, K. (2008) 'Education, Qualification and Employment: Hungarian Experiences', in: Bendit, R. and Hahn-Bleibtreu, M. (eds) *Youth Transitions: Processes of Social Inclusion and Patterns of Vulnerability in a Globalised World.* Leverkusen Opladen: Barbara Budrich Publishers, pp. 97–114.

Geertz, C. (1973) 'On Thick Description: Toward an Interpretive Theory of Culture', in: Geertz, C., *The Interpretation of Cultures.* New York: Basic Books.

Giddens, A. (1991) *Modernity and Self-Identity: Self and Society in the Late Modern Age.* Cambridge: Polity Press.

Giddens, A. (1992) *New Rules of Sociological Method. (2nd ed.)* Cambridge: Polity Press.

Gilchrist, R., Phillips, D. and Ross, A. (2003) 'Participation and Potential Participation in UK Higher Education', in: Archer, L., Hutchings, M. and Ross, A. (eds) *Higher Education and Social Class: Issues of Exclusion and Inclusion.* London: Routledge Falmer, pp. 75–96.

Goldthorpe, J. (2007) 'Cultural Capital: Some Critical Observations', *Sociologica,* (online). Available at: www.sociologica.mulino.it/doi/10.2383/24755 (retrieved 5 July 2014).

Goldthorpe, J., Llewellyn, C. and Payne, C. (1980) *Social Mobility and Class Structure in Modern Britain.* Oxford: Clarendon Press.

Gorder, K.L. (1980) 'Understanding School Knowledge: A Critical Appraisal of Basil Bernstein and Pierre Bourdieu', *Educational Theory, 30* (4), 335–346.

Grenfell, M.J. (ed.) (2008) *Pierre Bourdieu: Key Concepts.* Durham: Acumen.

Grint, K. (2005) *The Sociology of Work (3rd ed.)* Cambridge: Polity Press.

Gudgin, (2008) 'The Importance of Qualification in Achieving High Wages and Productivity', in: Rodgers, D. (ed.) *Labour Market Bulletin 21: March 2008.* Belfast: Department of Employment and Learning, pp. 101–110.

Hakim, C. (1996) *Key Issues in Women's Work: Female Heterogeneity and the Polarisation of Women's Employment.* London: Athlone.

Halsey, A.H., Heath, A.F. and Ridge, J.M. (1980) *Origins and Destinations: Family, Class and Education in Modern Britain.* Oxford: Clarendon Press.

Hammersley, M. (2000) *Taking Sides in Social Research.* London: Routledge.

Hammersley, M. (2008) *Questioning Qualitative Inquiry: Critical Essays.* London: Sage Publications.

Hardy, C. (2008) 'Hysteresis', in: Grenfell, M. (ed.) *Pierre Bourdieu: Key Concepts.* Durham: Acumen, pp. 131–148.

Hargreaves, D.H. (1967) *Social Relations in a Secondary School.* London: Routledge and Kegan Paul.

Hartmann, H. (1982) 'Capitalism, Patriarchy, and Job Segregation by Sex', in: Giddens, A. and Held, D. (eds) *Unemployment: Personal and Social Consequences.* London: Tavistock.

Harvey, L. (2000) 'New Realities: the Relationship Between Higher Education and Employment', *Tertiary Education and Management, 6* (1), 3–17.

Heath, A., Sullivan, A., Boliver, V. and Zimdars, A. (2013) 'Education under New Labour, 1997–2010', *Oxford Review of Economic Policy, 29* (1), 227–247.

Hebson, G. (2009) 'Renewing Class Analysis in Studies of the Workplace: A Comparison of Working-Class and Middle-Class Women's Aspirations and Identities', *Sociology, 43* (1), 27–44.

Helyer, R. and Lee, D. (2014) 'The Role of Work Experience in the Future employability of Higher Education Graduates', *Higher Education Quarterly*, *68* (3), 348–372.

Henson, K.D. and Krasas Rogers, J. (2001) '"Why Marcia You've Changed!" Male Clerical Temporary Workers Doing Masculinity in a Feminized Occupation', *Gender and Society 15* (2), 218–38.

Hesketh, A.J. (2000) 'Recruiting a Graduate Elite? Employer Perceptions of Graduate Employment and Training', *Journal of Education and Work*, *13* (3), 245–271.

Higher Education Statistics Association (HESA) (2007) 'Destinations of Leavers: from Higher Education Institutions Longitudinal Survey of the 2002/03 cohort – Key Findings Report', National Centre for Social Research.

Higher Education Statistics Association (HESA) (2009) 'Destinations of Leavers: from Higher Education Institutions Longitudinal Survey of the 2004/05 cohort – Key Findings Report', National Centre for Social Research.

Higher Education Statistics Association (HESA) (2011) 'Destinations of Leavers: from Higher Education Institutions Longitudinal Survey of the 2006/07 cohort – Introduction', (online). Available at: https://www.hesa.ac.uk/dlhelong0607_intro (retrieved 25 June 2014).

Highfliers (2010) 'Key highlights: Researching the Class of 2010', (online). Available at: http://highfliers.co.uk/download/Release2010.pdf (retrieved 25 June 2014).

Hochschild, A. (1983) *The Managed Heart: Commercialisation of Human Feeling*. Berkeley, CA: University of California Press.

Hochschild, A. (1990) *The Second Shift: Working Parents and the Revolution in the Home*. London: Piatkus.

Hodkinson, P. (1998) 'Career Decision Making and the Transition from School to Work', in: Grenfell, M. and James, D. (eds) *Bourdieu and Education: Acts of Practical Theory*. Routledge: London, pp. 89–104.

Hodkinson, P., Sparkes, A.C and Hodkinson, H. (2000) 'Career Decision Making and Culture in the Transition from School to Work', in: Ball, S.J. (ed.) *Sociology of Education: Major Themes vol. 1*. London: Routledge, pp. 343–361.

Holmes, L. (2001) 'Reconsidering Graduate Employability: the "Graduate Identity" Approach', *Quality in Higher Education*, *7* (2), 111–119.

Holmes, L. (2013) 'Competing Perspectives on Graduate Employability: Possession, Position or Process', *Studies in Higher Education*, *38* (4), 538–554.

Horgan, G. (2007) 'The Changing Working Class in Northern Ireland', in: O'Sullivan, S. (ed.) *Contemporary Ireland: a Sociological Map*. Dublin: UCD Press, pp. 318–332.

Hutchings, M. (2003) 'Financial Barriers to Participation', in: Archer, L., Hutchings, M. and Ross, A. (eds) *Higher Education and Social Class: Issues of Exclusion and Inclusion*. London: Routledge Falmer, pp. 155–175.

Ingram, N.A. (2009) 'Working-Class Boys, Educational Success and the Mis-recognition of Working-Class Culture', *British Journal of Sociology of Education*, *30*, 421–434.

Ingram, N.A. (2011) 'Within School and Beyond the Gate: The Complexities of Being Educationally Successful and Working-Class', *Sociology*, *45* (2), 287–302.

Jackson, B. and Marsden, D. (1966) *Education and the Working Classes*. Middlesex: Pelican books.

Jenkins, R. (2002) *Pierre Bourdieu: Revised Edition*. London: Routledge

Keep, E. (2014) 'The Role of Higher Education within Broader Skills Policies, a Comparison of Emerging Scottish and English Approaches', *Higher Education Quarterly, 68* (3), 249–266.

Keep, E. and James, S. (2011) 'A Bermuda Triangle of Policy? "Bad Jobs", Skills Policy and Incentives to Learn at the Bottom End of the Labour Market', *Journal of Education Policy, 27* (2), 211–230.

Lahire, B. (2011) *The Plural Actor.* Cambridge: Polity Press.

Lamaison, P. (1986), From Rules to Strategies: An Interview with Pierre Bourdieu. *Cultural Anthropology, 1*: 110–120.

Lareau, A. (1997) 'Social-Class Differences in Family-School Relationships: The Importance of Cultural Capital', in: Halsey, A.H., Lauder, H., Brown, P. and Wells, A.S. (eds) *Education: Culture, Economy, and Society.* Oxford: Oxford University Press, pp. 703–717.

Lawler, S. (2005) 'Introduction: Class, Culture and Identity', Sociology, *39* (5), 797–806.

Leathwood, C. and Hutchings, M. (2003) 'Entry Routes to Higher Education: Pathways, Qualifications and Social Class', in: Archer, L., Hutchings, M. and Ross, A. (eds) *Higher Education and Social Class: Issues of Exclusion and Inclusion.* London: Routledge Falmer, pp. 137–155.

Lehmann, W. (2009) 'Becoming Middle Class: How Working-Class University Students Draw and Transgress Moral Class Boundaries', *Sociology, 43* (4), 631–648.

LiPuma, E. (1993) 'Culture and the Concept of Culture in a Theory of Practice', in: Calhoun, C., LiPuma, E. and Postone, M. (eds) *Bourdieu: Critical Perspectives.* Oxford: Polity Press, pp. 14–35.

MacDonald, R., Shildrick, T., Webster, C. and Simpson, D. (2005) 'Growing Up in Poor Neighbourhoods: The Significance of Class and Place in the Extended Transitions of "Socially Excluded" Young Adults', *Sociology, 39* (5), 873–891.

Mangan, J., Hughes, A., Davies, P. and Slack, K. (2010) 'Fair Access, Achievement and Geography: Explaining the Association between Social Class and Students' Choice of University', *Studies in Higher Education, 35* (3), 335–350.

Martin, P. (2013) 'Destination of Leavers from Higher Education – A Longitudinal Survey', in: Rodgers, D. (ed.) *Labour Market Bulletin 24: July 2013.* Belfast: Department of Employment and Learning, pp. 107–112.

Mason, G. (2002) 'High Skills Utilisation Under Mass Higher Education: Graduate Employment in Service Industries in Britain', *Journal of Education and Work, 15* (4), 427–456.

Mason, G., Williams, G. and Cranmer, S. (2009) 'Employability Skills Initiatives in Higher Education: What Effects do they have on Graduate Labour Market Outcomes?', *Education Economics, 17* (1), 1–30.

Maton, K. (2008) 'Habitus' In: Grenfell, M. (ed.) *Pierre Bourdieu: Key Concepts.* Durham: Acumen, pp. 49–65.

Merrill, B. and West, L. (2009) *Using Biographical Methods in Social Research.* London: Sage Publications

Merton, R. (1957) *Social Theory and Social Structure.* New York: Free Press.

Miller, R.L. (2000) *Researching Life Stories and Family Histories.* London: Sage Publications.

Miller, R.L. (2004) 'Social Mobility in Northern Ireland', in: Osborne, B. and Shuttleworth (eds) *Fair Employment in Northern Ireland: A Generation on.* Belfast: The Blackstaff Press, pp. 49–64.

Mills, C. (2014) 'The Great British Class Fiasco: A Comment on Savage *et al.*', *Sociology*, *48* (3), 437–444.

Mills, C.W. (1959) *The Sociological Imagination*. Oxford: Oxford University Press.

Mirana, A. (2008) 'Job Integration of Young People in Argentina', in: Bendit, R. and Hahn-Bleibtreu, M. (eds) *Youth Transitions: Processes of Social Inclusion and Patterns of Vulnerability in a Globalised World*. Leverkusen Opladen: Barbara Budrich Publishers, pp. 85–96.

Moore, R. (2007) 'Protestants and Protestant Habitus in Northern Ireland', in: O'Sullivan, S. (ed.) *Contemporary Ireland a Sociological Map*. Dublin: UCD Press, pp. 388–401.

Moreau, M-P. and Leathwood, C. (2007) 'Graduates' Employment and the Discourse of Employability: A Critical Analysis', *Journal of Education and Work*, *19* (4), 305–324.

Morrison, A.R. (2014) '"You Have to be Well Spoken": Students' Views on Employability within the Graduate Labour Market', *Journal of Education and Work*, *27* (2), 179–198.

Mountford-Zimdars, A., Jones, S., Sullivan, A. and Heath, A. (2013) 'Framing Higher Education: Questions and Responses in the British Social Attitudes Survey, 1983–2010', *British Journal of Sociology of Education*, *34* (5–6), 792–811.

Mouzelis, N. (1995), *Sociological Theory: What Went Wrong*? London: Routledge.

Mouzelis, N. (2007), 'Habitus and Reflexivity: Restructuring Bourdieu's Theory of Practice', *Sociological Research Online*, 12 (6), (online). Available at: www.socres online.org.uk/12/6/9.html (retrieved 15 June 2014).

Mullen, A.L. (2010) *Degrees of Inequality: Culture, Class and Gender an American Higher Education*. Baltimore, MD: The Johns Hopkins University Press.

Murphy, P. and Gawthorpe, D. (2013) 'Matching Graduate and Employer Expectations', *Graduate Market Trends, Summer 2013*, 14–16.

Murphy, R. (1988) *Social Closure: The Theory of Monopolisation and Exclusion*. Oxford: Clarendon Press.

Nash, R. (1999) 'Bourdieu, "Habitus", and Educational Research: Is it All Worth the Candle?', *British Journal of Sociology of Education*, *20* (2) 175–187.

Noble, G. and Watkins, M. (2003) 'So, How Did Bourdieu Learn to Play Tennis? Habitus, Consciousness and Habituation', *Cultural Studies*, *17* (3), 520–539.

Office for National Statistics (ONS) (2012) 'Statistical Bulletin: Labour Market Statistics: January 2012', (online). Available at: www.ons.gov.uk/ons/rel/lms/labour-market-statistics/january-2012/index.html (retrieved 25 September 2014).

Office for National Statistics (ONS) (2013a) 'Annual Survey of Hours and Earnings, Provisional Results', (online). Available at: www.ons.gov.uk/ons/rel/ashe/annual-survey-of-hours-and-earnings/2013-provisional-results/stb-ashe-statistical-bulletin-2013.html (retrieved 25 September 2014).

Office for National Statistics (ONS) (2013b) 'Full Report – Graduates in the UK Labour Market 2013', (online). Available at: www.ons.gov.uk/ons/dcp171776_337841.pdf (retrieved 25 September 2014).

O'Leary, N.C. and Sloane, P.J. (2006), 'Rates of Return to Degrees across British Regions', WELMERC Discussion Paper.

Oliver, C. and O'Reilly, K. (2010) 'A Bourdieusian Analysis of Class Migration: Habitus and the Individualising Process', *Sociology*, *44* (1), 49–66.

Osborne, B. (2004) 'Education and the Labour Market', in: Osborne, B. and Shuttleworth (eds) *Fair Employment in Northern Ireland: A Generation on.* Belfast: The Blackstaff Press, pp. 65–87.

Owens, J. and Tibby, M. (2013) *Measuring the Impact of Pedagogy for Employability on Employability Policy and Practice in Higher Education Institutes.* York: Higher Education Academy.

Parsons, T. (1966) *Societies: Evolutionary and Comparative Perspectives.* Upper Saddle River, NJ: Prentice Hall.

Payne, G. (1987) *Employment and Opportunity.* London: The Macmillan Press.

Payne, G. (2012) 'A New Social Mobility? The political redefinition of a sociological problem', *Contemporary Social Science: Journal of the Academy of Social Sciences, 7* (1), 55–71.

Pegg, A., Waldock, J., Hendy-Isaac, S. and Lawton, R. (2012) *Pedagogy for Employability.* York: Higher Education Academy.

Porpora, D.V. (2013) 'Morphogensis and Social Change', in: Archer, M.S. (ed.) *Social Morphogenesis.* London: Springer, pp. 25–39.

Purcell, K., Elias, P., Atfield, G., Behle, H., Ellison, R. and Luchinskaya, D. (2013) 'Transitions into Employment, Further Study and Other Outcomes: The Futuretrack Stage 4 Report', The Higher Education Careers Service Unit.

Quality Assurance Agency for Higher Education (QAA) (2014) 'Employer Engagement: Emerging Practices for QAA Reviews', (online). Available at: www.qaa.ac.uk/publications/information-and-guidance/publication?PubID=2865#.VJK41yusUec (retrieved 26 September 2014).

Reay, D. (1998) '"Always Knowing" and "Never Being Sure": Familial and Institutional Habituses and Higher Education Choice', *Journal of Education Policy, 13* (4), 519–529.

Reay, D. (2000) 'Rethinking Social Class Qualitative Perspectives on Class and Gender', in: Ball, S.J. (ed.) *Sociology of Education: Major Themes vol. 2.* London: Routledge, pp. 990–1008.

Reay, D. (2004a) 'Finding or Losing Yourself? Working-Class Relationships to Education', in: Ball. S. (ed.) *Sociology of Education.* London: Routledge Falmer, pp. 30–44.

Reay, D. (2004b) 'It's All Becoming a Habitus: Beyond the Habitual Use of Habitus in Educational Research', *British Journal of Sociology of Education, 25* (4), 431–444.

Reay, D. (2012) '"We Never Get a Fair Chance": Working-Class Experience of Education in the Twenty-First Century', in: Atkinson, W., Roberts, S. and Savage, M. (eds) *Class Inequality in Austerity Britain.* Basingstoke: Palgrave Macmillan, pp. 33–51.

Reay, D. (2013) 'Social Mobility, a Panacea for Austere Times: Tales of Emperors, Frogs, and Tadpoles', *British Journal of Sociology of Education, 34* (5–6), 660–677.

Reay, D. and Lucey, H. (2000) 'Children, School Choice and Social Differences', *Educational Studies, 26* (1), 83–100.

Reay, D. and Lucey, H. (2004) 'Stigmatised Choices: Social Class, Social Exclusion and Secondary School Markets in the Inner City', *Pedagogy, Culture and Society, 12* (1), 35–51.

Reay, D., Crozier, G. and Clayton, J. (2009a) '"Fitting In" or "Standing Out": Working-Class Students in UK Higher Education', *British Educational Research Journal, 32* (1), 1–19.

Reay, D., Crozier, G. and Clayton, J. (2009b) '"Strangers in Paradise"? Working-class Students in Elite Universities', *Sociology, 43* (6), 1103–1121.

Reay, D., David, M. and Ball, S. (2001) 'Making a Difference? Institutional Habituses and Higher Education Choice', *Sociological Research Online, 4* (5), (online). Available at www.socresonline.org.uk/5/4/reay.html (retrieved 5 June 2014).

Reay, D., David, M.E. and Ball, S. (2005) *Degrees of Choice: Social Class, Race and Gender in Higher Education.* Stoke on Trent: Trentham Books.

Redmond, P. (2010) 'Outcasts on the Inside: Graduates, Employability and Widening Participation', *Tertiary Education and Management, 12* (2), 119–135.

Rinehart, J., Huxley, C. and Robertson, D. (1997) *Just Another Factory? Lean Production and it Discontents.* Ithaca, NY: Cornell University Press.

Robbins, D. (1993) 'The Practical Importance of Bourdieu's Analyses of Higher Education', *Studies in Higher Education, 18* (2), 151–163

Robbins, D. (1998) 'The Need for an Epistemological Break' In: Grenfell, M.J. and James, D. (eds) *Bourdieu and Education: Acts of Practical Theory.* Routledge: London, pp. 22–51

Robbins, L. (1963) 'Higher Education: Report of a Committee (The Robbins Report)', London: HMSO.

Rodgers, D. (2013) 'The Northern Ireland Labour Market "At a Glance"', in: Rodgers, D. (ed.) *Labour Market Bulletin 24: July 2013.* Belfast: Department of Employment and Learning, pp. 12–15.

Rosenthal, G. (2003) 'The Healing Effects of Storytelling: On the Conditions of Curative Storytelling in the Context of Research and Counselling', *Qualitative Inquiry, vol. 9* (6), 915–933.

Rosenthal, G. (2005) 'Biographical Research' In: Miller, R.L. (ed.) *Biographical Research Methods Volume III.* London: Sage Publications, pp. 25–58.

Ross, A. (2003) 'Access to Higher Education: Inclusion for the Masses?', in: Archer. L., Hutchings, M. and Ross, A. (eds) *Higher Education and Social Class: Issues of Exclusion and Inclusion.* London: Routledge Falmer, pp. 45–75.

Savage, M. (2000) *Class Analysis and Social Transformation.* Buckingham: Open University Press.

Savage, M. (2003) 'A New Class Paradigm?', *British Journal of Sociology of Education, 24* (4), 535–541.

Savage, M. and Egerton, M. (1997) 'Social Mobility, Individual Ability and the Inheritance of Class Inequality', *Sociology, 31* (4), 645–672.

Savage, M., Devine, F., Cunningham, N. *et al. (2013)* 'A New Model of Social Class? Findings from the BBC's Great British Class Survey Experiment', *Sociology, 47* (2), 219–250.

Savage, M., Devine, F., Cunningham, N. *et al. (2014)* 'On Social Class, Anno 2014', *Sociology,* 1–20, (online). Available at: http://soc.sagepub.com/content/early/2014/06/06/0038038514536635.full (retrieved 15 October 2014).

Sayad, A. (1993/1999) 'Emancipation', in: Bourdieu, P. *et al. The Weight of the World: Social Suffering in Contemporary Society.* Stanford, CA: Stanford University Press, pp. 580–589.

Sayer, A. (2005) *The Moral Significance of Class.* Cambridge: Cambridge University Press.

Schultz, T.W. (1971) *Investment in Human Capital: The Role of Education and of Research.* New York: The Free Press.

Schütze, F. (1992) 'Pressure and Guilt: The Experience of a Young German Solider in World War Two and its Biographical Implications', *International Sociology*, *7* (2), 187–208; *7* (3), 347–367.

Schütze, F. (2008) Biography Analysis on the Empirical Base of Autobiographical Narratives: How to Analyse Autobiographical Narrative Interviews – Part I (online). Available at: www.biographicalcounselling.com/download/B2.1.pdf (retrieved 5 June 2014).

Scott, J. (2000) 'Class and Stratification', in: Payne, G. (ed.) *Social Divisions*. London: Macmillan, pp. 20–55

Scott, J. (2002) 'Social Class and Stratification in Late Modernity', *Acta Sociologica*, *45* (1), 23–35.

Shu, X. and Marini, M.M. (1998) 'Gender-Related Change in Occupational Aspirations', *Sociology of Education*, *71*, 44–68.

Sianou-Kyrgiou, E. and Tsiplakides, I. (2010) 'Similar Performance, but Different Choices: Social Class and Higher Education Choice in Greece', *Studies in Higher Education*, *36* (1), 89–102.

Skeggs, B. (1997) *Formations of Class and Gender*. London: Sage.

Skeggs, B. (2004) 'Context and Background: Pierre Bourdieu's analysis of class, gender and sexuality', in: Adkins, L. and Skeggs, B. (eds) *Feminism After Bourdieu*. Oxford: Blackwell Publishing, pp. 19–33.

Skeggs, B. (2005) 'The Re-Branding of Class: Propertising Culture', in: Devine, F., Savage, M., Scott, J. and Crompton, R. (eds) *Rethinking Social Class: Culture, Identities and Lifestyle*. Basingstoke: Palgrave Macmillan, pp. 46–68.

Smetherham, C. (2006) 'Firsts Among Equals? Evidence on the Contemporary Relationship between Educational Credentials and the Occupational Structure', *Journal of Education and Work*, *19* (1), 29–45.

Smyth, J. and Cebulla, A. (2008) 'The Glacier Moves? Economic Change and Class Structure', in: Coulter, C. and Murray, M. (eds) *Northern Ireland: After the Troubles*. Manchester: Manchester University Press, pp. 175–191.

Social Mobility Foundation (2014) 'Home Page', (online). Available at: www.socialmobility.org.uk/ (retrieved 25 October 2014).

Stokes, H. and Wyn, J. (2007) 'Constructing Identity and Making Careers: Young People's Perspectives of Work and Learning', *International Journal of Lifelong Education*, *26* (5), 495–511.

Tagoe, M. (2009) 'The Relevance of University Education and Fears of Unemployment: Perceptions of University Students Making Transitions to the World of Work in Ghana', in: Brooks, R. (ed.) *Transitions from Education to Work*. Hampshire: Palgrave Macmillan, pp. 113–135.

Teichler, U. (1999) 'Higher Education Policy and the World of Work: Changing Conditions and Challenges', *Higher Education Policy*, *12*, 285–312.

Thomson, P. (2008) 'Field', in: Grenfell, M. (ed.) *Pierre Bourdieu: Key Concepts*. Durham: Acumen, pp. 67–81.

Tibby, M. (2012) *Report on Teaching and Learning Summit*. York: Higher Education Academy.

Tomlinson, M. (2007) 'Graduate Employability and Student Attitudes and Orientations to the Labour Market', *Journal of Education and Work*, *20* (4), 285–304.

Tomlinson, M. (2008) '"The Degree is Not Enough": Students' Perceptions of the Role of Higher Education Credentials for Graduate Work and Employability', *British Journal of Sociology of Education*, *29* (1), 49–61.

Tomlinson, M. (2012a) *Exploring the Impact of Policy changes on Students' Attitudes and Approaches to Learning in Higher Education.* York: Higher Education Academy.

Tomlinson, M. (2012b) 'Graduate Employability: A Review of Conceptual and Empirical Themes', *Higher Education Policy, 25* (4), 407–431.

Tomlinson, M. (2013) *Education, Work and Identity: Themes and Perspectives.* London: Bloomsbury.

Tooley, J. and Darby, D. (1998) *Educational Research, A Critique: A Survey of Published Results.* London: Office of Standards in Education.

Tyler, W. (1977) *Sociology of Educational Inequality.* London: Egmont Children's Books.

Vallas, S.P., Finaly, W. and Wharton, A.S. (2010) *The Sociology of Work: Structures and Inequalities.* New York: Oxford University Press.

Wacquant, L. (1992a) 'In Notes – The Purpose of Reflexive Sociology', in: Bourdieu, P. and Wacquant, L. (eds) *An Invitation to Reflexive Sociology.* Cambridge: Polity Press, pp. 61–215.

Wacquant, L. (1992b) 'The Structure and Logic of Bourdieu's Sociology', in: Bourdieu, P. and Wacquant, L. (eds) *An Invitation to Reflexive Sociology.* Cambridge: Polity Press, pp. 1–59.

Wacquant, L. (1993) 'Bourdieu in America: Notes on the Transatlantic Importation of Social Theory', in: Calhoun, C, LiPuma, E. and Postone, M. (eds) *Bourdieu: Critical Perspectives.* Oxford: Polity Press, pp. 235–262.

Wacquant, L. (2005) 'Habitus', in: Berckert, J. and Zafirovski, M. (eds) *Encyclopaedia of Economic Sociology.* London: Routledge, pp. 317–320.

Walby, S. (1986) *Patriarchy at Work: Patriarchal and Capitalist Relations in Employment.* Cambridge: Polity Press.

Webb, J., Schirato, T. and Danaher, G. (2002) *Understanding Bourdieu.* London: Sage Publications.

Willis, P.E. (1977) *Learning to Labour: How Working Class Kids get Working Class Jobs.* Farnborough: Saxon House.

Wilton, N. (2008) 'Higher Education, the Knowledge economy and Knowledge Workers: Does Current Education Policy Make Sense?', (online). Available at: www2.uwe.ac.uk/faculties/BBS/BUS/Research/CESR/April%202008%20Wilton.pdf (retrieved 25 August 2014).

Wilton, N. (2011) 'Do Employability Skills Really Matter in the UK Graduate Labour Market? The Case of Business and Management Graduates', *Work, Employment and Society, 25* (1), 85–100.

Wolf, A. (2007) 'Round and Round the Houses: The Leitch Review of Skills', *Local Economy 22*(2), 111–117.

Wyn, J. (2008) 'New Patterns of Youth Transition in Education in Australia', in: Bendit, R. and Hahn-Bleibtreu, M. (eds) *Youth Transitions: Processes of Social Inclusion and Patterns of Vulnerability in a Globalised World.* Leverkusen Opladen: Barbara Budrich Publishers, pp. 73–84.

Young, M.F.D. (1971) *Knowledge and Control: New Directions for the Sociology of Education.* London: Collier Macmillan.

Zeuner, L. (1999) 'Review essay: Margaret Archer on Structural and Cultural Morphogenesis', *Acta Sociologica, 42,* 79–86.

Zweig, F. (1961) *The Worker in an Affluent Society: Family Life and Industry:* London: Heinemann.

Index